SOCIAL RELATIONS
and CUBAN HEALTH
the
MIRACLE

SOCIAL RELATIONS
and CUBAN HEALTH
the
MIRACLE

Elizabeth Kath

Transaction Publishers
New Brunswick (U.S.A.) and London (U.K.)

Library of Congress Catalog Number: 2010002367
ISBN: 978-1-4128-1417-1
Printed in the United States of America

Library of Congress Cataloging-in-Publication Data

Kath, Elizabeth.
    Social relations and the Cuban health miracle / Elizabeth Kath.
        p. cm.
    Includes bibliographical references and index.
    ISBN 978-1-4128-1417-1 (alk. paper)
        1. Social medicine--Cuba. 2. Medical care--Cuba. 3. Public health--Cuba. I. Title.

RA418.3.C9 K38 2010
362.1097291--dc22
                                                                            2010002367

Contents

Acknowledgments   vii

List of Interviews Conducted in Cuba   ix

List of Abbreviations   xi

Preface   xiii

1. Introduction and Background   1

2. Social Capital and State Capacity   31

3. Political Will and Cooperative Institutional Arrangements   73

4. The Limits of State Capacity and Social Capital in a   91
Top-Down System: Exclusion and Non-Participation

5. Underground Health Care Arrangements as   131
Temporary Solutions and Long Term Challenges to the
Formal System

6. Conclusion   165

References   179

Index   195

Acknowledgments

In completing this book, I owe most to Geoff Dow for his inspiring intellectual contributions, his unceasing generosity in dedicating time to read and comment on my drafts, and his support, good humor and encouragement throughout the entire research and writing process. I gratefully acknowledge the academic communities at the School of Political Science and International Studies at the University of Queensland, and the Global Cities Institute at RMIT University, who provided a supportive and accommodating environment in which to work.

Un millón de gracias a todos mis amigos y contactos en Cuba y a los cubanos que conocí fuera de la isla; agradezco no solo a quienes me brindaron su tiempo en entrevistas pero también a todos los que conversaron conmigo durante el proceso de investigación y escritura de este libro. Sin su contribución no me hubiese sido possible llegar a conocer y entender un poco de la realidad Cubana, ni mucho menos a realizar este trabajo.

I would also like to thank: Rachel Parker for her timely and valuable input; Andy Hindmoor to whom I am immeasurably grateful for his support, feedback and encouragement; Bronwyn Wex, David Hundt, and Jennifer Laakso for being terrific colleagues throughout the research process and for patiently listening to my ideas on many occasions; Tim Anderson, for generously devoting time in Cuba to discussions about my research; Katherine Hirschfeld, for whom I not only have great respect as a scholar, but to whom I am deeply grateful for the warmth and enthusiasm with which she has encouraged me to publish this research, shared her knowledge and experiences, and recommended my work to other scholars; Paul James for making the time to discuss my work on numerous occasions over the years, and especially for his mentoring, encouragement and pearls of wisdom over the past year; the staff at Transaction Publishers—particularly Irving Louis Horowitz, Mary E. Curtis, Jennifer Nippins, and Angel L. Soto—for their interest in this work and the time and effort they devoted to guiding the book through the editorial process; Tania Florez and Heike Kath, for general supportiveness, but more specifically, for providing helpful contributions of medical perspectives on various ideas and clarification of medical terminology; Jake Najman and Leonie Callaway for the advice they provided on maternal mortality causes; Johan Sæbø for the openness and collegiality with which he shared his knowledge and experiences relating to his research in Cuba; and to all those who took the interest and time to read and comment on the manuscript in the lead up to its completion.

Thank you to my family, especially Mum, Father, Arthur, Henry, Sebastian and my fantastic cousins for their support and for enduring my periods of absence while writing this work. For their time and support, which I will never forget, I also wish to acknowledge: Barbara Sullivan, Daniel Syvertsen, Brett Thompson, Bill Ransome, Ben Gilna, Sally Queitzsch, Natalie Grzic, and the many others who helped in innumerable ways throughout the research and writing process. While I owe an enormous gratitude to all mentioned here, the responsibility for any error, omission or misinterpretation in this work is of course entirely my own.

Finally, but importantly, I am grateful to the other scholars whose previous work, acknowledged throughout, helped to inform and inspire this research.

List of Interviews Conducted in Cuba

NB. Although all but two of the respondents gave their formal consent to be identified by name, title and institution, as a precautionary measure all names have been coded to protect respondents' identities. Wherever possible, non-specific descriptions of job titles have been provided. Names of specific hospitals and clinics have also been omitted. This list is nevertheless intended to give some idea of the types of respondents who were involved.

Interview 1—*Dr. José Rivera.* Gynecologist/Obstetrician and Teacher. Interviewed 14 July 2004.

Interview 2—*Dr. Carla Lopez.* University Lecturer. Interviewed 19 July 2004.

Interview 3—*Prof. Sandra Blanco.* University Professor of Sociology (specializing in public health). Interviewed 20 July 2004.

Interview 4—*Sonia Fernández.* Social Worker from Havana's National Centre for Sexual Education (CENESEX). Interviewed 20 July 2004.

Interview 5—*Roberto Sanchez.* Social Researcher. Centre for Social and Psychological Research (CIPS). Interviewed 23 July 2004.

Interview 6—*Dr. Rodrigo Valdes.* Specialist in Internal Medicine. Interviewed 2 August 2004.

Interview 7—*Dr. Mario Almeida.* Cardiologist (Sub-Specialty in Pregnancy). Interviewed 2 August 2004.

Interview 8 (Joint Interview)—*Marina Delgado* and *Josefina Suárez.* Representatives from the Federation of Cuban Women (FMC). Interviewed 10 August 2004.

Interview 9—*Dr. Pablo Ramirez.* Representative of the Cuban Ministry of Public Health (MINSAP). Interviewed 6 September 2004.

Interview 10—*Dr. Enrique Ramos.* Representative of the Cuban Ministry of Public Health (MINSAP). Interviewed 6 September 2004.

Interview 11—*Dr. Elena Castillo.* Medical Specialist and "Basic Work Group" (GBT) Superviser at a Policlinic. Interviewed 20 September 2004.

Interview 12—*Susana González.* Social Worker at a Maternity Home (*Hogar Materno*). Interviewed 21 September 2004.

Interview 13—*Dr. Fernanda Medina.* Paediatrician and Teacher. Interviewed 21 September 2004.

Interview 14—*Dr. Arturo Jiménez.* Director of Neonatal Department in a Maternity Hospital. Interviewed 22 September 2004.

Interview 15—*Dr. Isaac Herrera.* Director of Obstetrics in a Maternity Hospital. Interviewed 22 September 2004.

Interview 16—*Dr. Milagros Rios.* Family Doctor. Interviewed 23 September 2004.

Interview 17—*Dr. Lola Molinero.* Teacher of Medical Sciences. Interviewed 30 September 2004.

Interview 18—*Dr. Carlos Diaz.* Former Family Doctor (still living in Cuba). Interviewed 1 October 2004.

Interview 19—*Marta García.* Anonymous Citizen of Havana (respondent did not wish to be identified by name, work title or institution). Interviewed 4 October 2004.

Interview 20—*Dr. Samuel Vargas.* Director of National School of Public Health. Interviewed 4 October 2004.

Interview 21—*Celia Arango.* Representative of the Federation of Cuban Women (FMC). Interviewed 7 October 2004.

Interview 22 (Joint Interview)—*Josefa Espinosa* and *Adela Raiz.* Representatives of the National Commission for Social Prevention and Attention (CNPAS). Interviewed 7 October 2004.

List of Abbreviations

CDR—Committee for the Defense of the Revolution

CEDISAP—Cuba's Centre for the Development of Health Information

CENESEX—Cuba's National Centre for Sexual Education

CNPAS—Cuba's National Commission for Social Prevention and Attention

COMECON—Council for Mutual Economic Assistance

DNE—Cuba's National Office of Statistics

ECLAC—United Nations Economic Commission for Latin America and the Caribbean

FMC—Federation of Cuban Women

GBT—Basic Work Groups at Cuban Policlinics

GDP—Gross Domestic Product

HISP—Health Information Systems Program

IMF—International Monetary Fund

MINSAP—Cuban Ministry of Public Health

OECD—Organization for Economic Co-operation and Development

PAMI—Cuba's Maternal-Infant Health Program

PAHO—Pan American Health Organization

RRC—Process of "Rendering Accounts"

UNDP—United Nations Development Program

WHO—World Health Organization

Preface

The subject of health virtually always arises in conversations about Cuba. For the country's supporters, health is the most commonly-cited evidence of the socialist system's success. Even critics often concede that this is the country's saving grace. Cuba's health statistics are indeed extraordinary. This small island outperforms in many key health areas virtually all of its neighboring countries and all countries of the same level of economic development. Some of its health statistics even rival wealthy industrialized countries, a point which attracts regular praise internationally from journalists and scholars. Moreover, these health outcomes have resulted against all odds. For Cuba, the usual conditions of underdevelopment have been further strained by an ongoing U.S. embargo and by the collapse of the Soviet Union that was its main trading partner. The latter provoked a crisis throughout the 1990s so severe that its economic impact has been compared to that of the Great Depression of the 1930s. Despite these major external crises, the country has continued to perform well in the area of health, sustaining and often improving its statistical outcomes. So how has Cuba managed these results under such circumstances? This was essentially the question I set out to answer when embarking on this project.

This book is the culmination of around five years of research and writing, including nine months of fieldwork in Havana during 2003 and 2004. I began this project with a number of positive assumptions about the Cuban health system. Based on its statistical health outcomes, and the glowing accounts in the literature I had read, I anticipated drawing lessons from the Cuban case that might inform some of the theoretical developments in the social capital and state capacity literatures. These literatures have each presented challenges to the liberal development model that seemed compatible with the Cuban example. In turn, I imagined that these lessons might even turn out to be generalizable to other poor countries' health sectors.

xiv   Social Relations and the Cuban Health Miracle

Ultimately, however, the project's findings were not quite what I had expected. On the one hand, the new research methods and theoretical tools I adopted for exploring this case gave way to some important original insights into Cuba's capacity to perform so well in health. On the other hand they also shed light on some more problematic aspects of the health system that are rarely identified or discussed in the existing literature. Most researchers' accounts of health in Cuba seem to adopt the country's health statistics fairly uncritically as conclusive evidence of its success. Rarely is much attention paid to the measures through which these statistics are achieved or the aspects of health care that statistics fail to capture.

The main argument I present in this book is that Cuba possesses an unusually high level of popular participation and cooperation in the *implementation* of health policy. This has been achieved with the help of a longstanding government that prioritizes key health areas, and has enough political influence to compel the rest of the community to do the same. That many different institutions and sectors have maintained a long-term focus on certain health goals is itself a significant achievement to which the island owes much of its success in the health field. On the other hand, I argue that the degree of real popular participation in *decision-making* regarding health policy is minimal, which contrasts with the image of popular participation usually portrayed by the Cuban government. Political elites design and impose health policy, allowing little room for other health sector groups to contribute to or protest official decisions. This is a problem, I argue, because aspects of health care that are important to those who use the system or work within it can be neglected if they do not fit within official priorities. This research uncovered a number of problems within the Cuban health system that have been sources of frustration for patients and health workers.

The intense politicization of health in Cuba has not helped encourage participative arrangements. The regime's preoccupation with promoting a positive image of its health accomplishments, especially before the international community, has arguably lead to a fixation on statistical improvements sometimes at the expense of other aspects of health care quality. This can also have the effect of silencing discussion of the system's weaknesses; there is evidence that health workers fear political repercussions if they do not deliver statistical results or when they draw attention to problems they encounter with the system. Without effective avenues for evaluation of, as well as participation and negotiation in the shaping of health policy decisions by health sector employees and the public, certain problems in the health sector persist unaddressed, and thereby chip away at public confidence in the system. This is worrying, I argue, because it threatens the sustainability of the public health system and with it many of Cuba's most important health achievements.

That this research revealed certain areas of the Cuban health system that do not live up to its glowing reputation is not entirely surprising. No system is perfect after all. On a personal level though, these findings were somewhat challenging to accept. Having set out with extremely optimistic preconceptions and hopes based on the literature I had read, it was disheartening to admit that my findings did not entirely match my original projections. However, on both scholarly and personal levels, this process taught me a valuable lesson; to recognize the difference between my honest perception of a certain reality, and the way I would like to perceive it. In almost all subject areas related to Cuba, extreme pro and anti sentiments dominate the literature, usually making for predictable and unconstructive reading. Realizing that this was the result of researchers who allow their preconceptions, and usually ideological bias, to interfere with what is observed, I made the decision to try to avoid falling into the same trap.

Of course, it is unrealistic to expect researchers to approach Cuba (or any case) without some degree of subjectivity, preconception or bias. In my own case, the country's unusually positive health outcomes were initially a source of great interest and enthusiasm, amplified by my personal belief that quality health care should be available to all people as a human right. Here was a poor country under siege that had managed to produce better health outcomes than its entire region, including its neighboring superpower adversary! My initial research question was therefore one that made a number of positive assumptions about Cuba (especially assuming the country's statistics to be evidence of its success). Only when some of my interview material, along with personal observations during fieldwork, contrasted with my preconceptions, did I become properly aware of the potential for biases. This accompanied feelings of disappointment and disillusionment, and a sense that my critical abilities were lacking if I had been previously unable to perceive many of the less favorable subtleties—especially having visited the island twice before! Moreover, the realization that my research findings conflicted in many ways with my original hypothesis and assumptions was personally confronting as well as challenging to the research. A failure to recognize and acknowledge these sorts of biases, however, can lead to unproductive enquiries more focused on reaffirming a prior ideological position, than on genuine scholarship.

I do not profess to know all there is to know about health care in Cuba and am especially humbled by my position as an outsider—I cannot claim the same degree of familiarity with Cuban health system as those Cubans who work within it on a daily basis. However, I have tried in every respect to present this work with honesty; to describe the reality as accurately as possible, given the resources, experiences and information available to me. In doing so, my broader intention has been to contribute to discussions about Cuba that transcend the ideologically-driven, extremist arguments that tend to dominate the literature.

I remain, overall, supportive of the health achievements Cuba has made, especially given its arduous circumstances. The country's preventive arrangements, its collective prioritization of key health areas including maternal-infant health, and the improvements in public access to health services through the expansion of health facilities and the provision of free universal care are among the accomplishments that set it apart from most other countries in the developing world in the health sphere. At the same time, it is my view that the sustainability and further progress of these achievements must necessarily involve open recognition and public discussion of the weaker aspects of the health system.

This book, researched during the final years of Fidel Castro's presidency, documents the state of the health system at the end of the long era of his leadership. Cuba has recently entered a new historical phase with the resignation of Fidel and the transfer of leadership to Raúl Castro. It is yet to be seen how Cuba's health sector will fare under this new leadership, particularly after Fidel's death. The way in which the issues raised in this book are dealt with under Raúl is yet to fully unfold, but will be important in determining the future arrangements and performance of Cuba's health system.

1

Introduction and Background

Introduction

Cuba, one of the world's most globally-isolated countries with a generally poor record of economic development, has achieved exceptionally positive health indicators that are comparable with those of wealthy industrialized countries. Moreover, these outcomes have been sustained, and some improved, despite the severe external crises the country has faced including the collapse of the Soviet Union in the early 1990s and an ongoing U.S. embargo. The apparent miracle of the country's continued health improvements despite its troubled economic situation has sometimes been described as the "Cuban Paradox" (Spiegel and Yassi 2004; Dotres Martinez 2001; Birch and Norlander 2007; Field 2007). Cuba's post-1959 health achievements have won almost unanimous international praise. Glowing accounts of the country's health record have regularly appeared in academic literature from a range of disciplines, in reports from international agencies and in the Cuban and world media (Waitzkin et al. 1997; Lunday 2001; Coughlin 2005; Spiegel and Yassi 2004; Santana 1988; Feinsilver 1993; Nayeri 1995; Danielson 1981; Rodriguez et al 2008; Whiteford et al 2008). In addition, it has been frequently suggested that other countries could learn from Cuba's example (De Vos 2005; Dresang et al. 2005; Moore 2007; Yudkin et al 2008; Keon 2009; Grattan 2010). Even World Bank officials, despite a record of promoting market-led economic growth and supporting policies as the most reliable route from the problems of underdevelopment, have acknowledged some of the country's accomplishments. In 2001, World Bank President James Wolfensohn publicly congratulated the island on having done "a great job" in health and education (Climan 2001). The Bank's Vice President Jo Ritzen commended the country's

1

infant mortality and under-five mortality rates, encouraging other poor countries to study its social welfare policies. More recently, the United Nations Development Program (UNDP) praised Cuba's position in the Human Development Index (HDI)[1]; it ranked fiftieth (in 2006) amongst 177 countries around the world (Escambray Digital 2007).

Cuba achieved its health outcomes via an unconventional path that explicitly rejects the prevailing liberal development model favored by international development institutions including the International Monetary Fund (IMF) and World Bank. The liberal model has tended to view increased spending on health (seen as a natural progression from increased private investment and the GDP growth thereby expected) as the most effective means for countries to improve outcomes in social spheres generally. In Cuba, health and education and other social programs have been politically prioritized despite the country's poverty-ridden status, and even through the extreme economic crises the country has faced. Statistical outcomes indicate the country has been highly effective in implementing these political decisions, despite resource shortages.

However, since material resources alone cannot explain the country's achievements in health, there is reason to suppose more intangible elements have been involved. Although Cuba's unusual health outcomes are widely recognized and applauded, the academic literature on the subject is still somewhat limited. Most of the studies of Cuba's health system link the country's success to various health policies (including free health care, the emphasis on primary care, the expansion of health facilities and others). However, in order to fully understand these health policies, I contend that we need to know how they are designed and implemented. The arrangements for collective decision-making in the Cuban health sector are still relatively under-researched but warrant more attention given the country's apparent effectiveness in this area.

This book adopts a new approach to the puzzle of Cuba's health outcomes by drawing on findings emerging from two bodies of recent theoretical literature; those dealing with "social capital" and "state capacity." Each presents challenges to liberal conceptions of development and societal progress. The concept of social capital, which has generated widespread enthusiasm in recent decades, is fundamentally an attempt to augment the traditional conception of capital as a purely material phenomenon by drawing attention to capital's non-economic dimensions. This follows from earlier discussions of human capital and cultural capital. The essence of social capital is the recognition that societies' developmental capacities are inseparable from social relations and social structures. During the same period there has been a revival of interest in state capacity; this literature has argued that liberals and Marxists alike have underestimated the capacity for the political realm to achieve what constituents want it to do. This book employs some of these theoretical developments as a new way to understand the unusual case of Cuba's success in achieving its health goals. Drawing on elements of these literatures, it is hypothesized that Cuba's ability to improve its public health outcomes might be the result of effective public institution-building, particularly the development of formal structures permitting public participation in the processes of health policy design and implementation.

For the purposes of this project, a specific health program (the Maternal-Infant Program or PAMI) was chosen as a focal point to gain insights into the overall system. The PAMI was selected partly because it is recognized as Cuba's most prioritized program and has produced some of the country's more impressive statistical outcomes (especially maternal and infant mortality indicators). The focus on a discrete and delimited segment of the health system was also a way to permit a thorough study that nevertheless fitted within the project's scope. The empirical research for this project included a total of nine months of fieldwork in Havana. Key components of this work were qualitative interviews with 24 experts representing significant groups or institutions associated with the PAMI. These included representatives from the Ministry of Public Health, family doctors, medical specialists based at policlinics and maternity hospitals, representatives from the Federation of Cuban Women (the mass organization most directly involved with issues of maternal and infant health), social workers, teachers and researchers in the area of maternal-infant health, and employees from various other institutions linked to the program (see "List of Interviews Conducted in Cuba," pages vii-viii). The fieldwork in Havana also allowed considerable immersion, including ongoing informal conversations and personal observations, which informed the research. In addition to interview material, selected excerpts from my field notes have also been included in the book. The research also draws significantly on secondary literature related to Cuba and its health system, mostly from international sources, but also data and literature collected in Cuba. Some data has also been included from interviews conducted in Australia with Cuban expatriates in the period after my return from Cuba.

The findings of this research were unexpected in the sense that they present a significant challenge to the image of the country's health system as it is usually portrayed in both the Cuban and international literature. The qualitative research methods and specific attention to the social dimensions of the health system have led to some new explanations for the system's successful outcomes. However, they also uncovered a number of the system's weaknesses that are usually overlooked due to a common fixation on quantitative assays of population health as sole measures of the health system's quality.

Within Cuba's health sector, considerable institutional capacity has been built up through the formalization of cooperative relationships between various actors (for example, between health workers and patients, between different institutions and sectors). This, I have argued, is an aspect of social capital that is quite well-developed. The concerted and coordinated effort of these diverse participants towards common objectives has considerably added to the country's capacity to achieve national health goals. In line with this, the research found that the "state" in Cuba is in some senses fairly "embedded," particularly in its capacity to mobilize popular action to achieve health initiatives. Unfortunately, while there is a great deal of popular cooperation and participation in the *implementation* of health policy in Cuba, the contribution, either direct or indirect, of different social groups to policy design is quite underdeveloped. This lack of negotiation with social groups has indirectly produced a number of adverse consequences that detract from the quality of health care and threaten the sustainability of the country's health achievements. A summary of how each chapter develops these arguments follows.

Summary of Chapters

Chapter 2: Social Capital and State Capacity

The purpose of this chapter is to identify and explain the aspects of social capital and state capacity that will be employed in this book. Existing literatures will be examined in an attempt to find conceptual tools for approaching and understanding the Cuban case. Since social capital is still an unsettled and disputed concept, a significant part of the chapter is devoted to clarifying what is meant by social capital for the purposes of this project. This involves a critique of the prevailing treatment of social capital as "social connectedness," and a recasting of the concept more in line with the structurally-located work of Coleman and Bourdieu and in the light of earlier debates regarding the social dimensions of capital. This discussion leads into a summary of a recent revival of interest in positive theories of "the state," often rendered as the developmental capacities of the state. In view of previous academic investigations of Cuba's health system, the relevance and potential contribution of social capital and state capacity are explained. Drawing on this theoretical discussion of social capital and state capacity, the project's preliminary hypothesis and research questions and details of the research conducted in Cuba are outlined.

Chapter 3: Political Will and Cooperative Institutional Arrangements

The main aims of this chapter are to illustrate the political prioritization given to maternal-infant health in Cuba and to highlight a number of institutional characteristics of the Cuban health system that have directly improved the country's capacity to achieve its health goals. The first section provides a background explanation of the various reasons why Fidel Castro and his government maintained a prolonged commitment to population health improvements (particularly in maternal-infant health), including its humanitarian, political, and symbolic motives. The following section details the nature of interaction between health workers and the Cuban population, particularly with regard to the PAMI. The design of health provision that prescribes regular contact between health workers (especially family doctors) and every citizen in their designated catchment area is quite unique to Cuba. This interaction is sustained through routine procedures for proactive, preventive monitoring of the population to avert factors leading to maternal-infant morbidity and mortality, as well as other health problems. That family doctors are required to serve long periods living in a defined community also allows long-term doctor-patient relationships, which improve doctors' knowledge of individual cases and assists with early diagnosis of health risks. A third section details a well-developed system of inter-institutional and inter-sectoral cooperation and the various ways in which this has facilitated Cuba's effectiveness in health policy implementation. Collaboration between different health institutions allows resource sharing and thereby increased public access to limited medical equipment and supplies. That family doctors, social workers and specialists work collaboratively on each pregnancy case (including regular communication and routine information sharing) improves the detection of risk factors and the general comprehensiveness of attention to each pregnancy case from its early stages. Furthermore, the contributions of sectors outside health reduce environmental, social and other factors that can detrimentally affect health outcomes. Considering that other countries have had limited success with inter-sectoral collaboration, the high level of public and systemic compliance with state health goals in Cuba is unusual. The final section of the chapter argues that this institutional cohesion—as well as popular mobilization and compliance with often interventionist measures to improve maternal-infant health outcomes—is the result of an organizational hierarchy controlled by a politically dominant and long-standing government that exerts pressure on all other levels of the system to ensure that its health goals are met.

Chapter 4: The Limits of State Capacity and Social Capital in a Top-Down System: Exclusion and Non-Participation

As Chapter 4 explains, the various institutions of the Cuban health system operate with unusual cohesion and unity in the pursuit of clear health goals, and this has been a significant contribution to state capacity. That this cohesion is maintained is largely attributable to the Cuban government. Its political dominance in the health sector has ensured health improvements remain a priority and that health goals are clearly defined. This is one aspect of state embeddedness that seems to be well-developed in Cuba's health sector; that is, the ability of state elites to marshal widespread cooperation and participation in the implementation of health plans. It was initially hypothesized that popular participation in the health policy-making process might have been part of the explanation for this effectiveness in implementation. As is outlined in this chapter, however, the research found very little evidence of negotiation between state elites and other social groups involved (patients who use the system and professionals with technical knowledge) in the process of health policy design. Rather, central state authorities were found to retain a monopoly over decisions regarding public health goals and policies; compliance is, for the most part, imposed rather than negotiated. These paternalistic arrangements contribute to a number of adverse consequences which are outlined in this chapter. Moreover, many of these consequences counteract the government's proclaimed health goals by undermining the quality of health care and threatening the system's chances of long-term sustainability. Lack of negotiation in the policy-making process can therefore be construed as a state weakness. I argue therefore that state capacity has not been satisfactorily consolidated in Cuba. From the analysis it can be inferred that for political principles and public policy competencies to be entrusted or embedded, collective decisions need to be whole-heartedly endorsed by the populace, not merely imposed.

Chapter 5: Underground Health Care Arrangements as Temporary Solutions and Long Term Challenges to the Formal System

The Cuban health system may therefore be less unified and concerted than it outwardly appears; when disputes or contestation over health policies erupt, they are often suppressed or silenced. The lack of institutionalized processes that would allow health workers and patients to influence health decisions perpetuates problems within the system and undermines its popular support. The impossibility of responding to problems via formal arrangements can provoke underground solutions. This chapter exposes an issue that is rarely mentioned in the academic literature on Cuba's health system: the existence of informal exchange practices that operates in the shadows of official health care delivery arrangements. Since this phenomenon is linked to a larger second economy in Cuba, the chapter begins by providing some background discussion of extant knowledge and debates regarding informal economies, drawing the distinction between informality in capitalist and socialist settings. It goes on to provide a profile of the second economy in Cuba, followed by a more specific discussion of informal practices in the health sector. In light of findings in the broader literature on second economies, it is argued that informal activity in the health sector "props up" and simultaneously threatens to undermine the formal health system. I argue that the phenomenon of informalization in the health sector signifies both a loss of state legitimacy and an erosion of social capital.

Cuba's Health Achievements

As can be seen on Table 1, Cuba has comparatively low expenditure per capita on health,[2] and health indicators that are uncharacteristically positive for a poor country, often comparing closely with developed-world outcomes. For example, while it spends only US$251 per capita on health as opposed to Brazil's $597, Mexico's $582, and the United States' $5,711, Cuba's infant and under-five mortality rates are lower than to those of the United States and more than three times lower than its Latin American counterparts. The country's doctor/patient ratio of 59 doctors per 10,000 people far exceeds the United States' 26, Australia's 25, and even Sweden's 33. Skilled health personnel attend almost 100 percent of births and maternal mortality indicators are considerably lower than in most other developing countries (UNDP 2006; 2009).

Table 1
Comparative Health Indicators

	Cuba	Brazil	Mexico	Haiti	China	United States	Australia	Sweden
Infant Mortality (0-1 year per 1000 live births) 2007	5	20	19	57	19	7	5	3
Under-five Mortality Rate (per 1,000 live births) 2007	5	22	21	76	22	8	6	3
Maternal Mortality Ratio Adjusted [3] (per 100,000 live births) 2005	45	110	60	670	45	11	4	3
Births Attended by Skilled Health Personnel (%)Most recent available data 2004-2006.	100	97	94	26	98	100	100	100
Physicians (per 10,000 people) Most Recent data available 2002-2004	59	12	20	3	14	26	25	33
Life Expectancy at Birth 2007	78.5	72.2	76	61	72.9	79.1	81.4	80.8
HIV Prevalence (% Age 15-49) 2007	0.1	0.6	0.3	2.2	0.1	0.6 [4]	0.2	0.1
Tuberculosis Cases (incidence rate per 100,000 people) 2007	6.4	48	20	305.6	98.3	4.2	6.2	6
Public Health Expenditure (as % of GDP) 2003	6.3	3.4	2.9	2.9	2.0	6.8	6.4	8.0
Private Health Expenditure (as % of GDP) 2003	1.0	4.2	3.3	4.6	3.6	8.4	3.1	1.4
Health Expenditure per Capita (PPP US$) 2003	251	597	582	84	278	5,711	2,874	2,704
Per Capita Government Expenditure on Health (PPP int.$) 2006	329	367	327	65	144	3074	2097	3533
Per Capita Total Expenditure on Health 2006	363	52.1	756	96	342	6714	3122	3119

Source: United Nations Development Report (UNDP 2006 and 2009 various tables; UNSD 2009 various tables; WHOSIS 2009 various tables).

With extremely limited access to internationally traded products, Cuba has also developed many of its own versions of vaccines and pharmaceuticals from scratch. For example, it was the first country to eradicate smallpox and polio. It eliminated numerous other diseases while denied access to internationally traded products. Additionally, despite its lack of access to materials or ideas from the rest of the world, it also produced many medical innovations—for example, the world's only meningococcal B vaccine (Carr 1999; Aitsiselmi 2001).

In addition to its achievements at home, Cuba provides medical aid to a long list of other developing countries and even to some developed countries. It frequently sends teams of doctors on medical assistance programs to its Latin American neighbors and other countries and provides medical scholarships to thousands of foreign students each year. It even offers 250 full medical scholarships per year to U.S. students from underprivileged backgrounds who cannot afford to study at home (Aidi 2001; Loose 2006; Marquis 2000; Feinsilver 2006). Furthermore, Cuba has invited many patients from neighboring countries who cannot afford treatment to travel to the island and receive free medical services (Williams 2007).

These outcomes are unusual for any context of underdevelopment. In Cuba's case they have attracted particular attention, considering the conditions of material shortage typical to developing countries have been exacerbated by an ongoing U.S. embargo on the island.[5] A 1995 study by the American Association for World Health found that the impact of the embargo on Cuba included:

- "a widespread shortage of nearly all pharmaceuticals, (only 889 of the 1,297 medications available in 1991 were available, some intermittently);
- degradation of the island's water supply due to a lack of access to water treatment chemicals and spare parts, which resulted in a rise in mortality and morbidity;
- serious nutritional deficits, particularly among pregnant women, due to the ban on foodstuffs;
- constraints on the exchange of information due to travel restrictions" (Aitsiselmi 2001).

In the context of these problematic circumstances, how was it possible for Cuba to perform so well in some areas of health? This was the very general question that this project set out to answer. Cuba's case ostensibly indicates that positive health indicators are technically possible for developing nations and, more significantly, that the more crucial factors in achieving them are probably not economic ones (see also Spiegel and Yassi 2004).

As mentioned, in recent decades, efforts by international development institutions to improve health outcomes in developing countries have assumed that increasing spending on health would flow from private investment and the GDP growth that was thereby expected (World Bank 2004a). Important research recently, however, has shown that neither increased per capita income nor expenditure on health is necessarily the most effective solution. A 1999 study by Wang et al. comparing the health performances of 115 countries found that increased income per capita was not the most significant determinant of improvements in health; other factors such as the education of women played a greater role. More recent research by Anderson (2005; 2006) compares the organizational approaches of Mexican and Cuban health systems in dealing with five major infectious diseases. The study found that organisational factors played a more important role in health outcomes than the overall investment of capital in health. Cuba's more positive performance than Mexico's, despite the limited material resources of the former, seemed to result from its more equal distribution of resources through the provision of universal access to health care and its well trained health workers. Hence, according to Anderson, OECD plans for "pro-poor" policies that aim to increase private investment, and thereby resources, in developing countries to improve health outcomes, may be missing the policy target.

Disparity between Cuba's Maternal and Infant Mortality Outcomes

That Cuba has managed lower rates of maternal mortality than most other countries in its region and developing status is a significant achievement. As one study notes, the percentage by which the maternal mortality ratio decreased in Cuba for the period 1959–2004 exceeds the progress of virtually all other Latin American countries (Cabezas Cruz 2006). Nevertheless, it is worth noting that, compared with the country's infant mortality rate, which is close to that of developed countries, maternal mortality outcomes are not quite as impressive. Cuba's maternal mortality ratio is almost double that of the United States and around four times that of Australia, for example.

The following table, containing provisional data relating to the various causes of maternal deaths in Cuba, suggests multiple contributing factors. Factors typically underlying these types of deaths include high rates of sexually transmitted diseases leading to fallopian tube dysfunction and subsequent ectopic pregnancies; inefficient contraceptive use; late diagnosis of hypertensive disorders other risk factors; high rates of rheumatic heart disease leading to death from circulatory disorders; thromboembolic disease leading to deaths around the puerperium; and a host of other possible factors including the pregnant women's age, weight, levels of alcohol consumption and so on (author's personal e-mail communications with Najman and Callaway 2007).[6]

While maternal mortality rates are low by comparison with other developing countries, the fact that the outcomes are not as positive as those for infants is an anomaly worth researching. Although a detailed examination of the biomedical and other causes of this disparity is not a principal aim of this project, the findings presented here may nevertheless contribute to discussion of the issue.

Table 2
Cuba's Maternal Mortality by Causes, 2007

Causes	Rate per 100,000 live births, 2007
Direct	21.3
Ectopic pregnancy	2.7
Abortion excluding ectopic pregnancy	3.6
Complications around puerperium	8.0
Obstetric embolism	3.6
Complications related to labor and birth	1.8
Placenta related complications/disorders	0.9
Other hemorrhages	1.8
Hypertensive disorders	1.8
Other complications	0.9
Indirect	8.9
Circulatory disorders	2.7
Parasitic and infectious diseases	0.9
Anemia	0.9
Other indirect causes	4.4
Maternal Mortality	30.2

Source: Cuban Ministry of Public Health (MINSAP). 2007. *Anuario Estadistico de Salud.*

Debates Surrounding the Reliability of Cuba's Infant Mortality Rates and Other Health Statistics

Although most foreign observers accept Cuba's official data as reliable, there has been some controversy surrounding the matter (Diaz-Briquets 1986: 8). Eminent expert on the Cuban economy Carmelo Mesa Lago (1969a) was one of the first to raise critical questions relating to the validity of Cuba's post-revolutionary health statistics. In relation to the reliability of socialist countries' statistics *per se,* Mesa-Lago identifies the two main viewpoints. The majority position accepts the reliability of the available statistics, arguing that any attempt by governments of socialist countries to deliberately misrepresent findings to the outside world would be easily revealed through cross checks of data. For example data made available internationally could be compared with the data used for domestic, technical purposes. The second viewpoint is that the official statistics from socialist countries should always be viewed with skepticism, since socialist governments have a vested interest in producing positive data in order to use them as an "ideological tool in the international politico-economic struggle" (1969a: 53-54).

One point that skeptical observers reiterate is that health care in Cuba pre-1959 was not as poor as the Castro government suggests. A number of scholars have questioned the Cuban government's account of drastic improvement in health since the 1959 revolution. Mesa Lago draws attention to some inconstancies and Cuban misrepresentations of the true health situation, clearly aimed at creating an impression that outcomes had steadily and continually improved since the revolution in 1959. In relation to infant mortality, for example, he points out that Cuba's Premier declared in 1967 that the country had improved its rate from 60 deaths per thousand live births in 1958 to a 1966 rate of 37 per thousand. However, according to UN statistics Cuba's infant mortality rate was 32.3 thousand in 1957 and 33 per thousand for 1958 (1969b: 48).

Nick Eberstadt, one of the more outspoken critics of Cuba's health statistics, also argues that infant mortality was already very low in Cuba before 1959, compared with the rest of the region, pointing out that death rates actually increased in the initial years of the revolution until a rapid decline that began in the 1970s (1988: 200). Hollerback, Diaz-Briquets and Hill agree that Cuba's health system and demographic profile were advanced for the region in the years directly leading up to the revolution and that the country had comparatively low infant mortality rates. They point out, however, that the initial worsening in mortality rates in the period directly after the revolution may have been due to improvements in the system for registering deaths (a claim that Eberstadt and others refute) or a result of the high numbers of doctors who left the island immediately after the revolution (1984: 13).

According to some estimates, around one-third, approximately 2,000 in total, of Cuba's physicians fled the country between 1959 and 1965 (Mesa Lago 1969b: 68). Others have estimated that half of—including many of the country's best—physicians left during this period (Diaz-Briquets 1986: 11). As a response, the entry-levels and course durations in medical schools were reduced in order to increase graduates and replace the loss (Mesa Lago 1969b: 68; Diaz-Briquets 1986: 11). It seems likely that this caused a temporary decline in the quality of health care service in the immediate post-revolutionary period, even though medical facilities were greatly improved, particularly in rural areas. An interesting point to note is that Cuba has sent around a fifth of its doctors away on its recent medical missions to Venezuela. According to an interview with a MINSAP official, Cuba's doctor-patient ratio includes those doctors on overseas missions. The respondent estimated Cuba's total number of doctors to be 64,000, its number of family doctors 36,000, and at the time of the interview he estimated the total number of doctors in Venezuela as part of the *Misión Barrio Adentro*[7] project to be 12, 000 (author's interview with Ramirez, September 2004). Especially considering Cuba's extensive web of overseas missions, the country's doctor/patient ratio is therefore not entirely accurate as a measure of the total number of doctors working in Cuba itself.

Some critics have argued that Cuba has a history of presenting misleading statistics. According to one former mid-level official from MINSAP who defected, medical records were altered during Cuba's 1981 dengue epidemic to create an exterior impression that the government had quickly brought the epidemic under control (in Diaz-Briquets 1986: 9). Eberstadt argues that a number of other inconsistencies in the country's health statistics invite suspicion. For example, he points out that, while Cuba reported a fall in its infant mortality rates of 45 per 1000 from 1969 to 1977, rates of morbidity resulting from parasitic diseases such as acute diarrhea, chicken pox, measles and hepatitis rose in the same period (1988: 202). Further, he argues that studies by foreign demographers show some inconsistencies throughout the 1970s between official and indirect methods for calculating infant mortality. Rates from the official birth and death registration were lower than those shown by indirect methods, such as the techniques used by demographers to correct for under-reporting of deaths (1988: 2001. See also Hollerbach,

Diaz-Briquets and Hill 1984: 13). Hollerbach, Diaz-Briquets, and Hill, on the other hand, endorse the official figures based on the consistency of statistics from direct and indirect reporting methods in previous years and the absence of any evidence that death registration had deteriorated in the 1970s. If in fact reliable, figures from the late 1970s place Cuba as the country with the lowest infant mortality rate in Latin America (1984: 14).

Against the skeptics, most experts in the field affirm the validity of the statistics. An article by McGuire and Frankel (2005) that is highly critical of the commonly-held belief that Cuba's high performance in health has been specific to the post-1959 period (see also Crabb 2001: 125-136) nevertheless endorses the completeness and reliability of the country's current health statistics. Other notable authors have provided a stronger defense of the country's outcomes. Sarah Santana (1988), for example, who spent four years in Cuba working with and assessing the country's statistical system concluded that Cuban data was reliable, complete and accurate. Feinsilver (1989a: 16) has supported Santana's position. She points out that the Pan American Health Organization (PAHO) has long considered Cuba's statistics reliable. Further, she argues that, unlike the Soviet Union that ceased to print its infant mortality and other statistics in order to hide negative trends, Cuba has not overtly concealed any unfavorable findings (1989b: 150). Similarly, Diaz-Briquets argues that the credibility of Cuba's reporting is strengthened by the fact that fluctuations in statistical outcomes have usually been reported honestly. For example, the government did not conceal the rise in infant mortality that occurred in 1985 (1986: 10).

It should be noted also that the controversial global position Cuba occupies undoubtedly has some influence on the way analysts approach the case. On the one hand it is arguable that the country's ideological isolation is itself an incentive for Cuban authorities to misrepresent health outcomes; in other words, as a means for defending the country's image before the international community. Some have argued that all socialist countries' statistics should be treated with caution for this reason. However, it should be acknowledged that deliberate misrepresentation of figures has occurred in many contexts other than socialist countries. Crabb (2001), for example, while critical of the Castro government's representation of health statistics, also points out that health was always a highly politicized domain in Cuba, even long before Castro.

> [E]ach political faction in Cuba (aware of the necessity of engineering support of the United States) took great pains to generate a positive image of its accomplish-

ments. Both office-holders and out-of-power coalitions tried to silence their critics by generating extensive political propaganda detailing the virtues of his (or his party's) administration and criticizing his rivals for being "undemocratic" and "corrupt." One of the most consistent themes in these propaganda wars was health and sanitation. Newly empowered caudillos took care to produce favourable health statistics, ostensibly reflecting great progress and humanitarian achievement (Crabb 2001: 111).

It is also worth bearing in mind that no country's health statistics are completely reliable. Registration of health-related cases is rarely if ever comprehensive; methods and guidelines for calculating (for example infant deaths) can vary. In light of this, when assessing the reliability of a country's health statistics, the question should really always be "To what *extent* are the figures reliable?", rather than "Are the figures reliable or unreliable?" It is certainly arguable that, as a result of its socialist and isolated position, any inconsistencies in Cuba's statistics are likely to attract more scrutiny and skepticism than would the inconsistencies of less-controversial cases. Ultimately, though, as both critics and supporters of Cuba's health system have acknowledged, no definitive conclusions can be reached by foreign researchers, especially given the restrictions they face when conducting research in Cuba.

This project began as a study of Cuba's positive aggregate health indicators, focusing especially on maternal-infant health improvements. Before conducting fieldwork in Cuba, my perspective on these outcomes was informed mainly by official data and secondary literature on Cuban health, most of which either assumes or accepts reliability of official data. As the research progressed, I became more aware of the politicized nature of health in Cuba and of the concerns some researchers have expressed that Cuban authorities may have reason to deliberately misrepresent outcomes. My acceptance of the statistical outcomes as measures of the country's success has changed somewhat, especially after the fieldwork process revealed aspects of health care quality that statistics do not seem to capture. Therefore, through the research process, the project evolved to focus more generally on health outcomes without assuming them to be entirely positive.

Conducting Health Research in Post-Revolutionary Cuba

As one of the world's few remaining "socialist" states, Cuba attracts a good deal of attention from scholars around the world. Its longevity as a self-proclaimed socialist nation and resulting global distinctiveness, its apparent success in some key areas of social development (via this unconventional path), and its problematic relationship with the United States are particularly interesting from a political science perspective.

However, despite its appeal as a subject of study, conducting research in Cuba is fraught with obstacles, many of which are well-concealed and invisible to foreign researchers, even when perceived first-hand.

At the outset, one of these challenges is navigating the literature. Especially in the earlier stages of research, filtering through the literature to identify key, worthwhile publications is difficult. For the researcher starting out with relatively little knowledge of the case, part of the difficulty is precisely distinguishing over-optimistic or pessimistic rhetoric from worthwhile research. Of the voluminous material written about Cuba, much is polarized between extreme pro- and anti-Castro positions; accordingly much is unconstructive. Hardline critics of the regime frequently direct attention to the country's negative human rights record, its lack of "freedom" and "democracy" without unpacking these concepts or comparing with other contexts, and assuming that the only political model compatible with real freedom is a U.S.-style liberal democracy (for example, Blum 2005). Many criticize the island's poverty and shortage by comparison with developed countries rather than in the context of its region and developing status. On the other hand, much of the literature produced by uncompromising Cuba supporters is equally unconstructive, painting a romantically glowing picture of the revolution's history and contemporary reality and presenting rationalized justifications for any "negative" aspects of the country's political or social reality. Even for researchers with origins outside the United States and Cuba, a moderate position can meet with hostility from both poles. Even constructive and substantiated criticism of "the revolution" can attract aggressively defensive responses from the more radical Cuba enthusiasts, who sometimes interpret criticism as evidence of "right wing bias," support for the U.S. trade embargo, endorsement of economic liberalization, and a lack of concern with social justice. Expressions of support for any aspect of the Cuban system can attract similarly one-dimensional assumptions regarding one's political persuasion. The polarization of debate is regularly reiterated when authors depict a good/bad dichotomy between Cuba and the United States, highlighting the vices of one case as a means for bolstering the virtues of the other and *vice versa*. As mentioned, criticism of the undemocratic aspects of the Cuban system is regularly treated as conclusive evidence that the country needs a market economy and U.S.-style democracy (for example, *Contacto Magazine* 2007). On the other hand, supporters of Cuba often point a finger at the U.S. democratic model's inadequacies to reinforce claims that "real" democracy has been achieved in Cuba (for example, Anderson 2007).

Many researchers embark on research in Cuba with an already firmly-set ideological position, proceeding to gather evidence that supports this position—a methodologically unsound approach for any research project. If one sets out on a mission to find positive aspects in any society, one is sure to find them; but this approach invariably distorts the accuracy of research findings. The following excerpt from a 1969 publication by prominent expert on the Cuban economy, Carmelo Mesa Lago, is still relevant today.

> After a decade of revolution, Cuba is more than an open question to be answered, an experiment to be observed. It has become an exciting research topic which appeals to social scientists throughout the world. Yet several problems have obstructed the scholar in his research on Cuba and its revolution.... Even where travel barriers are overcome, free movement and inquiry are not always possible. The government's screening of visitors to Cuba introduces another problem, i.e., the ideological bias of the outsider has often been a distorting factor in the search for truth. In a sizeable number of cases, articles and books written by the visitor or observer are frustrating: either the author has been limited in his information and therefore does not present a total picture of the subject in question, or he is biased either in favor of or against the socialist regime of the island, and has allowed this to interfere with an accurate presentation of the facts (Mesa Lago 1969a: 53).

Although the same can be said of extremist critics of the island, there is a peculiar militancy with which many sympathetic foreign (especially Western) observers attach themselves to the Cuban revolution. The island has long been the darling of the European left which, as Cornwell (2006) points out, is due to a number of factors. Fidel Castro's personal charisma has played some role, including his legendary image as leader of the revolution in connection with other symbolic figures such as Ernesto "Che" Guevara. Moreover, Cuba's hostile bilateral relations with the United States place it in a unique position to publicly criticize U.S. policy (by contrast with other Latin American nations that are constrained by dependence on U.S. aid and trade relations). As a result the country is an icon of anti-Americanism and anti-imperialism, a position that won increasing support in the climate of widespread global discontent during the years of George W. Bush's administration. Coupled with the failure of liberal economic reforms throughout the developing world in recent decades, this is one possible explanation for the enthusiasm with which many latch on to Cuba:[8] the country is taken to represent an alternative to Western society and the liberal development model. However, the problem with this approach is that it frequently leads to a partial blindness on the part of the observer, who perceives only positive evidence while conveniently overlooking (either consciously or subconsciously) unfavorable aspects of Cuban society. Although more extreme critics of left wing intellectuals' enthusiasm for socialist countries have referred to Lenin's well-known term "useful idiots"[9] (see Charen 2003), the reality is that many of the foreign observers who adopt an uncritical approach to Cuba are otherwise perceptive and experienced intellectuals.

One explanation for this puzzling inconsistency can be found in Paul Hollander's *Political Pilgrims,* which examines Western researchers' perspectives on communist countries throughout the period from 1928-1978. According to Hollander, many of these researchers appeared to adopt overly idealistic approaches towards foreign socialist countries, which contrasted with a highly critical approach towards their own societies. Hollander (himself an escapee of communist Hungary) argues that the researchers' heightened enthusiasm for communist countries was often linked to dissatisfaction with or estrangement from society at home. Countries perceived as "revolutionary" were held up as examples of viable alternatives that highlighted the problems of their own societies (Hollander 1981: ix). In the following passage, the author describes the double standards he perceived as associated with many Western researchers' perspectives on the communist countries they visited.

> Why was it that sensitive, insightful, and critical intellectuals found societies like the USSR under Stalin, China under Mao, and Cuba under Castro so appealing—their defects so easy to ignore (or, if observed, to excuse)—and so strikingly superior to their own societies?... How was it possible for many of them to have visited these societies often at their most oppressive historical moments (as was clearly the case of the USSR in the 1930s and China during the Cultural Revolution) and yet *not* notice their oppressiveness? Or, if they did, what psychological and ideological mechanisms enabled them to take a tolerant view? One's sense of bewilderment deepens, since it is usually taken for granted that a key attribute of intellectuals is a keenly critical mind, fine tuned to every contradiction, injustice, and flaw of the social world. ... Not surprisingly, my inquiry found that alienation from one's own society and susceptibility to the attractions, real or imagined, of others are very closely linked (Hollander 1981: 5-7).

For the ideologically convinced researcher, there can be an emotional resistance to acknowledging unfavorable findings of the revolutionary society in question; constructing rational justifications can be less confronting than compromising one's position. As Hollander argues, "The recognition that other social systems represent little or no improvement to one's own dilutes moral outrage; if social injustices and defects are endemic and discernible even in "new" revolutionary societies, it becomes difficult to sustain an impassioned criticism of one's own" (1981: 9).

While a commitment to research honesty is paramount to producing constructive work, in Cuba researchers have more to contend with than their own ideological biases. External factors, such as the role of the Cuban government, can also influence findings. The ability for foreign researchers to conduct genuine academic inquiry in Cuba is limited by a number of factors. The more obvious of these are travel and visa restrictions. For U.S. researchers, this is particularly complicated due to U.S. sanctions on Cuba. For those from other parts of the world, the major obstacles are within Cuba. Research of any kind—including interviews and visits to libraries—can only be legally conducted on a research visa. Obtaining one of these requires the work to be officially overseen by a Cuban institution. This in itself can act as a screening process, whereby the employees of the Cuban institution informally verify that the research project portrays Cuba in a positive light before approving the research project. Furthermore, once the research visa is issued, written permissions from the overseeing institution (and often also from the appropriate ministry) are required in order to visit librar- ies, hospitals and other centers. In this way, the Cuban institution and ministries are usually able to keep track of the researcher's movements and can also influence where he or she goes to seek information. In the following passage from her doctoral dissertation based on anthropologi- cal research exploring Cuba's health system, Mary Katherine Crabb also reflects this point.

> [Researching] health and medicine in Cuba following the revolution of 1959 is seriously hampered by the powerful ideological controls put in place by the social- ist regime. These controls are uniquely problematic in that they are pervasive and often covert. In fact, many researchers have described spending months conducting fieldwork, only to discover later on that their results had been covertly manipulated by the authorities in order to make sure that research findings would conform to the ideological mandate of the regime (Crabb 2001: 242).

It is fairly common for researchers to experience various forms of harassment or interference from Cuban officials.[10] However, many refrain from public criticism of such intrusion for fear of retribution from authorities, who have been known to punish informants or deny researchers access to research sites (Hirschfeld 2007: 100-101).

An awareness of cultural context, particularly relating to conversations about the regime, is an important prerequisite to conducting research interviews in Cuba. Interviewing on subjects of even remote political sensitivity can be met with guardedness from respondents, especially questions that could appear critical or judgmental of the regime. Dual discourses pervade virtually any political discussion in Cuba, and this can sometimes obscure intended meanings. It can require a period of immersion in Cuba before an outside researcher perceives the general atmosphere surrounding criticism of the regime. In my own case, while this was not apparent to me in my first months on the island, I gradually became aware of a degree of paranoia affecting many Cubans in relation to discussing Fidel Castro or the system generally. As time went by, I too found myself afflicted by the same paranoia. While people were often more open in the relative privacy of their homes, even there most criticism was expressed in codes. For example, rather than stating Fidel Castro's name, most people would make a gesture under their chin miming the shape of a beard, often while their eyes darted about to assess who was watching or listening, or refer to him with names like *"El Máximo"* or *"El Señor."* On some occasions, people who openly expressed criticism in private, warned me that it was best not to discuss these issues in public (see also McGeough 2005, 22) and I witnessed that the face they themselves displayed in their workplace and in public was very different from when they were at home.[11]

In her dissertation, Crabb describes how, for her too, "it became painfully apparent that a dual system of discourse pervades Cuba ... even "private" conversations can be conducted cryptically, with a special vocabulary used to blur meanings and render talk of politically sensitive topics unintelligible" (2001, 17). Like my project, Crabb's focused on the country's health system. In a narrative I could identify with, she describes how the intentions of her research at the outset were largely to explore and publicize Cuba's successes, however throughout her fieldwork she experienced periods of disillusionment at finding that many aspects of the health system did not seem as positive as she had expected. More uncomfortable than disillusionment, though, was the subsequent realization that she did not feel free to openly and publicly discuss these more unfavorable findings. Within a broader discussion of the fear and paranoia researchers can experience in Cuba, Crabb recounts an incident during her fieldwork where two members of *"la Juventud"* (a Cuban communist youth organization) arrived mysteriously at her door requesting with "aggressively friendly smiles" that she accompany them for a "cultural interchange." They drove her to a location where they proceeded to question her on a range of issues, particularly her political views.

[The member of the communist youth] wanted to know everything about how I happened to come to Cuba. Who did I know in Atlanta? Who were my contacts in Havana? Who had sent me? What were my motives in coming to Cuba? What was I going to do with the data I was collecting? I answered these questions with my usual research spiel, intentionally framing all of my answers to reflect the positive international reputation of the Cuban health care system (criticizing anything, under the circumstances, seemed unwise).... Several days later, I had an appointment with a friend at the University who had been somewhat indirectly connected with my project. I had always instinctively trusted him, and since we were alone at the meeting I hesitantly mentioned my recent encounter with State Security. There was no mistaking the momentary flash of terror in his eyes. *"So they got you?"* he whispered incredulously, so low to be practically inaudible. I looked back at him, suddenly mute with fear myself. It was the first time I had ever heard anyone speak of "Them".... My friend quickly recovered his composure, then made a gesture that indicated it would be unwise to talk of such things in the current surroundings... He then suggested we arrange to meet "by accident" in a public spot downtown several days later where we could presumably talk for a few minutes without raising suspicions.... [There is a] psychological deterioration that these kinds of encounters with the Cuban State Security have been known to provoke. There is something vaguely terrifying about this kind of invisible surveillance—one feels oneself persecuted by imaginary beings (2001, 254-265).

The fact that my project (as with Crabb's) initially set out to explore Cuba's *successes* (in my case, particularly its low infant and maternal mortality rates) undoubtedly facilitated my relatively easy entry to the island for research purposes. Although I didn't realize it at the time, in retrospect it seems less likely that Cuban institutions would have authorized my research had it been focused on some of the country's more unfavorable aspects. Many researchers, even some who have written very *uncritical* work on Cuba, have experienced extreme hostility from Cuban state security (including being banned from further research on the island) once they were perceived to be expressing even mild criticism of the revolution. Hirschfeld[12] outlines a number of these cases in her book, *Health, Politics and Revolution in Cuba since 1898* (2007). The prominent anthropologist Oscar Lewis, for example, began a research project in Cuba in the 1970s at the personal invitation of Fidel Castro. Subsequently, "authorities abruptly revoked his research permission, expelled him from the country, denounced him as a "counterrevolutionary," and arrested at least one of his informants who criticized the regime" (Hirschfeld 2007: 100. See also Lewis, Lewis and Rigdon 1977: vii-xxx). Hirschfeld also provides an account of the difficult no-win dilemma researchers commonly face following fieldwork in Cuba. This is a choice between self-censoring criticism to maintain friendly relations with the island (thereby misleading readers) or presenting both negative and positive findings openly with the risk of jeopardizing the possibility of returning to conduct further research in the future. The latter option also carries risks for interviewees, hence why I have coded the names of respondents to maintain their anonymity.

While my project primarily sought lessons from some of Cuba's positive health achievements, there were of course critical questions that needed to be addressed. I soon discovered that these were best treated with care. There was a clear sense in many of the interviews (especially the formally arranged ones) that the respondent wanted to verify that I was "on Cuba's side" before agreeing to the interview. Aside from the customary information provided about the research project, there was a usual process I had to undergo at the beginning of most interviews of assuring the respondent that a Cuban institution was supporting my project, showing an official letter from my supporting institution and generally demonstrating it was "safe" to be interviewed by me.

It was usually quite easy to gauge from the beginning of an interview how receptive the person would be to critical questions. In most cases, questions that were unfavorable to the regime had to be phrased in a highly cautious and non-aggressive way if they were to result in any kind of cooperation and constructive response. A number of interviewees simply stuck to a strict "party line" and ran off a seemingly rote-learned monologue I had already heard repeatedly, even using the same phrases in many cases,[13] while others were more forthright and constructive in their responses. After the first few interviews, it became fairly clear to me what type of "speak" the respondent was using. In a few cases, interviewees would refrain from saying anything controversial during the "official" interview, but then spoke more freely to me of their opinions once the tape recorder was turned off. In one case, for example, when I asked a doctor whether his US$20 a month salary was sufficient for him to live on, he became very defensive and refused to answer, saying the question was not relevant. Once I turned the tape off, however, he openly told me of his economic struggles and the hardship experienced as a result of rapidly increasing living costs and a salary that had not been adjusted for some years. Overall, the point of this discussion is to illustrate that an awareness of the peculiarities of the research context, such as those outlined here, is important when conducting research into the Cuban health system, as well as any aspect of Cuban (or any other) society.

The Structure and Development of Cuba's Health System

What follows is a general overview of the Cuban health system's structure. Cuba has maintained a state-funded public health system with universal and free access to health care since shortly after its 1959 revolution. As shown in Table 3, the system is organized into three basic levels (national or directing level, provincial or intermediate level and municipal level) (Mario Bravo 1998, 16).

Table 3
Cuban National Health System

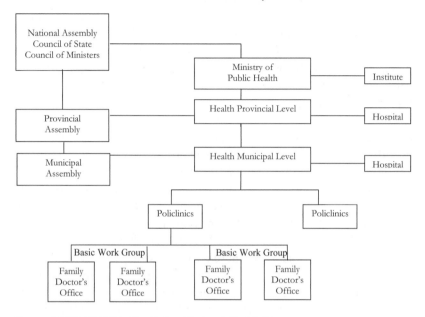

Source: MINSAP. 2004. *The Cuban National Health System.*

Ernesto Mario Bravo[14] provides some historical perspective from a Cuban point of view in his book *Development within Underdevelopment*, explaining that the process of establishing the health system in Cuba after 1959 took place in the following three stages:

- foundation (1960s)
- consolidation (1970s)
- takeoff (1980s)

In the *foundation* stage, private hospitals and pharmaceutical companies were nationalized, admissions to medical schools were increased, costs of medicine were lowered, new medical institutions were established (with particular attention the creation of a rural medical service) and medical coverage was made universal (Cole 1998, 16). The *consolidation* stage focused on improving work methods and the quality of medical training. New policies were also implemented including the establishment of policlinic program that would ensure all patients saw the same doctor, thereby improving doctors' knowledge of patients and their environment (Sixto 2002). In 1982, during the *takeoff* period, Cuba announced that it intended to become a world medical power. This period saw the beginnings of biomedical research in Cuba. Frustrated with the cost and inefficiency of the former Soviet style health system, the Cuban government embarked on a complete restructuring to focus on primary care in the early 1980s and the further expansion of medical coverage for the population through the "Family Doctor Program" (Dotres Martinez 2001).

After the collapse of the Soviet Union in 1991 and breakdown of the Council for Mutual Economic Assistance (COMECON), Cuba quickly entered a period of extreme and prolonged economic crisis and a program for crisis management referred to as the "Special Period in Time of Peace." The disappearance of favorable trade relations with COMECON countries and Soviet aid, exacerbated by the strengthening of the U.S. embargo with the introduction of the Torricelli Act of 1992 and the Helms-Burton Act of 1996 forced Cuba to re-enter global markets, meaning drastically increased prices and limited availability of exports. This led to a GDP decrease of over 35 percent with an 88 percent contraction of imports, which eased later in the decade but GDP was still below 1989 levels in 2000 (Sixto 2002: 328; Carranza Valdes and Valdes Paz 2004; Mesa Lago 1998: 858). Cuba began a series of reforms to survive the crisis, most notably including the opening up to foreign trade, introduction of tourism, legalization of foreign currency (first U.S. dollar, now only a convertible peso) and the legalization of some micro-enterprises. While at the end of the 1990s Cuba was one of the world's most egalitarian societies in terms of income distribution, the reforms of the 1990s generated increasing inequalities, especially between those with and without access to U.S. dollars (Mesa Lago 1998).

As with other sectors, the health sector was affected by the severe shortages during the crisis. Cuba had previously relied on the Soviet Union to supply materials for 85 percent of drugs consumed in Cuba and its collapse led to a shortage of around 300 medicines and a dramatic drop in importations of medical equipment (Sixto 2002: 333). From 1990 to 1996 the country's importations of medical and pharmaceutical products dropped from US$55 million to US$18 million (Brotherton 2005). Shortages in medicines and equipment were exacerbated by more general deterioration of infrastructure. Worsening standards of sanitation and access to potable water saw the increase of some contagious diseases such as tuberculosis, acute diarrhea and hepatitis, but these improved again by the end of the decade (Sixto 2002; Anderson 2002; PAHO 2001). Further, the reduced food production and imports led to a decline in quantity and quality of nutrition for the population that had a negative health impact, the most notable case being an epidemic of neuropathy beginning in 1992 affected mainly by dietary deficiencies (PAHO 2001; Brotherton 2005).

Nevertheless, despite the crisis and modest economic liberalizations, throughout the 1990s the government continued to prioritize the key social areas that have defined its socialist project, notably health and education (Carranza Valdes and Valdes Paz 2004; Spiegel and Yassi 2004; Anderson 2002; ECLAC 2004). Paradoxically, despite the compromises to country's ability to provide health care during the crisis period, most of its basic indicators remained the same or improved. Most notably, infant mortality decreased overall throughout the 1990s as did maternal mortality, and life expectancy increased (Carranza Valdes and Valdes Paz 2004; Brotherton 2005; PAHO 2001; Chelala 1998).

Primary Care: Family Doctor and Nurse Teams

The Family Doctor Program involves a team of a doctor and a nurse living in a specific community and servicing approximately 140 families or 700 people. Its design was highly innovative in its focus on preventive medicine and was the first of its kind internationally (Eckstein 1994: 131). According to one Cuban medical specialist (author's interview with Almieda, August 2004), the program emerged from an idea of Fidel Castro's. The concept was first put into practice with one experimental group in the municipality of Lauto, where the resulting health outcomes were so positive that the program went on to be generalized. The program was launched in the mid-1980s and by the end of that decade there were around ten thousand family doctors set up throughout the island. The goal was to bring medical services to the people, making it less likely that people would avoid visiting the doctor (Oppenheimer 1993: 159). All Cuban doctors now begin as family doctors and either continue in that position or move on to undertake a specialization.

The family doctor is officially the first port of call for patients, after which follows a highly coordinated system of referrals depending on the need for specialized care. Family doctors live at the same location where they work (the state provides this surgery/residence). Combined with the fact that doctors serve such small communities, this means that people's local doctor's surgery is rarely further than walking distance from their home. Health care services are therefore highly accessible.

Most preventive procedures, such as checkups, pap smears, breast examinations, some injections and so on are carried out at this local level. The equipment and facilities in a family doctor's surgery are very limited but in recent years some changes have been made to bring resources closer to the population (author's interview with Ramirez, September 2004). Nonetheless, doctors have a wide network of support facilities including referral centers, policlinics, hospitals, and laboratories.

In most cases, when a patient from a family doctor's community is referred to hospital or another health institution, the doctor is required to travel to the hospital (except where provincial and national hospitals are out of the local area) to speak in person with specialists and coordinate appropriate inpatient services. Family doctors also closely follow the case thereafter ensuring that records are kept and treatment is continued. Even in emergency cases when patients bypass the family doctor's office and go directly to a hospital emergency department, the staff there are usually expected to contact the patient's family doctor to arrange follow ups (Waitzkin et al. 1997). Hence, while family doctors serve relatively small communities, they have a high level of responsibility, as will be elaborated in Chapter 3.

The Maternal-Infant Health Program (PAMI)

Cuba's PAMI was originally conceived and designed by a small group of doctors in the Ministry for Public Health (MINSAP) (author's interview with Ramirez, September 2004). The written program states that the PAMI's goal is to "contribute to elevating the level of health of the population through prevention, promotion, protection and recovery of pregnant women and children, implemented by the National Health System in coordination with the rest of the state's institutions, mass organizations and the active participation of the community" (Leonard Castillo, Ermeso Rivera, and Sosa Marín 1985: 1).

The provision of medical attention in Cuba is organized into programs based on high-risk groups. Aside from the Maternal-Infant Program, these include the Program for Attention to Infectious Diseases, Program for Attention to Non-infectious Diseases and Program for Attention to the Elderly (these are the four most prioritized programs) (CEDISAP 2001). According to respondents interviewed in Cuba, the Maternal-Infant Program (PAMI) is given precedence over all Cuba's other health programs (author's interviews with Blanco 2004; Castillo 2004; Molinero 2004). A number of doctors attested in interviews that during inspections of family doctors' offices, the closest attention is always paid to ensuring all pregnancies are closely monitored (author's interviews with Castillo 2004; Herrera 2004).[15]

Among the different programs, the PAMI is also the most successful, to judge from the reduction of maternal and infant mortality figures. It therefore seemed the most appropriate focus for a study of the factors important to the achievement of positive health outcomes. Moreover, with approximately half a million women dying globally each year (around one death every minute) from preventable problems related to pregnancy and childbirth (WHO 2004a),[16] this choice of focus also reflects an awareness of the urgent need for attention to the issue of maternal-infant health in developing countries. While there has been extensive biomedical research into the causes of mortality and morbidity related to childbirth, there is still little understanding of the links between these individual-level factors and broader social, political and economic factors (Janes and Chuluundorj 2004).

While there is clearly a connection between poverty and maternal and infant mortality rates, and the situation is most critical in developing countries, these indicators have been shown to vary considerably independently of economic resources.

Most maternal deaths do occur in poor countries, and it is well known that poor countries are also the ones with the highest maternal mortality rates. In analogy to the link between poverty and infant mortality the relation poverty-maternal mortality has become part of common wisdom. This being said, there are considerable differences, even among countries that carry similar burdens of poverty, and much of this seems related to poverty constrained access to care.... The good news is that even in poor countries health services can make a difference ... the bad news is that resource mobilisation alone, however necessary, is not enough (De Brouwere and Van Lerberghe 2001, 2-4).

Table 4
Progression of Cuba's Infant Mortality Indicators

	1980	1985	1990	1995	2000	2001	2002	2003	2004	2005*
Infant Mortality (per 1000 live births)	19.6	16.5	10.7	9.4	7.2	6.2	6.5	6.3	5.8	6.2

* provisional

Source: MINSAP (2007). Various Tables.

Given that Cuba has managed its outcomes on the basis of limited internal economic resources and sustained external hostility, the case would seem to support these authors' observations that countries' capacity to devote material resources to maternal-infant health is not the only factor determining mortality outcomes. Therefore, in this work I look beyond material resources to explore some of the non-economic factors that played a role in the improvement of maternal-infant health outcomes in Cuba. I first build a theoretical framework for approaching this task, drawing upon findings in the literature on social capital and state capacity.

Notes

1. The HDI is a composite index that was adopted in 1993 by the United Nations Development Program as part of its annual Human Development Report. The index measures countries' achievements in three basic dimensions of human development: a long and healthy life, education, and a decent standard of living (UNDP 2006).
2. In its World Development Report 2004, the World Bank argues that Cuba's health system is expensive. "Cuba spends substantially more of its gross domestic product on health than other Latin American Countries: 6.6 percent in 2002," the report points out. Indeed Cuba's expenditure as a percentage of GDP (although not as an absolute amount) is greater than most other Latin countries for public health. When private health expenditure is added, however, most countries spend a larger proportion of GDP on health overall than Cuba does.
3. This ratio for maternal mortality is adjusted to account for problems such as mis-classifications and underreporting
4. Figure for 2003.
5. The U.S. embargo on Cuba that began in the early 1960s is the only embargo in recent history that explicitly includes food and medicine (Aitsiselmi 2001).
6. These were raised in a general sense only as examples of possible factors contributing to the different causes of maternal death listed.
7. A social program introduced by the Chávez government in 2003 that aims to provide free public health services to the Venezuelan population.
8. The Latin American left has tended to take an ambivalent approach to the Cuban case. Despite a widespread perception since the 1960s that revolutionary ideals had been betrayed in Cuba, "there was a reluctance to criticize the Revolution lest this gave succour to the United States' ongoing onslaught against radical movements and their demands for social justice in the Americas" (Lievesley 2005). Interestingly, a poll of 18 Latin American nations by Latinobarometro grouped George W. Bush, Fidel Castro and Hugo Chávez together as unpopular leaders (Hennigan 2007).
9. The term "useful idiots" was coined to describe Western travelers who gave unrealistically glowing reports based on visits to the Soviet Union.
10. On a number of occasions I heard first hand accounts of hostility to and censorship of criticism at international conferences.
11. In *Domination and the Arts of Resistance: Hidden Transcripts* (1990), James C. Scott provides an enlightening perspective on this type of disparity between official and unofficial discourse resulting from unequal power relations. "Every subordinate group creates, out of its ordeal, a "hidden transcript" that represents a critique of

power spoken behind the back of the dominant ... the process of domination generates a hegemonic public conduct and a backstage discourse consisting of what cannot be spoken in the face of power" (1990, xii).

12. Formerly Crabb.

13. Yin (1994: 85) recommends special attention and extra probing in such cases, which he describes as interviewees "corroborating one another but in a conspiratorial way."

14. Bravo has taught biochemistry at Havana's College of Medical Sciences since 1963 and has been closely involved with the development of Cuba's health system.

15. Family doctors have a minimum of twelve checkups with women throughout a pregnancy (MINSAP 2004), and some of those checkups are conducted in the pregnant woman's home.

16. De Brouwere and Van Lerberghe point out that abortion-related complications account for around 15 percent of maternal deaths (2001). Abortion is free and legal in Cuba.

2

Social Capital and State Capacity

Social Capital

"Social capital" as a concept is potentially one of the most radical developments in recent social science because it promises to overturn conventional notions of socioeconomic development. Therefore this chapter is intended to elucidate some of the factors affecting societies' developmental capacities. Social capital in its contemporary incarnation emerged in the social sciences, but went on to generate widespread enthusiasm and discussion across a broad range of disciplines. This includes, predictably, its re-incorporation into quite conventional discourse. Social capital has been characterized in innumerable ways (as networks, norms, trust, cooperation, reciprocity, institutions, voluntary association) and claims have been made that it contributes to all kinds of positive outcomes, including better health and education, economic growth, and more effective political systems (Edwards 2006: 21; Cullen and Whiteford 2001: 4; Fukuyama 1999, 1995; Poverty Net 2004; Putnam 2000; Coleman 1988; Knack 1997; Whiteley 2000; Kawachi, Kennedy and Loochner 1997; OECD 2001; Fukuyama 2001; Kawachi et al. 1997; Newton 1997; Putnam 1995). Perhaps due to a combination of its definitional haziness and an uncritical perception that it is a "good thing," the concept has also been used instrumentally to advance diverse political agendas. Varied interpretations mean that the mechanisms by which social capital is beneficial for health are disputed (Edwards 2006: 22; Baum 1999). The disparity in definitions and interpretations has only increased confusion about what social capital is, leading some to dispute its usefulness in social science (Scanlon 2004a; Ponthieux 2004). Despite the unsettled literature though, the essential lesson from the re-discovery of social capital is still a valuable one. It points out that "capital" has a social dimension.

This chapter begins by providing a critique of those prevailing approaches to social capital that treat "social connectedness" as the key to a society's capacity to produce desired development outcomes. It goes on to revisit earlier debates regarding the social dimension of capital and re-examines the structurally-located approaches of Coleman and Bourdieu, who were the first to reintroduce social capital into academic discussion. These authors are regularly cited in the more recent social capital literature but the more important implications of their work are often overlooked. The discussion in this chapter will aim to extract from the literature a more meaningful definition of social capital which, alongside compatible theoretical developments in recent literature on state capacity, will form the basis for an hypothesis that can be operationalized in the Cuban case as a way of explaining the country's unusual health outcomes.

The emergence of interest in social capital followed a series of re-conceptualizations in recent decades, among these human capital and cultural capital, aimed at improving traditional economic model by incorporating non-economic factors into the understanding of societies' developmental capacities (Edwards and Foley 1998a, 128; Portes 1998). These attempts aimed to amend previous conceptions of capital as a purely material phenomenon by adding new non-material categories. The importance of social capital's contribution was the recognition that capital is in fact inseparable from social relations and social structures (Fine 2001, 33; Bourdieu 1986). Broadly speaking, the concept refers to the non-material, social dimension of capital; it draws attention to the aspects of societies' wealth that arise from relations between people.

The recognition of social capital can be traced back at least as far as classical works such as Alexis de Tocqueville's *Democracy in America,* Durkheim's *The Division of Labour in Society* and (by inference) Marx's *Capital,* however its recent rejuvenation began with the work of French sociologist Pierre Bourdieu (1986). Bourdieu's discussion of cultural and social forms of capital was based on his recognition that it is "impossible to account for the structure and functioning of the social world unless one reintroduces capital in all its forms and not solely in the one form recognized by [mainstream] economic theory" (1986: 242). Bourdieu rejected the narrowly-defined liberal conception of capital as material capital generated through self-interested mercantile exchange oriented towards profit maximization. Mercantile exchange is just one form of exchange, he argued, but is not a complete explanation for the structure of the social world or the creation of capital. For Bourdieu social capital is "the aggregate of the actual or potential resources which are linked to possession of a durable network of more or less institutionalized relationships of mutual acquaintance and recognition." While social capital cannot be measured as or reduced to a material resource, it is inextricably linked to economic capital (1986: 248).

Soon after, in the English-speaking world, sociologist James S. Coleman reignited discussion of the concept when he published "Social Capital in the Creation of Human Capital" (1988). While accepting the aspect of economic theory that sees individuals as capable of rational, purposeful action, Coleman employed the concept of social capital as a way to use "the paradigm of rational action but without the assumption of atomistic elements stripped of social relationships" (1988: 118). For Coleman, social capital "inheres in the structure of relations between actors and among actors"; it belongs to a group and benefits individual members of the group, but cannot be solely owned or possessed by an individual (1988: 98).

> Like other forms of capital, social capital is productive, making possible the achievement of certain ends that in its absence would not be possible…. [T]he kinds of social structures that make possible social norms and sanctions that enforce them do not benefit primarily the person or persons whose efforts would be necessary to bring them about, but benefit all those who are part of such a structure (1988: 98-116).

Coleman examined the concept mainly in light of the social structures in a family or community that contribute to the creation of human capital. His work illustrates ways in which individuals and communities draw upon resources other than economic ones to facilitate action. He mentions obligations, expectations, information channels, and norms and effective sanctions as examples of social capital.

More recently Robert Putnam launched a new wave of debate when he argued there had been an erosion of social capital in the United States. His general argument in *Bowling Alone: The Collapse and Revival of American Community* (2000) is that populations engaged in voluntary association and social networks are likely to have a higher level of generalized social trust, which contributes to a better working democracy and greater efficacy in collective decision-making (see also Putnam, Leonardi and Nanetti 1994), and that this type of civic engagement is worryingly decreasing in the United States. Putnam measures five dimensions of social capital (community or organizational life, engagement in public affairs, community volunteerism, informal sociability, and social trust). For him the main factor was voluntary civic engagement. Under each of the five broad categories he constructed indicators ranging from "mean number of group memberships," to "percentage of individuals who agree that 'I spend a lot of time visiting friends'." Rather than focusing on social structures or relations located within a specific group, Putman characterizes social capital more as a cultural phenomenon generated by individuals. His work had a profound influence on the direction of contemporary discussion and understanding of social capital. It gave way to a landslide of literature that followed suit, generally involving survey data designed to count and aggregate individuals' social connections as a measure of social capital.

The sheer volume of literature claiming to identify correlations between such aggregated social connections and positive societal outcomes in numerous contexts arouses curiosity about whether the phenomenon might also exist in Cuba. Could Cuba's unusually positive health outcomes have something to do with social connections? It could be postulated, for example, that individuals in Cuba have good health because they are socially engaged or well connected. Or, that a high level of social connectedness in Cuba contributes to effective collective decision-making processes in the health sector (and hence good policy outcomes). However, postulations of this kind appear less compelling upon closer examination and scrutiny of the literature on social connectedness.

Problems with Prevailing Treatments of Social Capital

The tendency of the new research following Putnam's interventions into discussion of the concept has been to conceive of a society's stock of social capital as a quantifiable number of social linkages between its citizens, or density of voluntary associations, often termed "social connectedness" and measured by survey instruments. This approach has produced a range of interesting data linking social connectedness or civic engagement to broader positive societal outcomes including economic performance, health outcomes, and government efficacy. However, despite the popularity of the model and growing body of findings supporting the role of social connectedness, it has also attracted criticism mainly for identifying only correlations between social engagement and certain outcomes but falling short of identifying the actual process through which the former influences the latter. The area of health provides an example of this quandary.

The Example of Social Connectedness and Health Outcomes

The link between health and social connectedness is one of the most documented in recent social capital discussion. On the surface, if only judging by the sheer density of literature on the topic, it would appear there is overwhelming evidence to support the theory that improved health ensues from being socially well-connected. Levels of social support (Coulthard, Walker and Morgan 2001; Tomaka 2006; Lutgendorf et al. 2005), involvement in networks and associations and civic engagement (Kennedy, Kawachi and Brainerd 1998; Cullen and Whiteford 2001; Seeman 1996; Zunzunegui et al. 2003) have all been found to correlate with health and wellbeing. However, as Scanlon points out, such studies tend to arrive at a common unsatisfactory endpoint.

> [A]lthough study after study confirms a correlation between social connectedness and good health, the precise mechanism by which social connectedness impacts on health has yet to be identified (Scanlon 2004a).[1]

Many researchers have found that social isolation increases individuals' likelihood of morbidity and mortality (Cacioppo and Hawkley 2003; Orth-Gomer, Unden and Edwards 1988; Murberg and Bu 2001; Fang et al. 1998; Berkman et al. 2004). But others have concluded that there is still no real evidence to explain how an absence of social connections actually translate into morbidity and mortality. For example, recent work by Cohen that reviewed a 1979 study which found links between social connectedness and mortality rates concluded that "we are still reaching to understand how these social factors 'get inside' our bodies" (in Scanlon 2004a). Further, it would seem that even if social isolation worsens health outcomes for individuals, counting and aggregating social interactions of an overall society does not produce a measure that corresponds with aggregate morbidity or mortality indicators. For example, one of the few national-level studies on health and social capital (Kennelly, O'Shea and Garvey 2003) found that factors such as density of membership in civil associations in fact had very little connection to national health outcomes. Rather, other factors such as income and percentage of government-funded health expenditure had greater influence.

Therefore, it seems unlikely that an hypothesis correlating Cuba's positive maternal-infant mortality statistics with the social connectedness of Cuban women, for example, would yield constructive research outcomes. Even if high levels of social connectedness were found, the correlation would not be enough to draw meaningful conclusions regarding a causal connection to health outcomes, especially given the myriad other possible variables. However, given that much literature has alluded to a connection between social connectedness and good governance, it may be that social connectedness has contributed to effective governance in the health sector. This too seems a fragile conjecture though, especially given the problems associated with attempting to measure, define or capture social connectedness.

As tends to be the case in the literature generally, there is vagueness surrounding what social capital or even social connectedness actually means, and this often results in researchers choosing whatever social factor has the most positive correlation with good health outcomes and counting this as another victory for social capital. Amid the excitement of ongoing findings that support the case, the darker side of social relationships is usually overlooked. Little attention is paid to factors that would, by definition, count as social connectedness that are antithetical to achieving positive health outcomes. A few such examples are outlined by Cohen below:

> Social networks provide emotional, informational, and material support; regulate behavior; and offer opportunities for social engagement. They also provide modes of contact to spread disease and the opportunity for conflict, exploitation, stress transmission, misguided attempts to help, and feelings of loss and loneliness. These potentially negative aspects of networks can act as psychological stressors resulting in cognitive, affective, and biological responses thought to increase risk for poor health (2004: 680).

Some researchers have produced study results that contradict the theory that social connectedness improves health and wellbeing. A study surveyed children's levels of anxiety and depression along with parents' general sense of community and knowledge of their neighbors in diverse socioeconomic neighborhoods (O'Brien Caughy, O'Campo and Muntaner 2003) is one example. The study found that in wealthy areas parents' attachment to the neighborhood community was associated with lower levels of child depression and anxiety, but in poorer areas the reverse was true.[2] Other authors focussing on social capital and health have argued that broader economic and political structures should be given more attention since they shape levels of social engagement (Wakefield and Poland 2005; Marmot and Wilkinson 1999; Pearce and Smith 2003). In a review of literature on social capital and health, House et al. conclude the following:

> The extent and quality of social relationships experienced by individuals is ... a function of broader social forces. Whether people are employed, married, attend church,

belong to organizations, or have frequent contact with friends and relatives, and the nature and quality of those relationships, all are determined in part by their position in a larger social structure that is stratified by age, race, sex, and socioeconomic status and is organized in terms of residential communities, work organizations, and larger political and economic structures (in Scanlon 2004a).

In exploring possible non-economic foundations of Cuba's unusual health outcomes, the social connectedness/civic engagement model did not seem overly promising as an explanatory tool despite the volumes of literature adopting such an approach. Attempting to measure some aspect of general civic engagement in Cuba would not necessarily identify a precise causal connection to the country's health outcomes, even if a positive correlation were to be identified. Furthermore, beyond the area of health, the general social connectedness approach has been widely criticized. Critics have mainly targeted the limitations of attempts to empirically measure social capital and deeper issues associated with conceptualizing social capital as social connectedness or civic engagement.

Measuring Social Capital

Some authors have objected to measurement attempts that survey individuals, arguing that social capital can only belong to groups and therefore cannot be empirically measured as an aggregate of individual responses (Edwards and Foley 1998a). Another common complaint is that the choice of variables used to measure social capital tends to be illogical; a problem which increases confusion in the literature. Countless measurement models have been adopted, including combinations of different variables or sometimes just one variable. There is great variation between different researchers' measures and often inconsistencies within these measures. Many measures jumble together supposed indicators of social capital with measures of the outcomes these are claimed to produce. For example, trust is often considered alongside the networks and relationships that are supposed to create trust (see for example Putnam 2000). Furthermore, most empirical studies that claim to measure social capital in fact only measure one aspect of what is essentially a complex and multifaceted concept (Paxton 1999; Australian Productivity Commission 2003; Stone 2001; Portes 1998). Observing this problem, the OECD's report on social capital notes:

Much of what is relevant to social capital is tacit and relational, defying easy measurement or codification. Individual attitudes (e.g. trust) or behaviour (eg. joining organisations or voting) provide proxy measures of social capital, but these measures

should not be confused with the underlying concept (in Australian Productivity
Commission 2003: 45).

Clearly, methodological disputes pervade discussions of social
capital. As noted, the direction of causation between social capital and
the outcomes it supposedly produces tends to be vague. Many studies
have linked civic engagement with effective government or other positive societal outcomes. However, there is often no concrete evidence
to demonstrate whether civic engagement preceded and produced the
favorable outcomes or *vice versa*. For example, do more bowling clubs
and other such associations create trust and other positive societal effects,
or are populations with higher levels of these outcomes more likely to
socially engage with others? Studies of social capital also often lacks
consideration or control for external variables that could explain both the
civic engagement and its proclaimed outcomes (Australian Productivity
Commission 2003: 45; Portes 1998). Pointing out the circularity of most
attempts to measure social capital, Portes remarks, "the quest for the
prime determinant often ends up by relabeling the original problem to
be explained ... cities where everyone cooperates in maintaining good
government are well governed" (1998: 20). In relation to this project,
even if problems of measurement were resolved and a method were
designed that could adequately capture civic engagement, and high
levels of such engagement were found to exist in Cuba, this would not
necessarily tell us anything meaningful about health outcomes.

Social Capital as Social Connectedness: Conceptual Problems

Disquiet concerning the role of social capital in the contemporary
literature has often targeted the futility of combining a broad, all-in-
clusive definition of the concept with an assumption that it represents
something inherently positive (Woolcock 1998: 158; Australian Productivity Commission 2003: 20). This has contributed to one of the most
commonly-cited criticisms of social capital—that it has become "all
things to all people and hence nothing to anyone" (Woolcock 2000: 7).
Social connectedness (often, though inadequately, equated with social
capital) is regularly treated as a blanket concept without critical examination of whether all associations really do create trust or improve
positive societal outcomes. Much of the contemporary research seems
to imagine a society's stock of social capital to be calculable if only it
were possible to aggregate a sum total of social linkages or interactions.
As Ponthieux skeptically observes, the social connectedness approach

works on the assumption that if one wants to calculate the "amount of social capital available to a society, there's just to count the number of [horizontal] civic associations … the more of them, the higher the taste of the population for cooperation and the public good" (2004: 7). While often citing Coleman's work, proponents of the social connectedness theorization "stretch [social capital] to an aggregated level absent from Coleman's approach" (Ponthieux 2004: 12). The avoidance of structural context implicit in this approach obscures the link between social connectedness and the outcomes it supposedly affects. Defining a society's stock of social capital as all social interactions falling under a broad umbrella of "civic engagement," "social connectedness" or "voluntary association" is problematic because it doesn't account for associations that have negative effects on societies development outcomes and it neglects any element of investment (of time, money, energy) in social capital creation.

A number of authors have pointed out that many types of social relationships, groups and civic activity do not increase levels of trust and social cohesion at all, but are in fact antithetical to societies' democratic goals. Cullen and Whiteford (2001: 13) observe that "merely creating civil society groups does not automatically lead to the concurrent creation of social capital within and among these new civil society groups." In the case of Rwanda (an example a number of authors have raised including Colletta and Cullen 2000; Uvin 1998), the establishment of many NGOs and other community-based organisations throughout the 1980s does not appear to have constituted social capital, in view of the rapid spread of genocide throughout the country (Cullen and Whiteford 2001: 13). "Social capital" may have existed among Hutus, but the case is a clear example of the conflict and violence that can result where factors described as social capital exist only in exclusionary groups. As the Rwandan case suggests, membership in some types of social groups is motivated by, and in turn can promote, distrust, racial hatred and other antisocial tendencies. Neo-Nazi groups, the mafia, terrorist groups, drug cartels are other examples that fit the description of social associations motivated by goals to harm or exclude other societal groups (Cullen and Whiteford 2001; Streeton 2002; Portes 1998; Szreter 2002; Baum and Ziersch 2003; Mustafa 2005). They neither promote social cohesion, identification with others, nor trust. Rather, the social threat they embody is likely to erode trust amongst those they target, and reinforce prejudice, exclusion and antisocial tendencies amongst those involved. In the following passage, Streeton makes a similar observation:

["Social capital"] can be put to bad uses as well as good ones... Networks and social interaction can cause illegitimacy, bribery, corruption, nepotism, cronyism and crime. These can involve vast inequities. Civil society cannot only mean membership of choral societies and football clubs, but can be another name for lobbyists and rent seekers. The purpose of some of these groups, such as the Ku Klux Klan, is to suppress other social groups (2002: 44).

Other forms of social interaction, although not directly motivated by exclusionary goals, have also shown a correlation with low levels of generalized trust. For example, as Eva Cox (2002: 344) points out, although there is evidence that participation in religious groups is correlated with trust and tolerance of diversity between members of the same faith group, religious groups with theological attitudes that criticize non-members correspond with lower levels of more generalized trust. A study by Hughes and Bellamy of different Australian communities found that religious belief did not contribute to higher levels of general trust—atheists were in fact found to be more likely to trust others. Christian groups that make a strong distinction between themselves and non-Christians tend to be distrustful of those who do not conform to their faith (Cox 2002: 344). In a similar vein, social groups organized around male-dominated sports such as football can sometimes reinforce a culture of hegemonic masculinity that excludes women and endorses violence (see for example Burges, Edwards, and Skinner 2003). The exclusionary impact some isolated social networks have on outsiders is a point also noted by Portes, who provides several examples including the dominance of Cubans over some sectors of Miami's economy and the control by white ethnic groups over New York's fire and police unions and construction trades (1998: 10). Since some groups can be exclusionary and antisocial, privileging those who belong at the expense of those who do not, attempting to quantify general levels of civic engagement in groups and associations is a problematic means for gauging social capital if the concept is intended to tell us something meaningful about the collective outcomes of a society, whether those be health outcomes, educational outcomes or any other area of collective governance.

This is not to say that the basic underlying phenomenon of social capital is not analyzable within groups with antisocial goals. Regular cooperative interaction between members of any group creates a capacity that is more than the sum of individual members' contributions.[3] It increases trust, familiarity, and reciprocity between members, results in formal structures for engagement (such as regular meetings, coordinated plans of action) that facilitate resource and information sharing between members. In the process, it reinforces certain norms, beliefs and thought patterns within the group. All of these factors increase the group's capacity to affect external outcomes embodying its goals or values. The point to observe here is that the "social resources" pertaining to a particular isolated group belong to that group, and can only be definitively said to improve the outcomes of *that group according to its goals*. Of course this does not automatically imply enhanced outcomes for the broader society. For instance, as Ponthieux points out, "the same strong norms that may lower transaction costs within a context can play as many entry barriers which limit or cancel out this benefit at a more aggregated level ... the conceptualization doesn't explain how what works on a small scale (that of a group) works also at on a larger scale (that of several groups)" (2004: 16-19). The lack of logic in assuming all groups will improve societal outcomes is a point also labored by the Australian Productivity Commission reviewing the policy implications of social capital. The report observed that the degree to which social capital *within a group* benefits the broader community depends on what the group's goals are (2003: 21). In other words, if a group's goals are hostile to broader community goals, it is unlikely to facilitate the latter. The existence of "antisocial capital" discussed earlier demonstrates that high numbers of social groups and associations could as easily indicate a fragmented, conflicted society as a unified, cohesive one. There are logical problems therefore, with adopting a general theory that societies with "socially engaged" populations (meaning a high sum total of civic associations) will be effectively governed, have good aggregate health and education outcomes, less violence and so on.

A further limitation of attempts to measure societies' stock of social capital as general civic engagement levels is the avoidance of context, which allows discussion to sidestep the concept's more radical implications. Social capital was first introduced largely as a critique of the atomistic liberal worldview, but in some ways the social connectedness model returns to this narrow conception. In a critique of current discussions of social capital defined as ethical interactions (that is, characterized by cooperation, trust and mutuality), Scanlon goes so far as to say that the concept circumvents the social altogether. He argues that the approach bypasses any meaningful understanding of community and reinvents social capital in a way that is conveniently compatible with the market, thereby defeating its proclaimed purpose. "Society is whittled down to a series of individuals interlinked within a network expanding remorselessly across a featureless landscape incapable of nurturing anything greater than the sum of its parts" (2004a). In this way, he considers current conceptions to have lost their original usefulness.

Defining social capital in a non-specific way and almost synonymously with the term "civil society"[4] disconnects social relationships from the situations, history and interests in which they are embedded, thereby neglecting precisely what is important about the social. This conceptualization loses much of the heuristic value of Coleman's approach; in particular, its lessons about what types of relations matter in connection with certain goals (Edwards and Foley 1998a). One can be especially critical of attempts to gauge societies' stock of social capital through broad surveys of individuals.

> Important parts of the social capital argument we have sketched above fall by the wayside as one begins to operationalize it, as Putnam and others have done, with extant survey research. Indeed, in doing so social capital is seamlessly transformed into a characteristic of individuals acquired through social networks— above all, the associations of civil society… [I]f social capital is as context specific as we have indicated then it cannot be measured directly in extant longitudinal survey data like that of the General Social Survey. Nor is it legitimate, as we argued above, to treat the resulting aggregate measures as reliable indicators of the social capital available to the polity (Edwards and Foley 1998a).

As noted, attempting to measure general levels of "trust," "reciprocity" and "social connectedness" isolates these factors from broader social structures such as class, ethnicity and gender in which they are situated. The treatment obscures, for example, the fact that populations with high levels of social connectedness tend to fit "a typical profile of a married upper-middle-class home-owner in professional employment," which contrasts with the lack of connections and social engagement typical of lower socioeconomic groups (Scanlon 2004a). This suggests that, even if there is a connection between civic engagement and positive economic, educational, health and other achievements, there are deeper social sources that influence and sustain social participation and these are often ignored in social capital literature (2004a).

Most of the recent social capital studies focus on associations in civil society but pay little attention the role of government-association relationships (Freitag 2006; Maloney, Smith and Stoker 2000; Evans 1997a). This is despite some authors drawing attention to evidence that institutional arrangements including the role of governments and public social programs are important factors determining levels of political activity and civic engagement (Freitag 2006; Mettler 2002; Heller 1997; Skocpol 1996). According to Skocpol, for example, the cause of (and therefore

the solution to) what Putnam identifies as the decline of civic engagement in the United States has been widely misidentified as spontaneous
"bottom-up" efforts at the local level. She argues that civic association
in America has historically been determined by "institutional patterns of
U.S. federalism, legislatures, competitive elections, and locally rooted
political parties" and that the withdrawal of elites from these institutions
has caused declining levels of association among average Americans.

> Throughout much of U.S. history, electoral democracy and congressionally centered
> governance nurtured and rewarded voluntary associations and locality-spanning
> voluntary federations. But since the 1960s, the mechanics of U.S. politics have been
> captured by manipulators of money and data. Among elites new kinds of connections
> are alive and well. Privileged Americans remain active in think tanks, advocacy
> groups, and trade and professional associations, jetting back and forth between
> manicured neighborhoods and exotic retreats. Everyone else has been left to work at
> two or three poorly paid jobs per family, coming home exhausted to watch TV and
> answer phone calls from pollsters and telemarketers. How ironic it would be if, after
> pulling out of locally rooted associations, the very business and professional elites
> who blazed the path toward local civic disengagement were now to turn around and
> successfully argue that the less privileged Americans they left behind are the ones
> who must repair the nation's social connectedness, by pulling themselves together
> from below without much help from government or their privileged fellow citizens.
> This, I fear, is what is happening as the discussion about "returning to Tocqueville"
> rages across elite America (Skocpol 1996).

It seems that Skocpol has identified one of the aspects of social capital
that really matters for the contemporary malaise in Western democracies: the need for engagement between different, rationally opposed,
social groupings. Each inevitably contributes to the social role and
macro-effects of the other; not just rich and poor, but also people who
provide money and means of production and people who turn them into
productive or wealth-generating capital. The same applies, of course, to
potential collaborations or linkages between suppliers and customers,
government and governed, experts and amateurs and service providers
and clients.

Clearly some discussion and use of the term social capital has fallen
short of identifying the precise causes of good development outcomes.
The inevitable end point of most social capital discussions recently seems
to be a return to the question of which types of societal relations matter—measuring ethical relations as a homogeneous feature of society is
not enough. The social connectedness thesis has been important in drawing attention to correlations between a social realm and developmental
outcomes, but has obvious shortcomings in terms of explaining precisely
what is important about social relations, resulting in frequent calls for

more attention to underlying social forces. However, the limitations of some notions of the concept (not just difficulties of quantification) should not preclude the recognition that there are always non-economic, non-material causes of good societal outcomes. Exploring such causes in the Cuban context appeared especially promising given the puzzle of the country's unusually positive health outcomes despite its material poverty. However, the problem of finding a meaningful framework for examining social relations seemed critical, given the fundamental limitations of so many other constructions of social capital adopted in the literature.

It is worth remembering that the basis for widespread excitement about social capital in recent decades has been the fact that it allegedly plays a role in society's capacity to achieve collective goals, to develop and produce (in other words its stock of "capital"). Surprisingly however, there seems to be little theoretical reflection in the recent social capital literature on why social capital is *capital*. Often discussion appears to be based on an incomplete understanding of what capital is. One way to resolve some of the confusion in the literature may be to revisit earlier insights regarding the social dimensions of capital. Discussions of this nature have mainly taken place in the field of political economy, where many disparate traditions have challenged the orthodox conception of societies' capacity for wealth and progress as determined by quantities of material and human capital. Although from different traditions of analysis, a long line of prominent political economists has perceived the productive power of a polity as having non-economic underpinnings. Probably the most monumental contribution of this kind, and therefore an appropriate starting point, is Marx's *Capital* (1894). Central to this critique of the classical political economists' worldview is an observation that social relations are always implicated in the phenomenon of capital.

Revisiting Capital as a Social Relation

Understandings of "capital" have changed significantly since early usage of the term. First adopted from the language of merchants to describe head of livestock, capital went on to signify "money." The liberation of the term from this narrow definition is generally attributed to Adam Smith, who used capital as a classification for overall stock of goods—money and other objects—that constituted the requirements for production. This included the employable skills of people, now referred to as "intellectual capital" or "human capital." Classical bourgeois economists explained capital as the accrued product of previous labour and production (Wolf 2005: 75). Within the contemporary social sciences, the term capital is now generally associated with the work of critical political economists, including Marx, Keynes and the economic sociologists. According to Marx, capital has always been a social relation allowing forces of production to be developed:

> [C]apital is not a thing, but rather a definite social production relation, belonging to a definite historical formation of society, which is manifested in a thing and lends this thing a specific social character. Capital is not the sum of the material and produced means of production. Capital is rather the means of production transformed into capital, which in themselves are no more capital than gold or silver in itself is money (Marx [1894] 1996).

In other words, the physical objects involved in production only produce certain outcomes as a result of their being enmeshed in social relations. Hence, capital is neither the means of production (machinery, technology, resources) alone, money (financial capital) alone, nor social relations alone, but a combination of all three. For example, a tool such as hammer, considered alone, is a piece of metal and wood, not capital. The hammer could potentially be involved in many different social contexts and different points in time to produce different outcomes. Itself the product of a combination of labor, means of production and social relations, the hammer's capacity to produce is similarly dependent on all of these three elements. Left alone lying on a shelf the hammer produces nothing and as such cannot be considered capital. Combined with labor to make a table, the hammer becomes part of the means of production. However, this process is necessarily situated within a social context that affects the nature of what it produces. The hammer could be used in a household to make a table for private use (in which case many hours of labor may be spent with the intention of ensuring the quality and durability of the product); or the same hammer could be combined with the same labor in a factory to produce tables intended to be sold for profit. The same means of production combined with the same labor can therefore produce different outcomes based on the social context in which they exist (Shaikh 1990: 72). Further, the same hammer could be deployed in ways that are destructive rather than productive. The hammer's possibilities are infinite. Whether or not a material object is capital has and will always depend on the social dynamics in which it is inserted into the production process. For Marx, the social relations at issue in the capitalist context are those implied by (a) market allocation of resources, (b) commodity production and commodification of labor power, (c) profitability as a criterion for production and (d) undemocratic control of the production processes. These all prescribe relationships between social groups—what Marx calls the social relations of capitalist production—(which would be different in any pre-capitalist or post-capitalist situation). What these insights imply is that a social dimension is necessary in all capital.

For Marx, a society's development stems from an ongoing process of production and reproduction necessitated by human biological needs and propelled by "the creative source of new needs and capabilities" (Marx in Giddens 1971: 35). Society (in both its material and social forms) is continually created and recreated by every individual at every moment; a necessary process in order to sustain human life. The sum of this process is a system of production which always entails a set of social relationships between the individuals involved. Hence, production is *always* social by nature. Herein lies Marx's criticism of utilitarianism—he argues that human beings never produce as isolated individuals, but always through interaction and mutual exchange of activities with others. In this way, individuals enter into relations and connections, and only through these relations is production possible. In contrast with the utilitarian conception of human beings as isolated and independent, Marx saw individuals' capacities to produce as inherently contingent upon their situation within a broader societal structure. Further, this structure or set of social relations is always the cumulative outcome of a history of former social relations and production (Giddens 1971: 35-36) and the social relations themselves may be exploitative, transitory and system-defining. Therefore, wealth is more than just an accumulation of things; it is an historically developed set of social relations. Social capital as a concept captures these considerations.

Drawing on these insights, it can be said that different social arrangements and circumstances have different consequences in relation to capital accumulation or societal wealth. If social relations determine the manner of production and the nature of what is produced, then these relations either facilitate or impede a society's capacity to achieve positive outcomes at different stages of development. In essence, this is the same insight that has re-emerged in discussions of social capital. Although Marx didn't use the term social capital, his reasoning about capital demonstrates a highly developed understanding of the non-economic (sociological, organizational and historical) aspects of capital which contemporary writers are just now discovering with somewhat less theoretical sophistication. As we have seen, advocates of social capital have argued that factors contained in social relationships (such as networks, reciprocity, group membership, norms and so on) contribute to societies' development outcomes, including economic performance, health and education outcomes, crime levels, and government effectiveness. However, contemporary social capital literature has become so bogged down in attempting to apply the same narrow conception of the production phenomenon that has previously limited understandings of capital to the apparently tangible and quantifiable, that it has lost sight of the concept's deeper significance. A new recognition that the social affects societal outcomes is important primarily because it informs our understanding of *the nature of capital generally*, including its financial, material and human components.

If all production is embedded in social relations, then what has been observed as "social capital" is not really a new form of capital as distinct from financial, material or human capital as it is often treated; *social capital is rather a dimension of the broader phenomenon of capital that is inseparable from its other dimensions*. It makes little sense to describe social capital in the way most of the literature does—as a less tangible type of capital, or as a metaphor for capital (assuming "real" capital to be material).

A failure to recognize this point often leads to the fetishism of commodities or "things" as the key to developmental outcomes. In other words, this fetishism gives way to the idea that societies' capacity to produce wealth depends on their accumulation of money and other objects alone and that the overall stocks of things can be measured and quantified. The inadequacy of this understanding of capital is precisely what has resulted in ongoing efforts to add new categories to explain the phenomenon. Yet, usually these new "types" of capital are treated with the same fetishism in the sense that they are seen to have an inherent value in themselves. This is essentially what has led to the current fixation in the literature on attempting to develop quantitative measures for social capital. The reason this task has proved to be messy and complicated is that the social relations that make up a society's capital are essentially not quantifiable or observable to the naked eye.

This is not to discredit all empirical studies of social capital. Much is owed to Putnam in particular for reinvigorating the social capital debate and drawing attention once again to the existence of a social realm that underpins and is always implicated in societies' more tangible developmental achievements. However, if a society's stock of social capital refers to the social dimension of its productive capacities, then any measurement intended to enumerate social capital, regardless of its complexity or the number of variables it includes, can at best only measure proxies for social capital but not the concept itself. As numerous authors have pointed out, attempts to quantify social capital *per se* by surveying individuals may be missing the point.

Most problematic is that such attempts usually fail to reveal anything meaningful about how social relations actually improve the outcomes with which they are correlated. Identifying social relationships without connecting them to particular contexts conveniently permits the avoidance of the more controversial lessons in recognizing social capital—(a) that capital creation cannot be explained solely as the product of calculated mercantile exchange between self-interested individuals oriented towards profit-maximization and (b) that there is something about cooperative structures that facilitates simultaneously the achievement of collective goals and the productive process. These are essentially the more radical theoretical implications emerging from the earlier work of Coleman[5] and Bourdieu in the 1980s.

Bourdieu and Coleman

Since the concept re-emerged in the 1980s, the structurally located approaches of Coleman and Bourdieu appear to have come closest to identifying how and in what context cooperative relationships produce favorable collective outcomes. Their observations of the increased productive capacities of groups to achieve common interests beyond those which individual members could achieve in isolation, provide the basis for a legitimate challenge to prevailing conceptions of development as best achieved through competitive, uncoordinated arrangements.

Rather than aggregating numbers of civic associations as measures for a society's total stock of social capital as Putnam and others have done, Coleman and Bourdieu discuss the benefits that can ensue from group membership *for the members of a specific group.* Coleman's case studies included: Jewish New York diamond wholesalers whose mutual trust permitted them to freely exchange bags of diamonds for examination without the need for expensive security measures; radical Korean students' "study circles"—an organizational structure that enabled the students to coordinate demonstrations and protests; and a Detroit mother of six who, upon relocating to Jerusalem, found it was safe to let her young children travel across town alone due to a norm in Jerusalem whereby adults took it upon themselves to "look after" unattended children in their vicinity (1988: 98-100). These and Coleman's other examples demonstrate in various ways the efficiency with which common collective goals are achieved if cooperative organizational structures exist; such structures produce positive externalities, reduce transaction costs and increase time-efficiency. Like Coleman, Bourdieu also observed that cooperative arrangements within a group are a source of capital (a constructive resource that can be drawn on) for the group and its members. His concept of social capital referred mainly to durable institutionalized arrangements that form the basis for lasting relationships.

> [The network of institutionalised relationships in a group] provides each of its members with the backing of the collectively-owned capital, a "credential" which entitles them to credit, in the various senses of the word. These relationships may exist only in the practical state, in material and/or symbolic exchanges which help to maintain them. They may also be socially instituted and guaranteed by the application of a common name (the name of a family, a class, or a tribe or of a school, a party, etc.) and by a whole set of instituting acts designed simultaneously to form and inform those who undergo them; in this case, they are more or less really enacted and so maintained and reinforced, in exchanges.... The profits which accrue from membership in a group are the basis of the solidarity which makes them possible (1986: 248-249).

Several developments emerge from Coleman's and Bourdieu's work on social capital. The first is of the basic principle of group cooperation or synergy. This is not especially new but also formed part of earlier critiques of liberal explanations for societies' productive capacities. It was the basic argument espousing the division of labor (and consequently the spread of markets) in Adam Smith's *The Wealth of Nations* in 1776. An essentially similar point is observed, also, in a section of Marx's *Capital*. Providing various examples, Marx explains how the productive capacity of labor is increased through cooperation for a range of logical reasons. Just as an army has a greater power collectively than individual soldiers taken separately, so cooperation between laborers produces a new productive power that is greater than the sum of its parts.

> [A] body of men working in concert has hands and eyes both before and behind, and is, to a certain degree, omnipresent. ...Whether the combined working-day, in a given case, acquires this increased productive power, because it heightens the mechanical force of labour, or extends its sphere of action over a greater space, or contracts the field of production relatively to the scale of production, or at the critical moment sets large masses of labour to work, or excites emulation between individuals and raises their animal spirits, or impresses on the similar operations carried on by a number of men the stamp of continuity and many-sidedness, or performs simultaneously different operations, or economises the means of production by use in common, or lends to individual labour the character of average social labour whichever of these be the

cause of the increase, the special productive power of the combined working-day is, under all circumstances, the social productive power of labour, or the productive power of social labour. This power is due to co-operation itself. When the labourer co-operates systematically with others, he strips off the fetters of his individuality, and develops the capabilities of his species (Marx [1887] 1999: Part 4, Chapter 13).

Second, consideration of social capital within a specific context allows an appreciation for the element of previous effort involved in the process of building structures that support lasting cooperative relationships. For Bourdieu,[6] social capital, like all capital, is a potential capacity that accumulates over time, producing and reproducing itself. Social capital is not a natural given; it does not spontaneously exist. Rather, it "is the product of an endless effort at institution...necessary in order to produce lasting, useful relationships that can secure material or symbolic profits" (1986: 249).

> [T]he network of relationships is the product of investment strategies, individual or collective, consciously or unconsciously aimed at establishing or reproducing social relationships that are directly usable in the short or long term, [that is,] at transforming contingent relations, such as those of neighbourhood, the workplace, or even kinship, into relationships that are at once necessary and elective, implying durable obligations subjectively felt (feelings of gratitude, respect, friendship etc.) or institutionally guaranteed (rights) (1986: 249).

These institutions (manifesting social capital) serve as a foundation that enables and facilitates the lasting relationships which sustain a collective. For example, group members organize *occasions* (such as scheduled recreational events, parties, rallies), *places* (schools, smart neighborhoods), and *practices* (cultural ceremonies, sports, games), all which serve to maintain the lasting relationships that are necessary in order for a collective to exist and persist. "The reproduction of social capital presupposes an unceasing effort of sociability, a continuous series of exchanges in which recognition is endlessly affirmed and reaffirmed." This process necessarily involves the investment of time energy and therefore also economic capital (Bourdieu 1986: 250). Logically, and necessarily, these occasions places and practices can be seen to include respectively policy debate, policy institutions and policy implementation.

Bourdieu's and Coleman's work on social capital presents a challenge to the standard view of group-formation in liberal theory—that social groups are largely a hindrance to rational, individual choices and are therefore an obstacle to economic efficiency (Storper 2005: 36). Moreover, the findings signify a legitimate challenge to previously conceived notions of development as a process best achieved through depoliticized and non-directive means: competition and the pursuit of individual interests and registered through market processes. Liberal political theory that advocates the market as the best means for achieving developmental outcomes is based on the assumptions that (a) economic wealth is the most important measure of a society's progress and development and (b) the combined decisions by self-interested, rational individuals automatically result in optimal economic outcomes, which is tantamount to the collective good. In other words, the best means for achieving economic wealth is the uncoordinated pursuit of individual interests. Theoretical and empirical evidence emerging from Coleman's and Bourdieu's discussions of social capital presents a challenge to these assumptions by providing evidence of non-market based coordination. Their work demonstrates (a) that the many non-economic inputs into and outputs of development and progress (b) that cooperative organizational structures produce better outcomes for their members than would be possible in their absence, and (c) that certain cooperative arrangements are necessary for the effective functioning of markets. These insights suggest that liberal theory has failed to recognize the full significance of capital and that the application of its model may therefore lead to less than optimal developmental outcomes.

However, while both Bourdieu and Coleman explain how social capital benefits groups and their members, they do not address the issue of how social capital could be built to facilitate national-level development goals such as improved aggregate health, education and economic outcomes. Even if the principle of group investment in collective practices with the aim of expanding collective achievements observed in small-scale examples such as building a wall or trading diamonds provides the basis for an anti-liberal hypothesis about the sources of social and economic capacity, what does this imply for the capacity of a society to achieve collective goals? Since cooperation in some groups doesn't necessarily translate into better outcomes for a society, the quest for social determinants of good national development outcomes needs to specify which social arrangements matter.

If we are to consider the insights emerging from Coleman's and Bourdieu's work in a way that says something meaningful about a society's social capital, then a logical starting point is to consider that the "group" in question is the society and the members of the group are its citizens. If we apply the concept of group synergy or the increased capacity of groups ensuing from cooperative structural arrangements, then rather than including *all* social relationships in a definition of social capital, it may be more worthwhile to focus on the social structures that bind together or maintain the solidarity of a citizenry. If a theory can be developed that links what Coleman and Bourdieu observed within small groups to a society's capital, then the institutions that matter are not particularistic arrangements belonging members of exclusive groups, but those arrangements which are commonly and universally owned by all members of a society.[7] In other words, if social capital in a small group is collectively owned, if it serves as potential or actual resources for members of the group, and is "the basis of the solidarity that makes them possible" (Bourdieu 1986: 249), then the same should apply to a large-scale collectivity. A society's social capital should refer to a collectively owned accumulation of potential or actual resources that are in some sense universally acknowledged by and available to citizens. This implies group investment in collective practices with the aim of expanding collective achievements.

Examples might include *occasions* such as national ceremonies or celebrations, election days, designated days for collective action to combat common problems (such as public health, litter and other environmental issues); *places* such as public parks, schools, universities, hospitals, parliaments, business districts, train-stations, court houses, museums; and *practices* (or institutionalized guidelines governing practices) such as elections, information-sharing networks, laws, systems for dealing with transportation, water supply, employment, dispute resolution, health care, education, rubbish collection, road works and so on. These structures and their common ownership rely entirely on collective knowledge and acknowledgement (Bourdieu 1986: 255), which presupposes a process of socialization that transforms collective agreements into norms of behavior. Social capital is thus essentially a set of collectively acknowledged structures which guide social exchange (including rights and obligations). Whether consciously acknowledged by individuals or not, these arrangements at once constrain certain behaviors[8] and make possible a higher level of sociability (thereby group action) than would otherwise have been possible.

Social capital as it is conceived here is an accumulated investment of time, energy and resources aimed at institutionalizing workable processes for problem-solving, collective decision-making and lasting, useful relationships. For example, publicly formalized processes for averting or resolving conflict that evolve through historical negotiations and agreements between different interest groups (between workers and employers or tenants and landlords), or publicly accepted laws and systems for dealing with problems that members of a society face in common (like health, environment, education and transportation). Social capital, like all capital, is an accumulated investment of social energy which lives on beyond its creation and, so long as it is collectively acknowledged by members of a collectivity, can progressively raise the threshold for what the whole can achieve.

A society's capital, in other words, can essentially be understood as its manner of asserting humans' "control over nature" or the ability to produce desired future outcomes against competing natural forces. At the heart of controversies over capital, then, have always been struggles over ideas about which arrangements best enable polities to effectively control humanity's life and destiny together with the capacity of politics to deal with the unwanted consequences of competitive "modes of regulation"—unemployment, inequality and the lack of democracy, as well as collective problems related to public health or any other sphere of collective decision-making. Ongoing debates about the relationship between the state and civil society are central to these questions. As suggested above, the liberal view has traditionally advocated an unrestrained civil society as the most practically effective sign of social and economic development. Public institutions have been seen as inefficient, easily corrupted, and prone to failure in terms of implementing and achieving collective goals. Aside from the early social capital literature discussed above, the most significant challenge to liberal conceptions of development in recent times has come from a resurgent interest in the developmental role of the state that has also advocated the expansion of public institutional capacity and "infrastructural power of the state" as a means for enhancing societies' collective capabilities. As will be elaborated, this literature—along with the social capital literature—provides a useful framework for examining the Cuban case, where positive developmental outcomes in the health field appear to have been achieved via an unconventionally state-led path.

State Capacity

During the same period as social capital was repopularised, political science and many other disciplines revived an interest in positive theories of "the state" (Skocpol 1985: 3; Burlamanqui 2000; Evans 1992, 1995; Hay and Lister 2006; Hay 2006; Huber and Stephens 2001; Jessop 2002; Jessop and Sum 2006; Levy 2006; Schmidt 2003; Streeck and Yamamura 2001; Weiss and Hobson 1995; Weiss 1998,

2003; Woo-Cumings 1999; Marsh 2002). Part of this was a school of "developmental statism" triggered to a large degree by rapid economic growth in East Asian countries including Japan, Taiwan and Korea. In reaction to claims that these cases supported liberal economies (more or less in accordance with neoclassical economics), developmental statists argued the countries' successes were linked to strong states that had managed significant autonomy in deliberately directing investment into chosen industrial sectors (Polidano 2001: 513). This work coincided with a compatible movement in political science to "bring the state back in" (Evans, Rueschemeyer, and Skocpol 1985), which advocated that politics should build the capacity to achieve distinctive outcomes that would not have been achieved without conscious political decisions and institutional development.

The re-emergence of positive theories of the state was a significant development in political theory considering that both liberal and socialist traditions—the dominant ideological traditions of the post 1945 era—have held pessimistic views of politics. Due to their skepticism and suspicion of state power, both liberals and Marxists alike have held little faith in the capacity of the political realm to achieve what constituents want it to do. Important to more recent discussion of the state has been the causal relationship between politics (collective decision-making) and other forces in society. That is, the current suggestion by modern statists is that politics is not completely subservient to class or socioeconomic forces, but may instead determine economic conditions such as industrial structure, trade patterns and economic growth. In other words, it is possible that the collective efforts of a citizenry to control its destiny, if institutionalized, competent and strategic, can overcome apparently inexorable economic forces.

Marxists have traditionally downplayed or denied the effectiveness and autonomy of the political realm, believing that the state could not act independently of social interests. Based on the *Communist Manifesto*'s assertion that the "executive of the modern state is but a committee for managing the common affairs of the whole bourgeoisie" ([1848] 1978: 475), they have argued that the state is a "capitalist state." In other words, the state is always an instrument for maintaining the capitalist mode of production (Miliband 1983). However, more recent Marxist work has conceded that the state has "relative autonomy," meaning it is not completely dominated by capital but can act independently to some degree. This retreat from determinism is attributed to different social groups or sections of capital that pressure and control the state but whose interests are conflicting. The state thereby acts as a mediator and, in certain circumstances, is said to have the capacity to secure cohesion if it has bureaucratic competencies. For Marxists, the state still serves powerful economic interests, and exercises autonomy only within the boundaries of the interests of the capitalist class as a whole; but the political sphere has other responsibilities as well. Modern statists have endorsed the concept of relative autonomy but have argued, among other things, that the capitalist class lacks the cohesion, consciousness and organization that would be required to "keep the state in line." Further, the capitalist class may not even be aware of what its own interests are (Block 1987: 83), being forever torn, for example, between the pursuit of control and the pursuit of profitability.

Liberals have traditionally insisted that the fact that the state can act autonomously does not necessarily imply that it *should,* because the political realm is corruptible, potentially authoritarian, inefficient and ineffective in achieving what it sets out to do. According to liberal theory, state intervention in the economy always tends towards bureaucratic despotism, mismanagement, rent seeking, and inefficiency (Jessop 1990: 175). Contemporary statist writers dispute liberalism's negative preconceptions about state power, namely that "all states are essentially alike —predatory and self serving in motivation, incompetent or inefficient in economic affairs" (Weiss 1998: 17). They have criticized liberal theory for failing to acknowledge the facilitative role of state power and the possibility that subordinating the state to market forces may obstruct the democratic process. Revisionists such as Skocpol and Weiss argue that politics itself should not be seen as inherently undesirable, because strong states don't necessarily threaten democratic freedoms or economic progress.

The revival of positive theories of the state had a considerable impact throughout the 1980s and 1990s and this appears to have played a role in a significant shift in thinking by key international policy-making institutions such as the International Monetary Fund (IMF) and the World Bank. Until the 1990s, these institutions insisted on pro-market "reforms" and economic growth as the only viable way to redress the problems of underdevelopment. Official institutions saw this as involving an environment where social, cultural, institutional and traditional "impediments" to market forces have been "reformed" away. Some poignant illustrations of a shift in development thinking in recent years were reported in various *World Development Reports*. These changes followed intense criticism of the Bank's and the IMF's self-defeating policy advice for numerous developing nations around the world, including Latin American nations, and growing international criticism of its over-reliance on market forces in combating poverty.

> Neoliberal adjustment applied to poor and unequal societies has not only failed to lift all but the largest boats; it has also deprived these societies of the few dynamic enterprises and the little economic autonomy achieved during the prior era. Latin American societies have lost quite a few babies with the bathwater in these years. It is time to restart anew, learning from the errors of the past, and reasserting the rights of these nations to pursue their own path toward social integration and economic development, rather than being controlled from the outside. No nation has ever been developed solely by external market forces. The illusion that the "magic of the markets" would accomplish this for Latin America in the late twentieth century was just that, an illusion (Centeno and Portes 2003: 28).

Failed predictions that free-market mechanisms would in many contexts relieve poverty and reverse underdevelopment, fuelled distrust in economists' capacities to critically analyze the causes of poverty in the developing world. The critics now notably include former chief economist and senior vice president of the World Bank, Joseph Stiglitz, who publicly pointed out "the devastating effect that globalization can have on developing countries, and especially on the poor of those countries." He criticized the IMF and World Bank for relying too heavily in their policy-making on the "outworn presumption that markets, by themselves, lead to efficient outcomes" and for failing to take into account the potentially important role of government facilitation in economic development (2002: xii). Stiglitz' suggestion is that liberal dogma has been much more damaging in poor countries than in the affluent West.

The World Bank has since conceded that some of its liberal, deregulatory policies have unnecessarily increased hardship and insecurity in developing countries while failing to eliminate familiar cycles of underdevelopment poverty and corruption. It has called for more attention to be paid to institution-building. For example, the 2002 issue of the *World Development Report*, subtitled "Building Institutions for Markets," acknowledges that weak institutions hinder development and worsen the conditions of poverty. The Report concedes that without effective institutions suited to local needs, poor countries may be excluded from the benefits of markets (World Bank 2002). This shift ties in with the emergence of a broader school of "New Institutionalism" which acknowledges social, political and historical institutions, but still seeks to explain these in terms of neoclassical economic theory. This school opposes the earlier American Institutionalist school that sought to incorporate into economics theories from other social sciences (Fonseca 2006b). In the case of the Asian "tigers," new institutionalists tend to argue that it was the role of private business that brought about the 40-year period of economic growth, not state autonomy (Polidano 2001).

In his review of recent literature on the state, Polidano outlines the essential conceptual debate between statists and new institutionalists as centered around the question: "does autonomy enhance or detract from a state's capacity and effectiveness?" (2001: 514). In opposition to the new institutionalists' view that it is private business and not state autonomy that produces better developmental outcomes, Polidano outlines two main statist perspectives. The first is that of developmental statists, who argue it is the degree to which states can act independently of social forces to prioritize economic growth and direct private investment that matters. Most advocates of this perspective view state autonomy as "a wasting asset: economic growth strengthens both capital and labour and gradually whittles away the state's freedom of action" (2001: 516).

Another school of statists (here termed the neo-statists) tend to differ on this final point; they argue that states' autonomy is in fact *enhanced* through cooperation and coordination with non-state actors. Developmental states do not undermine their own power but develop greater power and capacity through increasingly complex connections with civil society, usually referred to as state "embeddedness."[9] This line of thought derives largely from Michael Mann's pioneering work in *The Sources of Social Power,* which distinguishes two types of state power—despotic power (whereby the state can act arbitrarily, free from constitutional restraint) and *infrastructural* power (the state's ability to embed itself in society). In modern polities, infrastructural power is more prevalent and important than despotic power (1993: 53). Mann outlines three dimensions of infrastructural power. These are: "penetrative" power—the state's power to interact directly with the population; "extractive" power—its ability to reach into and extract resources from a society; and "negotiated" power—collaborations between political and industrial actors. Negotiated power is considered by contemporary state capacity theorists to be the ultimate form of state strength because it involves the coordination of activities that would not otherwise be subjected to authority. State strength, they argue, "increases with the effective embedding of autonomy, whereas state weakness ensues from despotic abrasion against society" (Weiss and Hobson 1995: 7). In other words, the more concentrated and arbitrary the state's power, the more it becomes isolated from social groups. However, when state power is integrated into society, its strength is increased with its greater capacity to generate and to focus economic and social energy (Krygier 1997: 115). Polidano makes the point that:

> [The neo-statist perspective] accepts that state agencies can develop policy preferences autonomously. But it argues that governments can achieve far more if they work with rather than against society. Institutionalized state-society linkages do not diminish the state's capacity to achieve industrial transformation; on the contrary they are the highest expression of that capacity (2001: 518).

So, as opposed to liberals who tend to view the state as an alien body that wields power over society, this view considers the state as capable of generating strength *through* society; that is, as the apparatus that enables collective decision-making. In this way state institutions or structures are perceived to both protect against unwanted change and facilitate desired change, thereby producing not only better outcomes but also *democratic* outcomes. The modern state, according to Mann and the neo-statists, is not a monolithic actor but takes the form of many institutions, often with divergent functions, which permeate and are permeated by other societal forces. There is a high degree of "interpenetration" between state and civil society in modern states as compared with earlier feudal states (1993: 61). The modern state's strength or capacity depends on the degree of this embeddedness—equivalent to its level of citizen participation—which limits its despotic strength or ability to act independently of the democratic will. In this way, formal institutions and other civil organizations incorporated in or endorsed by the state's apparatus activate collective decision-making and increase the capacity of a polity to influence future outcomes.

It is worth noting that, despite their divergent views on the instigators of political decision-making, one thing the new institutionalist and "state embeddedness" theorists have in common is that they emphasize (even if inadvertently) societal cooperation and cohesiveness (the incorporation of as many democratic inputs as possible into formal mechanisms for collective decision-making) as the keys to developmental success. In light of this, the focus (at least for the neo-statists) has shifted from political and institutional "actors" to the milieu of politicized and deliberated "capacity building" within the state sphere. Along these lines, particularly in the context of modern, developed polities, it is worth considering doubts Mann raises about the appropriateness of the eighteenth century convention of treating the state and civil society as distinctly separate entities.

[S]uch a clear distinction between society and state carries dangers. It is, paradoxically, highly political, locating freedom and morality in society, not the state.... This was so among the eighteenth-century writers resisting what they saw as despotism, and it has recently been so again as Soviet, East European, and Chinese dissidents sought to mobilize decentralized civil society forces against state repression. Yet states are not as distinct from the rest of social life as these ideologies suggest (1993: 23).

The state and civil society have always been interwoven, Mann argues, and the Western state became increasingly so through the process of modernization (1993: 42). He states that: "To understand states and appreciate their causal impact on societies, we must specify their institutional peculiarities" (1993: 88). In other words, broad questions about whether "the state" or "civil society" should control the process of collective decision-making may be founded on an overly simplistic conception of the state, especially given the high level of "interpenetration" between public and private realms (1993: 61). In light of this, rather than examining the relationship between state and civil society in a way that treats them as necessarily separate and singular actors, it may be more fruitful to examine instead the relationships (and divisions) between the multiple actors and groups that comprise and often overlap in these two spheres. Expanding on this, questions of how organizational structures and the relationships within them shape and determine the nature of collective decisions and their implementation are worth considering. In other words, which types of social arrangements are conducive to a polity producing, implementing and sustaining collective decisions and *vice versa?*

A Framework for Approaching the Cuban Case

Cuba's achievement of unusually positive health outcomes despite obvious deficiencies in economic development presents a puzzle that has attracted interest from observers around the world. However, there are still relatively few comprehensive academic investigations of the subject. The existing literature does postulate various explanations for the country's health success. These have usually focused on fairly palpable (if nevertheless important) health policies Cuba has adopted, including its emphasis on primary health care, the incorporation of alternative and complementary therapies (Dresang et al. 2005; Swanson et al. 1995; Waitzkin et al. 1997), the provision of free, universally available health services, well-trained health workers (Anderson 2005; 2006; Waitzkin et al. 1997), active participation of the community (Iatridis 1990; Susser 1993) and the political prioritization of health (Feinsilver

1993). Some have also pointed to the broader conditions of the socialist system, especially the guarantee of egalitarian access to basic services as contributing to the outcomes (Chomsky 2000; Feinsilver 1993; Navarro 1993; Spiegel and Yassi 2004).

Speigel and Yassi (2004) allude to "social capital" (conceived as social connectedness) as part of the explanation. Reporting on their research in two Central Havana communities (Cayo Hueso and Colón), the authors conclude that self-reported health improved with higher levels of social connectedness. However, they include only a very limited discussion of what social capital means and do not specify which measures were used and why. Nor do they directly discuss broader social and political factors that influence social connectedness in the Cuban context.[10] Referring again to social capital, the authors also report that "there is an extremely high level of social capability to undertake collaborative activity at a local level to address collective needs." They argue that this social capability was demonstrated during the 2002-2003 outbreak of dengue in Havana "which triggered widespread mobilization, volunteer labor and a high degree of cooperation and compliance" (2004: 101). Interestingly, most of the article is devoted to highlighting deliberate national-level health policies (including public funding and universal access) and policies in other sectors (including free education and food rationing) as explanations for country's health outcomes. Yet the tone adopted when social capital is mentioned suggests that local mobilization, compliance and cooperation in line with national health policies are part of a bottom-up phenomenon, which is spontaneously "triggered" when problems such as the dengue epidemic emerge. This not entirely sufficient explanation begs some important questions regarding the relationships between policy makers and local communities.

It is evident that the Cuban government has for decades deliberately and strategically pursued key health improvements (elaborated in Chapter 3). Furthermore, the existing literature has usually pointed in the direction of effective health policies as the key determinants of the country's health outcomes. Hence, it would seem that the question of how Cuba improved key health indicators is also importantly a question about the sources of state effectiveness. The country's experience of managing to design and implement deliberate plans for overcoming some conditions of poverty (such as high mortality and morbidity) *in the absence of* material affluence strongly suggests that social capital and state capacity may be relevant. Even for many statists, the conventional presumption until now has been that the material wealth created by liberalism is a precondition for the construction of a more democratic society where collective decision-making processes play a central role. In other words, social inequalities and limited participation produced by the market were viewed as an initial price a society needed to pay in order to generate enough wealth to build more productive and democratic conditions (Boreham, Dow, and Leet 1999: Ch 6). Much of the recent literature on state capacity has focused on already affluent countries, advocating a stronger role for the state as a progression from, but reliant on the building blocks of, previous liberal achievements such as material affluence and political democracy.

Cuba's significant developmental success in areas such as health and education despite an obvious lack of material wealth allows the speculative hypothesis that it may not be necessary for developing countries to sacrifice or downgrade social goals in order to achieve economic ones—the reverse may even be true. It is well-known that good health and education outcomes are important aspects of the human capital linked to economic performance. If these can be achieved even with very low levels of material affluence, they may serve as more than just achievements in themselves. For developing countries this is a particularly pertinent issue in light of the well-documented social impact of free-market development models.

The theories of social capital and state capacity discussed in this chapter provide an appropriate starting point in the search for an explanation for the successful outcomes of some sectors in Cuba, a country that since 1959 has explicitly rejected the prevailing liberal development model. Since material resources alone cannot explain the country's achievements in health, there is reason to suppose more intangible elements are involved. One of the fundamental points emerging from the discussion of social capital is that societies' developmental outcomes rely on more than stocks of material capital; different societal arrangements and circumstances have different consequences in relation to capital accumulation or to affluence more broadly. Even within the broad category of "capitalist" systems, societies with different sets of circumstances such as income distribution; information networks; health, education, transport, administrative, electoral and legal systems; degrees of class hegemony, institutional and infrastructural achievements; conflict resolution arrangements and so on, will have different developmental outcomes. The discussion in this chapter implies that the same could apply in countries (such as Cuba) where the main mode of production is "socialist." In the absence of a theory of "socialist accumulation" or "development under state auspices" (especially development in a context of blockage and shortage resulting from insignificant trade), it is reasonable to postulate that "non-economic" aspects of development have played an important role.

Moreover, given the country's declared socialist system, outward appearances allow for speculation that its health system may be a case where cooperative institutional arrangements have produced positive societal outcomes. Given that Cuban authorities and some international observers of the Cuban health system have suggested there is a high level of "community participation" in the health sector, there is room to postulate that this may have something to do with the country's positive health outcomes. It may be that community involvement in health policy-making and implementation has produced good policy outcomes. This hypothesis is based on the insights drawn mainly from Bourdieu's and Coleman's observations regarding social capital, as well as neo-statists' arguments about the desirability of state "embeddedness." An examination of what types of organizational arrangements comprise the country's health system is intended to add something valuable to existing knowledge about Cuba and may also contribute to current discussions of social capital.

Given the obviously central role of the state in Cuba, the debates within the statist literature provide the basis for speculation. The successful outcomes certainly appear to support the statists' optimism regarding the potential for state autonomy (the capacity for the state to achieve what it sets out to do, even against competing natural, economic or social forces) and successful political accomplishments. However, given that there are different perspectives in the state capacity literature regarding the sources of state autonomy in developing contexts, it would seem important to identify the more precise arrangements that have been the basis of state capacity in setting and implementing health policy in Cuba. It may be that a high degree of state embeddedness (interpenetration between the central institutions of the state and civil society groups) in the health policy-making process explains the apparent effectiveness in policy implementation. On the other hand, perhaps the more important factor has been the ability for central decision-makers to make independent decisions "over the top of or against" other social groups.

Research Questions

As mentioned, the impetus for this research was the general puzzle of how Cuba managed to achieve impressive health outcomes despite its problematic internal and external material circumstances. However, this puzzle is examined here through a fairly specific lens informed by some of the theoretical findings emerging from social capital and state capacity literature. Drawing from this literature, an hypothesis emerged that Cuba's health outcomes may have resulted from cooperative institutional arrangements in the health sector, and a high degree of state "embeddedness" incorporating the contributions of many social groups in policy design and implementation. Thus, the more focused questions the research set out to explore were: *What are the institutional arrangements of the health sector and to what extent do central state decision-makers engage with and incorporate the contributions of other social groups in the process of designing and implementing health policy?* In the process of exploring these questions, the research is both theory testing and theory building. The project began by extracting in this chapter various aspects of recent social capital and state capacity discussions to

Table 5
Key Components of Social Capital and State Capacity investigated in Cuba

Social Capital	State Capacity: State "Embeddedness"
Formalized arrangements that allow ongoing cooperative relationships between different groups/actors associated with the PAMI to be developed, for example: a) Health workers' relationships with patients which facilitate the delivery of health care services; b) Relationships between different health institutions (Family doctors, policlinics, hospitals, MINSAP), which allow health goals to be achieved despite resource shortages; c) Relationships between mass organizations and health institutions which improve community contributions to health improvement; d) State-society linkages which allow contributions of different sections of the community to health policy design and implementation. (This is what neo-statists have called "embeddedness").	Infrastructural (non-despotic) state capacity a) "Penetrative power" (the state's power to interact directly with all of the population and to have directives routinely, reliably heeded). b) "Extractive power" (its ability to reach into and extract resources from a society without risk of revolt or the need for extra-legal coercion). c) "Negotiated power" (collaborations between political actors and other actors associated with the health sector, particularly including health sector employees and patients, such that citizens understand and accept the viewpoint of state officials and *vice versa*).

build a theoretical framework to be "tested" with empirical research in Cuba. Although the project's main purpose is to understand the Cuban case, the empirical research in turn feeds back into the theories by adding some suggestive ideas to current understandings of social capital and state capacity. The following is a table that summarizes the main components of social capital and state capacity which formed the basis for the empirical research in Cuba.

The Research in Cuba

Broadly speaking, research for this project constitutes a case study. A case study, as Gerring defines it, is "an intensive study of a single unit for the purpose of understanding a larger class of (similar) units" (2004, 342). For this project, the single unit is a program within the Cuban health system (the Maternal-Infant Health Program, or PAMI). The study aimed to provide broader explanations for Cuba's positive track record in health in the context of material shortage, but used a discrete and delimited aspect of policy for deliberate reasons. In part this was dictated by financial and time limitations. Interviewing employees from every institution connected with the overall health system would have been impossible given the scope of the project. The actual result would have been random interviews with a scattered selection of loosely-connected institutions, which would have provided only a fragmentary picture. I therefore chose one "slice" of the health system. The PAMI was an obvious choice due to the particularly positive statistical outcomes associated with it.

As detailed earlier in this chapter, my interpretive framework draws upon conceptual controversies surrounding capital. I have postulated that "social capital" will provide important insights into my research questions because, as discussed earlier, the premise here is that non-material aspects of social development need to be constructed, or invested in, over a long period. The Cuban regime would argue that this has in fact been the case. Dispassionate inquiry equally suggests that the recorded health outcomes depend on cooperative organizational arrangements and community acceptance of official procedures that are reasonably interpretable as aspects of social capital.

"State capacity," insofar as it implies public procedures which have secured outcomes not otherwise imaginable without political will or effort, can also be postulated as a determinant of recorded health achievements. Like social capital, state capacity typically has observable effects, and can be understood as itself a product of deliberative, collective efforts.

State capacity therefore is hypothesised as facilitative of the public processes that have led to low infant and maternal mortality rates, while constituting the basis for further improvements in health.

The research approach is qualitative, combining a number of different types of qualitative data. These include primary sources such as interviews and recorded fieldwork observations, as well as secondary literature and statistics. The inclusion of multiple types of evidence serves as a means of verification. By triangulating different sources to explore the same research question, I attempt to verify the validity of my outcomes. This is particularly important when gathering what Denzin and Lincoln call "qualitative empirical materials," or the different types of information sources collected in the field (Punch 1998, 60). Where possible I verify official interviews against less formal sources such as personal observations and informal conversations, and *vice versa*. Secondary literature written by researchers outside Cuba also serves to corroborate formal interviews and secondary data collected in Cuba.

Fieldwork for the project was carried out during two main visits to Cuba. While I had briefly visited the island once before in 2001, the first trip for research purposes was made in 2003 for a period of two months. This was largely a preliminary phase that was spent becoming familiar with the location, establishing contacts with some research institutions, seeking informal advice on the direction of the project and collating a general indicative bibliography. The second trip involved a longer period of seven months based in the capital, Havana. The empirical research for the project was conducted throughout those seven months in 2004. Since research in Cuba required foreign researchers to be affiliated with a Cuban institution, my research was officially "overseen" by a Cuban academic institution. The role of the institution I was affiliated with in Cuba[11] however, was in practice largely a bureaucratic one. Staff there coordinated a small number of interviews but their main contribution was organizing a temporary residence visa on the grounds of research and providing official letters (affirming that my project was officially sanctioned by a Cuban institution) to present to interviewees at other institutions such as the Ministry of Public Health (MINSAP) and the Federation of Cuban Women (FMC).

Interviews

The major part of empirical research involved semi-structured, open-ended, face-to-face recorded interviews in Spanish[12] with 24 respondents.

Respondents were chosen according to their knowledge and expertise in relation to the PAMI and their connection to institutions linked to that program. The selection of interviewees, therefore, was not intended to achieve a random population sample but to collect advice and opinions from experts in the area in order to illustrate whether and how the underlying theoretical framework being deployed in this book (the creation and impact of social capital and state capacity) comes into play in the practical context of Cuba's PAMI. (For more details refer back to the list of interviewees on pages vii-viii). During the interview process, I was able to visit and spend some time in various health institutions including maternity hospitals, policlinics, family doctors' offices, the Ministry of Public Health, a maternity home (*hogar materno*), the FMC headquarters and centre for documentation, and the other locations where interviews took place. Particularly the health workers I interviewed usually offered to show me around and explain their workplaces.

I found that, as a foreigner, contacting a person directly for an interview via the institution in which they worked was in most cases met with suspicion, guardedness and requests for official letters of authorization, the reception was entirely different when a friend or a friend of a friend had sent me. I soon became aware of the underlying culture of informal networks in Cuba, commonly referred to as "*sociolismo*" [a popular Cuban play on words that sounds a lot like the word socialism (*socialismo*) but suggests a system where things are achieved through friends or "*socios*"]. I quickly discovered that when trying to achieve almost anything in Cuba, it was well worth mentioning immediately the person who had sent me. This seemed to produce a greater level of trust even than when I appeared with official letters from authorizing institutions and, hence, I found some of the most frank and forthcoming interviewees were those I contacted in this informal way. Most interviewees recommended me to other relevant contacts they knew and in this way I gained access to a range of specialists related to maternal and infant health.

Arranging interviews was far from simple, however. The general process of organizing an appointment in Cuba was often time-consuming and frustrating. I soon learned that carrying reading material in my bag at all times was necessary if I planned to avoid wasting most of the day waiting. Similarly, I discovered that telephoning a person during work hours did not mean they would be at their desk to answer the call, and that setting a time for an interview did not mean the interviewee would arrive on time or arrive at all.

In addition, innumerable other unforeseeable obstacles appeared on a regular basis to interfere with interviews. For example, I was in Cuba during Hurricane Charley and when Hurricane Ivan threatened to hit a month later. My first appointment for an interview with the Federation for Cuban Women (FMC) coincided with the morning after Hurricane Charley. My house had no telephone line, gas or electricity after the storm so I picked my way through the streets filled with fallen trees and other debris to find a public telephone that worked to call the FMC where nobody answered the call. As I discovered, it was taken for granted in Cuba that nobody goes to work the day after a cyclone. Despite these and many other unforeseen difficulties that were part of the normal rhythm of life in Cuba, however, I also met many helpful and obliging people who went out of their way to support the project.

The interview scripts were structured around similar themes and the general goal of exploring the non-economic factors involved in the development of the PAMI. The major purposes of the interviews were to obtain general information to build a profile of the health system generally and more specifically about the PAMI and to seek opinions about what were the main factors contributing to the country's health outcomes. In particular I sought information about the nature of relationships between the different institutions associated with the PAMI, their relationships to the government and their interactions with the public. Although exploring similar themes, interview questions were also adapted to each interviewee's area of expertise.

The qualitative nature of the research also allowed for respondents themselves to play a role in shaping the interviews. For example, later interviews were partly influenced by responses to previous interviews. If a series of respondents had difficulties understanding or answering a certain question, I would rephrase that question for following interviews in a way that made the issue more accessible. If a respondent raised any additional themes or issues that were relevant and interesting to the study, I would also explore those in subsequent interviews. Hence, I found that by the end of my research period in Cuba, my original interview framework had been considerably restructured and revised. Hence the project had elements of an iterative-inductive approach; its design and analysis evolved with the progression of the research (see O'Reilly 2005: 3, 23). Respondents also gave me an insight into the ways in which the themes addressed in my project were conceptualized from the Cuban perspective and what were some of the theoretical discussions underway in Cuba that related to my area of interest. While I found little evidence of the term "social capital" that has been so prolific in the English-speaking world in recent years, Cubans did seem to be addressing similar or compatible themes, albeit expressed in different terms and shaped more specifically to the Cuban context [the concept of *"intersectorialidad"* (inter-sectoral cooperation), for example].

Post-Fieldwork Discussions with Cubans in Australia

During the period of writing up this work (from when I arrived back in Australia in late 2004 after fieldwork until 2007) I engaged in many discussions with Cubans in Australia. Although these discussions were not originally part of my research plan and did not take place during the period of official fieldwork, they provided many additional insights that were relevant to my work. I initially had some doubts about including any of these, as they could be perceived as overly impressionistic sources. For example, in a critique of a journal article in which I had included some testimonies from expatriate Cubans, one peer reviewer declared: *"Anyone familiar with Cuban "expatriates" would know that they left for economic reasons rationalized as discontent with the Cuban socialist system. Their testimony can only be biased."*

However, I ultimately decided to include some information from these discussions.[13] I defend this decision by arguing that the Cubans with whom I conversed in this period found themselves in Australia for many different reasons and certainly did not all declare themselves political dissidents escaping from socialism. Some had immigrated to Australia for family reasons, others for one or a combination of work-related, economic or political reasons. Others were studying in Australia, and still others were temporarily visiting Australia, later to return to Cuba. Moreover, given the restrictions on the island that prevent criticism of the regime, it may be that many Cubans feel more comfortable speaking candidly about life on the island once outside that context. Furthermore, while the testimonies of some Cuban expatriates can be biased, the same potential for bias applies to many Cuban sources *inside* Cuba. As Fernández (1990) observes, researchers should be alert to personal or political agendas affecting responses relating to Cuban issues *generally.* They should also adopt a critical perspective when reading material published in the Cuban media and academic journals attached to certain research centers on the island. Although they often contain valuable information, the line between serious scholarship and echoes of the official party line is sometimes blurred in these publications. The same cautions should apply to interviews. The views expressed inside and outside the country sometimes vary, even when coming from the same source. "How should analysts interpret the statements of former Cuban officials (such as General Rafael Pinos)? Do we take their words at face value now or believe what they said before, when they held posts in the Cuban government? Where is the truth to be found among all these conflicting sources?" (1990: 238). Although this is largely an unresolved issue, the best a researcher can do—aside from maintaining a critical approach in relation to all sources—is to employ multiple sources of evidence. It was for these reasons that I decided to include the discussions with Cuban expatriates; they served as one way to corroborate certain details from the more formal interviews in Cuba.

Participant Observation

While in Cuba, I soon realized that, although formal interviews were important and central to my work, I would also need to triangulate these with other sources of evidence. This included finding some way to incorporate the myriad unofficial discourses I heard and observations I made, since these offered an important dimension to the study that official interviews couldn't always reveal. Throughout the total of nine months spent in Cuba for research, I engaged in countless informal discussions on a daily basis with friends, neighbors, other personal contacts, taxi-drivers, strangers on buses or in the street and so on. Needless to say, these interactions, while not formally tape-recorded, contributed to shaping my views and the overall outcomes of my research. I found different ways to incorporate these. One of these was to record many of the informal discussions and personal observations and experiences in a fieldwork summary. Another such technique was to try wherever possible in formal interviews to raise issues that had emerged from informal discussions. For example, I might ask an official interviewee something like: "I have heard some people in general discussions on the street commenting that they feel doctors don't give them enough information in consultations. Do you think this is true?" This proved to be a useful way to broach sensitive questions without appearing too aggressive or critical. Official respondents seemed more willing to respond when they knew the questions had been sparked by what I had heard *Cubans* say, rather than something I had read in the foreign press, for example.

Even so, many of my field observations could not be captured in interviews in this way but nevertheless had a significant influence on the evolution of the project. Indeed, Karen O'Reilly, in her book on ethnographic methods, emphasizes that even in the process of conducting interviews, it is often the case that much of what is learned goes on "behind the scenes" and is not captured in the data collected from respondents:

> I would like to argue that many people who do research using interviews would benefit from actually permitting themselves to realise that as well as learning from the data they are collecting as people speak to them, they are also learning through participating and observing, and could learn more if they allowed themselves to do this more freely (O'Reilly 2005: 101).

At the outset, my methodological fieldwork plan resembled that of a traditional case study. I set out with the plan of conducting formal tape-recorded interviews with employees of as many as possible of the institutions directly involved with the PAMI. I also envisaged this to be achievable in a relatively short period (less time than I ultimately spent on the island). As it turned out, the achievable pace for organizing and conducting the formal interviews was far slower than I had anticipated. The appearance of myriad obstacles including bureaucratic procedures, transportation, natural disasters, power cuts and corruption hampered my intended research schedule and I ultimately spent seven months on the island (nine months including my initial research trip in 2003). What became apparent after the first few months, however, was that this delay had definite indirect advantages for my research. The longer period of time I spent on the island in 2004 permitted a level of immersion that had not been possible in my earlier visits (two weeks in 2001 as a tourist, and two months in 2003 for initial research). I became aware of more subtle aspects of Cuban culture, society and politics that could not have been perceived through formal interviews alone. In this sense, living in the place of fieldwork for a longer period allowed some degree of "participant observation"—the research took on an ethnographical dimension I had not planned but that enriched the research considerably.

Notes

1. Where page numbers are not supplied for direct quotes, this is due to the document not containing page numbers, as is the case with some electronic versions of articles.
2. While not related to health specifically, a study of Swedish municipalities by Lundasen (2005) also produced contradictory evidence to the civic engagement thesis; it found that density of voluntary associations was in fact negatively correlated with socioeconomic development.

3. This point is demonstrated in the work of Bourdieu, Coleman, and other theorists who draw attention to the resources generated through group membership which enhance the social power and economic rewards. I will return to these authors later in this chapter.

4. Indeed, in the recent literature, "social capital" and "civil society" are frequently treated as interchangeable. This not entirely appropriate association appears to have played some role in shaping discussions of the directions and implications of social capital. Civil society has historically been a concept used to support the liberal model and, in particular, has been employed to support the anti-state position. This dates back to its earlier modern usage that presented the concept as one part of a state/civil society dichotomy (Edwards and Foley 1998b). Civil society has traditionally represented a spontaneous realm of social order and has served as a point of contrast with the more formal, political institutional arrangements within society (Ahrne 1996: 110) but that nonetheless is held to reconcile individual interests with the collective good (Tonkiss and Passey 2000: 8) in the absence of government. As a result, it has been associated mainly with those advocating a realm of informal collective action separate from the more formal, authoritative institutions in society. Thus, in the 1990s it was frequently adopted by libertarian movements reacting against oppressive governments demanding a realm of voluntary collective action in the absence of the state. Correspondingly, in its more recent usage, the term has been associated with neoliberal economics and been employed by the Western right to complement its anti-statist agenda (Edwards and Foley 1998b: 6). However, conceptually, civil society and social capital are not the same thing; they emerged from different histories with different purposes. There is a basic inconsistency between the treatment of social capital as the interactions of civil society and the reason the concept (re)emerged in the first place, which was to demonstrate something about societies' developmental capacities that the market model fails to capture.

5. Despite Coleman's description of social capital as a separate type of capital, his general treatment of the concept seems more fruitful than more recent approaches.

6. Coleman also portrays social capital as durable social structures, but unlike Bourdieu does not explain how these structures are created.

7. Of course, this is not to say that the only type of social capital that improves collective decision-making and societal outcomes is that which is universally owned and accessible. Many particularistic civil society groups can of course also have indirect benefits on countries' outcomes. However, the fragmenting and anti-social effects of some groups call for a narrower specification of what forms of social capital can be more definitely linked to societies' development outcomes. The construction of social capital proffered here is an attempt in this direction.

8. For a detailed discussion of how public institutional arrangements can act as "beneficial constraints," see Streeck (1997).

9. This is not incompatible with the construction of social capital developed earlier as social investments in cooperative, inclusive institutional arrangements.

10. The authors do not acknowledge either, the dual discourses that are often adopted Cuba in relation to health or the possibility that political factors could have influenced interviewees' responses. For example, it is conceivable that individuals who have strong ties to the Communist Party are comparatively socially "well-connected." This is especially likely considering the Cuban laws prohibiting non-government association and the social pressures to politically conform. Furthermore, most Cubans are very aware of the political importance of the country's health outcomes, particularly the image of the country's health system as it is portrayed to the international community (see Chapters 3 and 5 for elaboration of all of the

above points). As the authors were foreign researchers in Cuba, it is imaginable that "well connected" respondents may have had a greater interest in transmitting a positive image of the country's health situation, which might have influenced the higher levels of self-perceived health and well-being they reported. The authors may have controlled such factors but this cannot be judged given that they neither mention these issues nor provide information regarding their variables and methods for measuring social connectedness.

11. For the purposes of maintaining the anonymity of staff at the institution, its name is not included here.

12. Although my Spanish is fluent and I had visited the Cuba prior to the research period, it should be acknowledged that being an "outsider" always has some bearing on the nature and quality of data collected. Although I became fairly 'immersed' during the period I spent on the island, the act of conducting research in a foreign context inevitably carries some linguistic and cultural barriers. In a similar vein, being a "foreigner" in Cuba can also have an influence on the types of responses informants provide. For example, many Cubans can be wary of expressing critical views about Cuba's political or social situation to foreigners they do not know well. As is discussed further later in this chapter, I compensated for this somewhat by adopting various measures for gaining interviewees' trust and by combining interview material with other sources of evidence. Nevertheless, the possibility should be noted that some interviewee responses may have been influenced by my identity as a foreign researcher.

13. As with all other interviews, sources' names have been coded to maintain anonymity. Consent was obtained from these sources for the inclusion of all material referenced to them.

3

Political Will and Cooperative
Institutional Arrangements

Introduction

This is the first of the chapters in this book which relate findings from
the research conducted in Cuba. The main contributions of the chapter
are to highlight the deliberateness with which the maternal-infant health
improvements are collectively pursued in Cuba, and to draw attention to
a range of institutionalized arrangements which coordinate and integrate
diverse sections of the community into the process of implementing the
goals set out in the PAMI. It is argued that the unusual cohesion and
coordination of the system in the pursuit of improved maternal-infant
health outcomes can be explained as the outcome of an organizational
hierarchy wherein the Cuban government is the most powerful and
influential actor.

There is nothing accidental or spontaneous about Cuba's maternal
and infant mortality outcomes. What became apparent, especially in
many of the formal interviews, was the remarkable intent with which
the Cuban government and all institutions—both in and outside the
health sector—pursue certain health objectives, notably the reduction
of maternal and infant mortality. Behind the unusually positive indicators are the exhaustive preceding efforts on the part of all sectors and
institutions of a regime that has often been described as "obsessed with
maternal-infant health."

Preventive health care as it is practiced in Cuba involves proactive
efforts from health workers at all levels of the system, as well as other sectors of the bureaucracy, to identify and avert potential risks contributing
to morbidity and mortality. This entails regular and ongoing interaction

between health workers and all of the population aimed at public health surveillance and the modification of lifestyle and behavioral factors associated with health risk. The latter can sometimes involve significant intervention into Cuban citizens' private lives. Surprisingly, there appears to be little public contestation around the PAMI or health goals generally. The cohesion and cooperation that generally characterize the Cuban health sector, particularly in relation to the pursuit of prioritized health programs such as the PAMI, have afforded significant effectiveness in improving health outcomes compared with other countries at a similar level of economic development.

The Cuban Government's Humanitarian, Political, and Symbolic Motives for Prioritizing Health Outcomes

Rarely did Fidel Castro make a speech during his presidency without some mention of the Cuba's infant mortality rates and the superiority of its indicators over those of the United States. The following excerpt from a speech delivered at Havana's Plaza de la Revolución on 1 May, 2004 for International Labor Day is a typical example:

> They [the United States] know that, despite their criminal blockade and the obstacles they put in place to prevent us obtaining medicines, equipment and medical technologies, in our country infant mortality is lower than in the United States (Applause); maybe they ignore the fact that we are going to reduce this infant mortality to less than 6, and maybe in the near future, to less than 5. Let's make the conviction—one that I never talk about—that in no more than five or six years, the life expectancy in our country will reach no less than 80 years (Applause), and that the country will become the most advanced centre of medical services in the world (Castro 2004).[1]

The sustained precedence given to health, particularly maternal-infant health, above many other collective concerns in Cuba can be accurately understood only in the light of its role in the history and contemporary reality of the country's socialist project, the latter being inseparable from its bilateral relations with the United States. Protecting the health of the population for ethical reasons has been a cornerstone of the revolutionary regime's declared project from the outset (see Castro [1953] 2001). Delivering its promise of improved health outcomes is therefore significant for the government's legitimacy within Cuba. Performance in health and education is still the point most commonly cited by the revolution's supporters as evidence of the system's success, despite its failures in other areas (Oppenheimer 1993: 158). Beyond the realm of domestic politics though, health indicators are employed as powerful symbolic, ideological tools in the regime's struggle to win international support for its project and to prove its humanitarian superiority over the United States.

As any student of Cuba has learned, to understand any facet of the revolution, it is critical to first investigate how Fidel Castro sees an issue and how his views about the issue have changed over time. This is evident in health matters. Castro's concern with health and health care antecedes the revolution. His position, stated as early as in his well-known defence during the trial following the 1953 Moncada attack, was unequivocal. Access to health care should be universal. His objective since coming to power has been to fulfil this populist promise. Few efforts have been spared to do so despite the fragility of the Cuban economy, and the many crises it has faced. What is extraordinary about the Cuban health system is it serves as a political and ideological weapon. Castro, in his compulsive desire to confront the U.S. decided long ago to challenge "imperialism" in the statistical "health battlefield." Castro believes that some day Cuba will attain better health indicators than the U.S. and that such achievements will convincingly prove the moral and political superiority of the revolution.... It is no exaggeration to state that Castro, and hence the rest of the revolutionary leadership, is obsessed with health...and especially [with] maternal-child health... [W]hat is unique about Cuba is the zeal with which it is pursued (Diaz-Briquets 1986: 39-40).

The following excerpt from an interview with a gynecologist/obstetrician in a Cuban hospital demonstrates a clear awareness of the way health outcomes are used to defend the regime's image before the international community. The respondent explained that Cuban doctors are educated and socialized to understand the political importance of health statistics and to incorporate this understanding into the way they approach medical practice.

Those working in the system have to comply with and maintain the same results because these are the flags [the government flies]; they are what is promoted to the world as the good aspects of this system. If we don't have [our good health results] then we could come under even more scrutiny. Other things about our system are questioned, but in health we can't be questioned because we have the results and with few resources.... Here they educate us with this conception (author's interview with Herrera, September 2004).

Brotherton has described Cuba's socialist health ideology as using "measures of the health of individuals as a metaphor for the health of the body politic, effectively linking the efficacy of socialism and its governmental apparatus to the health conditions of the population" (2005: 348). In her study of the use of symbolism associated with the Cuban health system, Feinsilver explains the process through which health in Cuba is used to gain what she calls "symbolic capital." Beyond achieving positive health statistics, Cuba engages in an extensive operation of medical diplomacy whereby it sends teams of doctors to developing countries in its region and even offers scholarships to underprivileged U.S. medical students (2006; 1989b; Loose 2006). This medical diplomacy plays an important role in winning Cuba support from abroad, which translates into more tangible benefits (Feinsilver 2006). For example, Cuba sends teams of doctors on missions to Venezuela to work in Chávez's health programs. In exchange, Venezuela provides Cuba with around ninety thousand barrels of oil per day (Williams 2007). Despite Fidel Castro having publicly admitted the symbolic role health plays in Cuba as a "challenge and a battleground between imperialism and ourselves" (quoted in Feinsilver 1989b), Cuban officials have tended to deny that the country's generosity in providing medical treatments, medical scholarships and teams of doctors to neighboring countries has political or economic motives (see Marquis 2000; Williams 2007).

Institutional Developments Ensuring Access to Health Facilities and Regular Contact between Health Workers and the Population

Attention to expanding health coverage and the establishment of health as a state responsibility has been common to socialist systems (Chen and Hiebert 1994; Navarro 1993) and Cuba is no exception. Cuba's Public Health Law, adopted in 1983, specifies that the state has a fundamental and permanent obligation to protect and improve the health of the Cuban population. Furthermore, the law stipulates that institutions forming part of the national health system should give high priority to preventive actions and measures (Evenson 2005). Superficial indicators suggest Cuba's preventive approach has contributed to its positive health outcomes. The country's rate of vaccination is close to 100% of target populations. Following mass vaccination programs that were some of the country's first preventive health measures after 1959, the prevalence of infectious diseases preventable by vaccines has been reduced to a level below all other nations at similar levels of economic development (Waitzkin et al. 1997).

A closer examination of the way health care is delivered in Cuba reveals a collective effort on the part of medical professionals at all levels of the health system to foresee and avert potential health risks before they become major problems leading to morbidity and mortality. This takes the form of a comprehensive system of registration, surveillance and monitoring of the population[2] involving institutions at all levels of the system beginning at the community level with the Family Doctor Program. As part of their role, the family doctor and nurse are required to see each person in their catchment area at least twice a year and to keep complete and updated health records (Waitzkin et al. 1997). A focus on preemptively addressing *potential* rather than *actual* health problems entails a level of official involvement in patients' lives virtually unheard of in most other global contexts. As one interviewee observed, Cuba is the only country he had seen where it is normal for a family doctor "to knock on the door, to make sure the children are bathed and check that the bathroom and sanitary service are in a reasonable condition" (author's interview with Herrera, September 2004). In Western liberal contexts, by contrast, the expectation that doctors will actively contact or pursue patients rarely extends beyond sending an occasional reminder letter for appointments or checkups. It is easily conceivable for patients to live periods of months or even years without seeing a doctor. Even in countries where national universal schemes exist, health services are rarely delivered automatically but depend on the initiative of individual patients to solicit them. A recent newspaper report comparing U.S. and Cuban health expenditures and life expectancy indicators points out that part of the reason for the United States' comparatively low life expectancy is a lack of preventive screening. This is especially the case for uninsured patients who, for financial reasons, tend to delay treatment for a condition until it becomes a serious illness (Dorschner 2007). By contrast, the Cuban system is designed to prevent anybody from "falling through the cracks" of the program. In addition to the Family Doctor program, in house physicians either reside in or regularly visit government offices and factories to make routine health checks; this implies that if patients escape family doctor visits they will be screened at work (Oppenheimer 1993: 160).

The Cuban health system is characterized by health workers' practical intervention into patients' lives on a frequent and ongoing basis. The Cuban family doctor, upon arriving in a new community, begins a process of proactively surveying and classifying the population with the goal of detecting early signs or risks of preventable health problems. In the case of the PAMI, this involves automatically scheduling consultations and keeping comprehensive sexual health records for all women in the catchment area from when they reach reproductive age. Through this process, it is usual for health institutions to become closely involved in pregnancies at early stages. Once a pregnancy is registered, the pregnant woman's *libreta*[3] food rations are adjusted to include special dietary requirements such as calcium, vitamins, and extra milk (author's interview with Ramirez, September 2004). Then a series of scheduled consultations with the doctor automatically begins.[4] By contrast with most Western contexts, the doctor is the party responsible for initiating and continuing this process.

Family doctors are required to serve the same community for a minimum period of five years, meaning that when a pregnancy is diagnosed, the pregnant woman's general medical history is already well known to the doctor from previous routine health checks.

> If I arrive as a new family doctor to a community, and say it has 1500 people, the first thing I have to do is characterize that population. Here we characterize into four groups: healthy patients, patients at risk, group three is sick patients and group four is patients with disabilities. I start visiting the patients or they come to the *consultorio* and as I do this I am also classifying.... Looking at the family all together in the home environment allows us to decide whether that family is at risk.... Doctors here have to walk a lot to visit all the families [which is important] because this allows us to observe and modify their lifestyles.... Suppose there is a family in my community that has a man and a woman and they have a daughter and the daughter has reached reproductive age; let's say she is 22 years old. The girl gets married, wants to have a child and falls pregnant. At this point I already know this girl because I visited her family's house while she was growing up so I already know if this is likely to be a pregnancy with risks, or a normal pregnancy.... It is much easier this way than if a [pregnant woman] arrives who I don't know (author's interview with Castillo, September 2004).

Cuba's approach to health care has been described as an integral one that "combines prevention with cure and treats the individual as a bio-psycho-social being, living and working or studying in a given environment" (Feinsilver 1993, 29; see also Pietroni 2001). Since doctors reside in the same community they serve, doctors and patients interact with one another in a range of situations and contexts; in the *consultorio* (doctor's office), in the patient's household and around the neighborhood where both live. The doctor-patient relationship is also highly social and informal by contrast with a typical Western context. There is a noticeable absence in Cuba of the bureaucratic formalities typical of U.S. or Australian health services; patients are not separated from doctors by receptionists, insurance forms, or strict opening hours, but simply turn up at the doctor's office and wait in a line. Doctors regularly consult with more than one person at once in the same room and in many cases patients even approach doctors in the street to ask medical questions (see also Hirschfeld 2006). Aside from improving doctors' ability to observe patients and therefore anticipate their health risks, the close and ongoing doctor-patient relationship also improves trust between the two parties (author's interview with Almeida, August 2004; see also Lunday 2001). This leads patients to be more forthcoming in seeking help and providing doctors with information.

[The fact that doctors live in the community] has a positive influence on everything because the doctor comes to be seen as part of the family. If you are a young person who comes to see me for the first time you might not feel comfortable telling me, for example, that you are sexually active. So you might hide it or deny it, meaning that I am not aware I should be taking care of your reproductive health, making sure you don't fall pregnant too early and that you don't have a sexually transmitted disease.... On the other hand, when your doctor is the same doctor who attended your mother in childbirth, gave you your vaccines when you were small and watched you grow up, you can go to this doctor without any difficulty and say "look, I have this problem, could you help me?" (author's interview with Almeida, August 2004).

Doctors' close contact with patients usually continues when patients are referred to other health institutions such as hospitals or maternity homes. Family doctors are also responsible for post-natal care and keeping a close watch on the progress of new infants. They schedule regular appointments and visit the infant's household to administer vaccinations, monitor hygiene conditions, identify risk factors, and educate parents on how to care for the child. This close observation of patients and attention to preventing health problems during and after a pregnancy would appear to have a profound influence on the health of the mother and child. As a member of the Cuban Federation of Women put it, the likelihood of maternal and infant mortality "has to do with the whole trajectory of a woman's sexual and reproductive health. A woman who, for example, doesn't carry out regular sexual health checks will have a higher possibility of developing health problems that could later lead to a maternal death" (author's interview with Delgado and Suárez, August 2004).

Supervision of health services in Cuba is centrally coordinated and based on an organizational hierarchy. The records family doctors keep are monitored by and answerable to a "Basic Work Group" (GBT) based at the local policlinic. Policlinics control more resources than family doctors' offices and each one services around twelve family doctor communities. A GBT is made up of the twelve doctor/nurse teams (known as a "Basic Health Team") along with three specialists who worked from the policlinic—a gynecologist/obstetrician, a pediatrician and an internist (author's interview with Castillo, September 2004). Policlinics report to health organizations at the municipal level. These report to the provincial level, which in turn reports to the national Ministry for Public Health (MINSAP). At the local level, policlinic supervisors place considerable pressure on family doctors to sustain routine observation of their local communities. When any preventable health problems emerge in their community, family doctors are held accountable and the same follows suit through to the national level (author's interviews with Herrera 2004; Valdes 2004; Castillo 2004).

Information regarding chronic and acute illnesses is transferred sequentially up this ladder via a computerized surveillance system that enables health surveillance at the national level of factors such as changing patterns in the spread and distribution of diseases, as well as the emergence of any new epidemics (Waitzkin et al. 1997). The Cuban health system has a large team of health statisticians compared with most other countries in the world. The responsibility of statisticians at all levels of the system is to report information to the level directly above them, meaning that information travels vertically upwards to MINSAP. This system bears resemblance to earlier Soviet health models, with a strong reliance on statistics as a means for controlling mortality and morbidity (Braa, Titlestad, and Sæbø 2004).

Inter-sectoral and Inter-institutional Cooperation

Aside from these organizational structures aimed at integrating the population into the medical system, the health system is also arranged in such a way that a high level of collaboration between its different institutions, fulfilling the objectives set out in the PAMI, is secured. Cuba also seems to have managed to incorporate contributions to the program from sectors outside health. As will be detailed in this section, these arrangements have been significant in reducing the multi-factoral contributors to maternal and infant deaths.

Moves to a more multi-sectoral approach to health have recently been seen in some European nations (Vega and Irwin 2004). Sweden and the UK are among those endeavoring to increase responsibility for population health amongst government agencies outside the public health sector. This comes with the recognition that the causes of many public health problems are multi-factoral, meaning that no single organization or sector contains all of the relevant information, expertise and resources required to sustain significant public health improvements (Mays 2002). Vega and Irwin call for similar initiatives to be implemented in developing countries, arguing that OECD pro-poor policies that target low-income groups (see OECD 2003) are insufficient because they overlook factors other than income that influence health outcomes. While in most countries the administrative and budgeting structures in the public sector still discourage inter-sectoral cooperation, there is a growing body of evidence suggesting its importance to the improvement of population health (Vega and Irwin 2004: 3,11; Holveck et al 2007).

An assessment of health policy reform in Russia, for example, suggests that the absence of a "coordinated national effort" was responsible for a decline in health outcomes (Duffy 1997). Previously favorable health trends throughout the 1970s were reversed during Russia's political transition period of the 1990s. Throughout this period, infant mortality rates were among the indicators that dramatically worsened, with the number of deaths increasing by 50 percent from 1980s figures. According to Duffy, contributors to the problem were the deliberate moves throughout the democratization process to decentralize decision-making and increase competition between regional government actors. This led to a polarization of these actors who became more occupied "with lobbying for funds and cultivating personal contacts (as in the Soviet period), [than] developing innovative programs." This fragmentation, combined with underdeveloped institutional conduits between citizens and the state, limited the possibility of formulating workable and coherent health policies, exposing the need for a more proactive effort at the national level (1997: 541).

In an abstract sense then, Duffy's account of the Russian experience suggests that government actors, when working alone (or in competition with one another), can become so preoccupied with trivial problems confined to their jurisdiction that broader problems are ignored or perpetuated. The Cuban case appears to demonstrate that, when sectors of the bureaucracy work together collaboratively towards predetermined goals, a broader contribution to the improvement of population health is possible. The following excerpt from an interview with a representative from the Cuban Ministry of Public Health (MINSAP) is illustrative of what was a common overall theme emerging from the interviews; formal institutionalized cooperative relationships between different sectors of the bureaucracy were considered one of the important organizational factors contributing to the country's low levels of maternal and infant mortality.[5]

> I would say that the *key* factor contributing to the reduction of infant mortality in Cuba is inter-sectoral cooperation, that is, the role exercised by governments and parties at the level of every municipality in the country to unite all sectors of the community in prioritising the Maternal-Infant Program (author's interview with Ramirez, September 2004).

This respondent went on to emphasize the need for maternal and infant health outcomes to be viewed as results of the collective efforts of a society rather than related only to the sector, or to institutions or individuals directly involved in the field [a point also emphasized by interviewees Castillo (2004) and Blanco (2004)].

The indicator maternal mortality is a *social* indicator.[6] There cannot be good maternal mortality rates if, for example, there are not good roads where an ambulance has to travel to bring a woman with complications in labor from Maici to the province's capital, Guantánamo. There cannot be good maternal mortality rates if there is no decent communication system that allows one to call intensive care to tell them to prepare a bed for the child that is on the way ... if we hadn't built roads years ago, houses, hydro systems and aqueducts, children now would be dying of diarrhea (author's interview with Ramirez, September 2004).

From even before a woman falls pregnant in Cuba, she comes into contact with a range of institutions that contribute either directly or indirectly to the outcome of her potential pregnancy. When she reaches reproductive age, the woman is scheduled a "preconceptional reproductive risk consultation" with her family doctor. This consultation assesses her general health and aims to modify factors such as her diet in order to preventively minimize risks associated with pregnancy (author's interview with Ramirez, September 2004). A woman's compliance with the routine schedule of consultations that begin from the outset of her pregnancy, along with other preventive requirements throughout the pregnancy, is largely viewed and treated as a social responsibility. In other words, ensuring the outcome of a healthy child is not solely her task. Arguably, neither is it solely her *choice*. Decisions about her diet, lifestyle, the medical attention she receives and so on are (at best) facilitated and (at worst) coerced[7] by a wide societal network acting collaboratively to minimize the number of maternal and infant deaths.

Initial visits with the family doctor establish whether a pregnant woman is a low or high-risk case and she is referred accordingly to appropriate specialists and scheduled the required number of prenatal consultations. At the community level, the family doctor works in conjunction with the local branches of two of the country's principal mass organizations, the Federation of Cuban Women (FMC) and the Committee for the Defense of the Revolution (CDR). Both of these organizations also have responsibilities in connection with the PAMI. For example, the FMC representative and the family doctor have regular meetings to discuss the pregnant women in their area. Combining the FMC representative's knowledge of the population's social conditions and the doctor's medical assessment, the two parties make decisions about the social and physical requirements of the pregnant women in the community and how to address these. If, for example, a woman has not been attending her scheduled consultations with the doctor, the FMC representative will usually go to the woman's house to find out why this is the case and, if necessary, convince the woman to attend (author's interview with Castillo, September 2004).

Aside from these more targeted home visits, *brigadistas sanitarias* [brigade workers (a branch of the FMC)] make general visits to all of the population. Their role includes identifying health hazards in households, educating the population about how to manage them and helping administer public health campaigns. For example, brigade workers may give children vaccination injections or point out to parents health hazards such as smoking inside, cooking with boiling water near where children are playing and so on. Public health authorities also visit all households to carry out regular hygiene checks including routine publicly-funded fumigations and inspections of water tanks. All of these efforts contribute, either directly or indirectly, to the reduction of maternal and infant deaths (author's interviews with Arango 2004; Medina 2004; Delgado and Suárez 2004). Cubans appear fairly socially accustomed to these regular visits to their home (normally without forewarning) and to complying and cooperating with public health initiatives (field notes 2004).

Cooperative relationships between different institutions within the public health sector also help to overcome problems of resource shortages, by permitting and encouraging resource sharing that effectively maximizes the population's access to medical equipment and supplies. For example, as one doctor explained, regular meetings held between the directors of different Cuban hospitals in conjunction with health authorities seek, among other objectives, to ensure that scarce resources are used to their optimum capacity.

> Right now, for instance, there is a meeting in the province where all the hospital directors are present. There they will be discussing things like, for example, how many units of cefazolin each has in their warehouse. One might have 1000, so the health authorities tell them to send 200 of those to a hospital that has more limited supply... At the level of the Ministry for Public Health, they devise political strategies or programs that seek to optimize material resources. What does this mean? We have, for example, very few ultrasound machines. Therefore [we make arrangements so that] ... patients from the municipality of Marianao can access the equipment on Mondays, those from La Lisa on Tuesdays, from Playa on Wednesdays, and on Thursdays the high risk cases from all of those zones (author's interview with Herrera, September 2004).

Diaz-Briquets points out that no developing country aside from Cuba has been able to afford the "desirable but expensive luxury" of having most childbirths occur in hospitals with specialized equipment and personnel (1986: 40). The resource limitations with which health professionals work are blatantly observable in Cuban health facilities. Since

Cuba has extremely limited access to internationally traded disposable health supplies such as syringes, tubes, sample taking devices and so on, these are substituted with Cuban-made or resterilizable items. Much of the medical equipment still in use in Cuban hospitals and clinics is many decades old and no longer used in any other part of the world with maternal-infant mortality indicators comparable with Cuba's (author's interview with Jiménez, September 2004). As a number of interviewees pointed out, many nations with access to far superior medical supplies and equipment have far inferior health indicators to Cuba's (Rios 2004; author's interviews with Castillo 2004; Herrera 2004; Ramos 2004a). The cooperative system of resource sharing described above may go some way to explain how this was possible in Cuba. The overall cost of providing high-quality facilities to the population is significantly reduced where limited resources are shared.[8]

Institutions outside the public health sector are also expected to contribute to the PAMI when called upon. One example of this raised in an interview was that workplaces are required to provide lunches to pregnant women in their geographical area who do not have the economic means at home for a satisfactory diet. In Cuba, workplaces provide lunch for their employees. Family doctors with high-risk pregnant women in their community make arrangements with local workplaces in order that these women be given a lunch pass to eat every day alongside the workplace's employees (author's interview with Valdes, August 2004). Similarly, agricultural cooperatives are required to make food donations to maternity homes (author's interview with Ramirez, September 2004).

According to the Director of Cuba's National School of Public Health (author's interview with Vargas, October 2004), the role of sectors outside public health is fundamental to the achievement of positive health outcomes. He said part of the role for a public health director should be communication with the directors of other sectors to make them aware of the importance of public health goals and persuade them to contribute.

The first thing I have to achieve as Director of Public Health is to sensitize others who should participate.... I might call, [for example], the Director of Hydraulics and Aqueducts, who deals with water supply, and I explain the importance of water to population health. I explain how many areas have sick babies dying of diarrhea from drinking unhealthy water. I make him sensitive to the issue. It's not that I call him to a meeting and order him to fix the water, no. I make him aware of the problem and I say "look, I need you to make a plan for next year to ensure the water is not contaminated"... It's important that the Public Health Director understands how inter-sectoral cooperation works and that he or she is not the director of other sectors—they are partners (author's interview with Vargas, October 2004).

Mays (2002) explains that, in many of the countries where inter-sectoral collaboration has been attempted, one of the main obstacles has been a lack of willingness on the part of institutions outside the health sector such as business, education, human services, criminal justice and so on to collaborate. Non-health actors are often reluctant to contribute efforts and resources to initiatives they do not control and where no obvious benefits will result for their own institution or sector. Given these experiences of other countries, that Cuba has managed such a degree of cooperative involvement in public health endeavors is unusual. According to Mays, another factor that often interferes with multi-sectoral initiatives is change in political leadership or political priorities. The sustained leadership of the Castro government, the nationalization of all health services and the government's commitment to public health since its inception for the reasons outlined above may explain why multi-sectoral collaboration has so far been sustained in Cuba. The respondent Vargas (author's interview, 2004) argued that the existence of a single health system in Cuba had unquestionably facilitated the coordination of different institutions within the system.

Political Will

The respondent (Vargas) went on to argue that the primary factor involved in Cuba's success in maternal-infant health was the existence of initiative on the part of the government to achieve those outcomes or, as he termed it, "the existence of political will"[9] (see also Spiegel and Yassi 2004). He argued that the cooperative relationships between sectors and institutions in Cuba, although facilitative of positive health outcomes, would have been ineffectual in the absence of a clear political prioritization of maternal-infant health.[10]

> Prioritizing health needs to begin not in the public health sector but at the level of the government. Yes, the public health sector is the coordinator; it partly leads the way because it has the technical knowledge of health that corresponds with its sector.[11] However, it has to be guided by the overarching direction of the state and government (author's interview with Vargas, October 2004).

It is worth noting that the World Bank also recently in its 2004 *World Development Report* the importance of "political will" in the context of Cuba's health outcomes, particularly its low infant mortality rates. Returning to the "Cuban puzzle" of good health outcomes despite low economic growth and low per-capita incomes, the bank notes that "sustained focus of the political leadership on health for more than 40 years surely played a big part" (2004b: 157).

In Cuba, reducing levels of maternal and infant mortality is, along with other health results, an explicitly stated goal outlined in the Maternal-Infant Health Program (PAMI). The written program that articulates the PAMI's purpose and goals clearly implies multisectoral involvement, stating that the prevention and protection of pregnant women and children is to be "implemented by the National Health System in coordination with the rest of the state's institutions, mass organizations and the active participation of the community" (Leonard Castillo, Ermeso Rivera and Sosa Marín 1985: 1).

Several of the doctors interviewed also attested that the positive performance of Cuban health workers is to a great extent attributable to the priority health is given at the national level. Health professionals work under constant demands from above to fulfill targets and monitor a range of programs—these demands determine to a large extent the order of priority given to different health problems. One doctor gave the following explanation:

> Since the first years after the triumph of the revolution it has been a number one priority of the country's leadership, in our case Fidel Castro, to make the health professionals aware of the important role of those who work with mothers and babies. This conditioning is transferred from generation to generation. What is it that makes us arrive at a satisfactory final result? [It is] the strict demand and compliance with all of the programs, norms and procedures that are established to improve those results.... If you decide to become a doctor here there is simply no other option. You cannot make demands or petitions as an individual or group that could go against the development of the work you are doing [because] that doesn't exist.... There are plenty of other countries that have better resources than we do but do not achieve the same results. I think the sociopolitical system is the determining factor here ... the strictness, the demand from above (author's interview with Herrera, September 2004).

As this passage suggests, Cuban health workers have limited political and economic power compared with their counterparts in, for example, the United States, Australia or European countries. As a professional group, doctors and nurses have little recourse to challenge the government's monopoly over health decision-making.[12] Almost all doctors [aside from a small number who received their medical training before 1959 and are permitted to continue private practice (author's interview with Almeida, August 2004)] must work for the state; they have no alternative employment options in health. General restrictions on non-government voluntary associations limit the ability of doctors to join professional associations that could provide leverage to negotiate work conditions or affect health policy.[13] The government's stranglehold over the national media similarly restricts health sector employees from publicizing opposing views on health policy. This ability of the government to restrict the political influence of other groups is clearly part of the explanation for the coordinated and collaborative effort towards the goals of the Maternal-Infant Program and the health system more generally. As Diaz-Briquets observes, the totalitarian nature of the state's influence in Cuba has facilitated its decisions to allocate scarce resources to prioritized areas of health. Decisions about resource allocation can be made with relatively little concern for competing interests (1986: 42).

Discussion

One of the more conspicuous characteristics of the Cuban health system is a high level of cohesion and collaboration between different institutions within the health sector regarding the country's health goals and priorities. This extends beyond the health sector to involve also actors within sectors outside health that regularly contribute to prioritized health programs such as the PAMI. The sustained participation by non-health sectors is particularly notable, especially considering that this often involves resource sacrifices without any immediate trade-offs or material incentives (for example, agricultural cooperatives could sell the food they donate to maternity homes but agree to the latter). On the whole, according to the accounts provided by many of the Cuban interviewees, there would appear to be relatively little contestation surrounding the decision to collectively prioritize health over other sectors, the PAMI over other health programs, or a preventive approach as the means for achieving the goals of the PAMI. Furthermore, the successful implementation of Cuba's proactive health policies also depends on the achievement of public compliance with health care delivery methods, involving close and regular monitoring of every citizen and often fairly interventionist measures to modify behavior and lifestyles.

Given that health systems elsewhere have encountered difficulties sustaining coordinated initiatives involving commitment from multiple institutions, this cohesion and sustained multi-institutional, multi-sectoral devotion of energy to specific health goals is unusual. How did Cuba manage this high level of societal integration and cooperation in the pursuit of certain health objectives, which has clearly increased its effectiveness in accomplishing those objectives? The short answer to the puzzle is that the collaboration is the result of an organizational hierarchy, headed by a politically dominant and long-standing government with an ongoing commitment to health and clear health priorities. The source of state capacity and effectiveness in the health sector then—or the ability of the system to deliver its goals—would appear to derive from the autonomy of central state institutions. In other words, state elites have managed to prioritize certain goals *independently of* competing interests and to pull other actors into line in cooperation with the implementation of those goals.

Even taking into account the authoritarian aspects of this power dynamic, it is arguable that the hierarchical arrangements underpinning the Cuban health sector have been effective in that they have delivered the results. As a means for efficiently reducing maternal and infant mortality, there are advantages to central control in the context of resource shortages. The incorporation of all institutions, services and facilities into one nationalized sector has especially improved resource-sharing, which allows optimal public access to the country's limited health facilities and supplies. Moreover, the ability of state elites to achieve the compliance of multiple institutions and sectors, apparently in the absence of significant challenges from opposing interest groups in the private sector, simplifies the process of policy implementation. These attributes of the top-down system have worked to Cuba's advantage in its quest for improved maternal and infant and other prioritized health indicators.

Based on the surface-level profile of the Cuban health system presented so far, the case appears to support the social capital argument that (expressed as a rudimentary abstraction) cooperative organizational arrangements involving different sections of the community in public policy (at least its implementation) provide an important and relevant explanation for Cuba's ability to improve population health outcomes despite limiting material resource shortages. More specifically though, the case allows for preliminary postulation that the "vertical" or hierarchical types of social relations that have been "looked down upon" in much of the social capital literature (Scanlon 2004a: 3) are conducive to greater bureaucratic cohesion and cooperation concerning development goals, and this can contribute to developing countries' capacity to achieve good health outcomes in the face of material underdevelopment. Importantly, the "social" aspects of this social capital discussed here in relation to Cuba's health sector have required considerable *investment* of time, effort and resources—thus showing that the social capital is "capital" too.

Considered in terms of state capacity, the deliberateness with which the Cuban health improvements were pursued allows for certain optimism in terms of the potential for developing countries to set and achieve their developmental priorities. The centrally coordinated hierarchy of the Cuban system may have developmental advantages over development goals oriented around depoliticized and non-directive processes, since what has been achieved has depended on a political capacity to effect outcomes not easily imaginable otherwise. More specifically though, this chapter finds evidence of some aspects of state "embeddedness" (interpenetration between the state and civil society) which neo-statists have argued increases political effectiveness. In particular, central state elites have managed significant "penetrative power" (the ability to interact with the population to achieve compliance with state directives) and "extractive power" in the sense of being able to direct the country's resources towards specific goals fairly unproblematically, with little need for direct force or coercion. On the other hand, the findings so far also seem to support the arguments of developmental statists that state autonomy, or the ability of central state institutions to set the agenda and prioritize certain programs independently of other social forces, increases state effectiveness.

However, these preliminary deductions are based on limited information. This chapter has provided a broad outline of the approach to health in Cuba and the organizational arrangements that have facilitated public policy implementation (examined in relation to the goals of the maternal-infant health program). No reliable conclusions can be drawn though, regarding the sources of the Cuban health system's effectiveness, without first examining the extent of "interpenetration" between state elites and other sections of the community in the process of health policy *decision-making*. That is, the extent to which actors outside central state institutions influence or directly participate in the decisions taken at the national level is as important to this inquiry as the implementation process. Furthermore, beyond the improvements in broad aggregate health outcomes that are so often under the spotlight, other secondary consequences of the system should also be considered—particularly compromises and conflicts of interest involved in the process of policy implementation.

Notes

1.   Author's translation.
2.· In its World Development Report 2004, the World Bank revisits the question of how Cuba performed so well in health despite its low levels of growth. It concedes that one of the key factors contributing to Cuba's positive health outcomes, in particular its low infant mortality rates, is its close monitoring of the health system (World Bank 2004b).

3. Cubans are provided with a *libreta*, or ration book, which entitles them to monthly allotments of basic food supplies.
4. The average number of consultations throughout a pregnancy in Cuba is ten or eleven and normally around three or four of these are with a specialist (author's interview with Rivera, July 2004). One of the procedures included in these consultations, which appears to play a vital role in reducing mortality rates, is routine amino acid fluid testing for congenital abnormalities and the provision of free abortions. Where fetal abnormalities are detected, abortion is recommended and provided. Cuba is the only Latin American country where induced abortion is legal and, since congenital abnormalities are one of the main causes of infant death, preventive abortions have probably been partly responsible for mortality decline (Diaz-Briquets 1986: 40-41).
5. For the purpose of this study, the establishment of regular, official meetings between two or more parties (institutions or sectors) is considered one characteristic of a "formal" as opposed to an "informal" relationship.
6. An FMC representative, along with other interviewees, also emphasized this point. "Our concept of maternal-infant health is that it is not just a health problem; it is a social problem" (author's interview with Delgado & Suarez, August 2004).
7. This point is discussed in further detail in the following chapter.
8. Although not related so much to resource sharing, another interesting example of resource optimisation was raised by one of the doctors interviewed. The respondent described a small balloon device used for opening narrowed heart valves (in an operation called balloon valvuloplasty). This is a common but expensive procedure. Each balloon costs around $25,000 and the companies that produce them specify that the devices are for single use only. According to the respondent, Cuban doctors had managed to successfully resterilize and reuse these devices up to three or four times, thereby cutting costs enormously and providing the service to as many patients as possible (author's interview with Almeida, 2004).
9. This precise term (*voluntad política*) was proffered by at least four interviewees in describing the government's prioritisation of health as an important factor contributing to the country's health outcomes.
10. This was the case regardless of a privatized or state-led system, he argued. The existence of regulations obliging private tobacco companies to print health warnings on cigarette packets was one example he used of inter-sectoral cooperation that would not have been possible without political will (author's interview with Vargas, October 2004).
11. As is argued in the next chapter, this technical knowledge is sometimes underutilized due to the government's monopoly on health decision-making and insufficient consultation with health sector employees in the process of policy design.
12. See the next chapter for more discussion of this point
13. Cuba's Law of Association (Ley de Asociaciones) prohibits the legalization of any genuinely independent organization, including independent trade unions. In order to legally operate, organizations must collaborate with a state organization. The working conditions and pay for state employees are therefore determined by the state (Human Rights Watch 2007). The country's official mass trade union (the Cuban Labour Union Federation or CTC) is controlled by the Communist Party and is therefore not a real avenue for state-employed workers to protest work conditions (Pax Christi Netherlands 1999).

4

The Limits of State Capacity and Social Capital in a Top-Down System: Exclusion and Non-Participation

Introduction

The previous chapter presented a range of findings that generally supported the hypothesis with which this project began. It argued that a high degree of inter-sectoral and inter-institutional cooperation in the Cuban health system, steered and coordinated by a politically dominant government with clear health goals, enhanced the country's capacity to achieve broad improvements in a key area of public health. These findings correspond for the most part with the Cuban government's official depictions of the health system. The Cuban Ministry of Public Health outlines its governing principles as including a commitment to the provision of free and accessible health services, a preventive approach to health care, inter-sectoral cooperation and community participation, international collaboration, and normative centralization combined with executive decentralization (MINSAP 2007). The previous chapter outlined the broad structural arrangements between different institutions and sectors associated with the PAMI and showed how these arrangements contribute in a technical sense to the improvement of broad health outcomes. Based on this fairly macro-level assessment, the system was found to be characterized by cooperation, cohesion, and wide-ranging participation towards clearly defined goals.

This chapter is devoted, first, to a more micro-level examination of social relations underlying the Cuban health system, which presents many findings that challenge the usual portrayals of the system in the literature (and hence the assumptions with which the project began).

In particular it reveals the sometimes coercive means through which compliance with health goals is achieved and some of the adverse effects of this coercion affecting individual patients and health workers. These less favorable outcomes are rarely acknowledged or explored in studies of Cuba's health system, where broad statistical indicators are often used uncritically to herald the health system's quality and popular participation. Second, the purpose of this chapter is also to evaluate the extent of negotiation between central decision-makers and the Cuban population in the health decision-making process. In particular it examines participatory arrangements in the health sector (including patient involvement in medical decisions and the contributions of health workers and the community generally to health policy design). The aim is to explore the extent of "negotiated" state power in Cuba, or the degree to which state power and public decision-making are embedded in society itself. The findings presented in this chapter challenge not only my initial assumptions about the health system but also, to some extent, the tentative conclusions that could be drawn from the previous chapter. A lack of effective conduits for incorporating public responses and contributions into health decision-making processes (in health policy-making at the national level and, in turn, medical decisions at the local level) can negatively impact on important aspects of health care quality, thereby counteracting the government's proclaimed health objectives.

Limited Patient Autonomy and Participation in Health Decisions

As Hirschfeld observes, most studies of the Cuban health system continue to focus only on health statistics with little attention to the methods by which the statistics were produced (2007: 99). Cuba's health improvements are almost always "described quantitatively, in the form of improved population health statistics, but never qualitatively" (2007: 227). Similarly, Brotherton (2005) argues that many researchers approach Cuba's case with "statistical fetishism," treating statistics as a representation of reality without critically examining how the statistics were obtained or what they really reflect.

Cuba's health statistics become trapped in an epistemological conundrum, one which not only discursively, but also materially constructs certain realities, while at the same time it excludes others. In this process, we become blinded by what I argue here is a kind of *statistical fetishism*, a heightened focus on ideological models and measures of health, in place of more nuanced accounts of the complex interrelationships among the individual practices of health care professionals and ordinary people, health policies, and state power (2005: 340-341).

The author goes on to argue that there is a need to break away from the practice of measuring success through the polarized lens that distinguishes only printed numbers "in order to provide a more fruitful interrogation of how Cuba's health statistics are in fact part of a broader social and political project" (2005: 344-345). While it is difficult to dispute that lower rates of mortality and morbidity bring fundamental improvements to population wellbeing, it is important to remember that wellbeing is a complex and multidimensional concept linked to a myriad of factors. Statistical outcomes do not reveal, for example, patients' self-perceived needs or subjective experiences of the health system. In other words, it is conceivable to achieve a technically positive result in terms of physical health through means that isolate, humiliate or otherwise negatively impact on the patients' emotional or psychological wellbeing.[1] One Cuban doctor provided the following account as an example of the adverse consequences that sometimes result when patients are not involved in medical decisions.

> We had at one stage a problem with a nineteen-year-old patient who had a slight mental delay but she was in secondary school … [and she was] a patient with whom one could have a conversation. She fell pregnant with [a heart condition that prevented a normal pregnancy] meaning we had to order a termination. However, we knew the condition could then be corrected in an operation, after which the patient could fall pregnant again and have a child normally. So what happened? The patient came through the usual system in her local area[2] but the social worker in her community made an additional report saying that the patient had schizophrenic tendencies, that she had family members with schizophrenia. The social worker was trying to influence the doctors into sterilizing the patient using arguments that really were not valid.… Even if you are schizophrenic, when you are using medication and your condition is under control, there is no reason why you should be denied the right to have a child. If you can be a good mother, a dedicated mother, why should I deny you the ability to be a mother? Despite the fact that we recommended very specifically that this patient should *not* be sterilized, the obstetrician responsible for carrying out the pregnancy termination on this young woman went ahead and sterilized her, without our consent, without the patient's consent and without the family's consent. How did I discover this? By pure coincidence. The family wanted to bring the girl in to have tests done to find out whether, after all, she would be able to have children. When I examined her I discovered the doctor had sterilized her.… This example happened as a result of paternalism (author's interview with Valdes, August 2004).

It is not being suggested here that all experiences of the Cuban health system are unpleasant or isolating in this way. It is being argued, however, that some adverse effects on wellbeing at the individual level can result in a system where paternalistic decision-making processes prevail and patient participation in medical decisions is limited. Furthermore, these effects detract from the overall benefits to wellbeing resulting from improved health outcomes.

Some of the doctors interviewed said it is common for health practitioners in Cuba to make medical decisions based on what they believe will produce the best health outcome, without involving the patient in the decision-making process (author's interviews with Blanco 2004; Valdes 2004; Herrera 2004; Fernández 2004). In an anonymous interview[3] one Cuban respondent spoke from the perspective of a patient of her experience visiting a dentist in Sweden. She described how surprised she was when the dentist began explaining the treatment procedure to her—"now I am going to give you the anesthetic, then I will clear the canal of the tooth because you have a deep cavity" and so on. The respondent was completely unaccustomed to this. She said that in Cuba, by contrast, patients often felt confused when they came out of a medical consultation.

> Here doctors don't tell you what exactly they are doing and sometimes they give you a diagnosis in very medical terms from a medical text book and you come out of the consultation thinking "So what is it that I have?" The other day a neighbor of mine arrived at my house and asked me if I had a medical book. I said I didn't have one and asked her what was wrong. [She told me:] "The doctor diagnosed me with *lupos eritematoso* and said I have to take vitamin E but I want to know what it actually is that I have" (author's interview with García, October 2004).

The respondent went on to say she had spoken with others who were panicked after an HIV test because they had been told to come back and repeat the test in several months and they didn't know why. It had not been explained to them that there was nothing abnormal about their test results. It was simply standard procedure to test for HIV every six months because the virus had an incubation period before it could be detected (author's interview with García, October 2004). A study of female patients' views on antenatal care found that compared with other countries, a lack of information was not so much a problem in Cuba (the authors report that Cuban women "receive a good deal of information and reflect very much the technical language of doctors and nurses when they speak") but found that women were dissatisfied by the lack of information they received regarding "the psycho-social aspects of care." Furthermore, the study found that although women have relatively high educational levels and therefore the capacity to understand and use information about their health, they cannot necessarily question the doctor's decisions (Nigenda et al. 2003).

Based on the assumption that health professionals in developing contexts normally work with tighter resource constraints, more critical health epidemics and lower levels of public education[4] than those in the industrialized world, it is likely that the type of health care delivery practices the respondent (García) describes are more prevalent in such contexts. It is arguable, though, that in Cuba, a factor contributing to paternalistic patterns of health care delivery is the intense pressure on doctors to perform in highly politicized areas of health. Feinsilver alludes to the possibility that pressure to achieve statistically impressive outcomes leads doctors to force decisions on patients. She points out, for example, that the intensity of Cuba's campaign to decrease infant mortality gives some reason to believe that doctors may strongly recommend or even pressure women to abort in cases where an abnormal fetus is detected. This is despite the fact that the Cubans Feinsilver interviewed officially claimed there was no such pressure on women (1989a: 17). The previous account from Valdes' interview (concerning the patient who was sterilized without her consent) raises further skepticism regarding this issue. Hirschfeld's observations also point to the possibility that abortions are not always as voluntary as officials maintain.

> After observing one family doctor berate a pregnant woman for failing to show up for a scheduled ultrasound, for instance, I questioned her (the doctor) about Cuba's maternal health programs. "What happens if an ultrasound shows some fetal abnormalities?" I asked her.
> "The mother would have an abortion," the doctor replied casually.
> "Really? Why?" I asked.
> "Otherwise it might raise the infant mortality rate," she replied automatically.
> What this exchange reveals is the way in which this particular physician interpreted her role with respect to the dual obligations of patient care and political duty. If the mother in this case resisted or refused to terminate a potentially problematic pregnancy, it could negatively affect Cuba's infant mortality statistics. The national Ministry of Health in Cuba has made preservation of the infant mortality rate one of its most central goals for all medical personnel, and individual doctors are supposed to organize their clinical interventions to maximize these national public health goals. If the patient appears to resist these interventions, the doctor's role is ostensibly to resolve the issue in the interest of "the revolution" (i.e. as defined by the Ministry of Public Health) (2006: 343).

The seemingly compulsory nature of patient cooperation with the government's mission to prevent maternal-infant deaths also came to light during a visit to a Cuban *hogar materno* (maternity home) and in several interview discussions on the subject. The following section provides an outline of how these preventive institutions operate.

The Case of Maternity Homes

While family doctors usually succeed in monitoring the pregnant women in their community, they sometimes have trouble managing cases that fall into a "high risk" category but are not serious enough for hospitalization. Women who are severely underweight, those carrying twins and those with what interviewees referred to as "social problems" are amongst the cases family doctors, along with representatives from the local Federation of Cuban Women (FMC), have the option of sending to a maternity home (author's interviews with Arango 2004; Castillo 2004; Diaz 2004; Espinoza and Raiz 2004; Ramirez 2004).

Maternity homes in Cuba were first developed for women living in remote areas who did not have easy access to hospitals. The homes were situated close to maternity hospitals and pregnant women were sent to live there during the period directly leading up to the birth, to allow easy access to hospital once they went into labor (author's interview with González, September 2004). Maternity homes used for this purpose were a way to deal with the dramatically increased risks associated with births where medical assistance was absent. According to Bergstrom, "women living far away from health facilities may suffer a maternal mortality four times as high as similar women living close by." Maternity waiting homes or maternity villages of this sort have been used with varying success in various parts of the world to overcome problems of geographical isolation (1994, 313).

In Cuba, this idea has been expanded to include women from major centers, incorporating services as a preventive measure for a variety of other situations; this has also contributed to the improvement of maternal and infant health indicators (Perez 2002). The time women stay in these homes ranges from short periods to entire pregnancies, depending on individual circumstances. Family doctors make decisions about the length of stays and usually continue to visit and monitor the woman throughout this period. During the time spent in these homes, women are provided with measured diets and close observation. Aside from the occasional excursion, they are required only to rest, eat and listen to educational talks from nurses on topics such as adolescent pregnancy and risks associated with smoking. Women admitted to maternity homes are not free to enter and leave as they please but require official passes[5] (author's interview with González, September 2004). When questioned about the apparently compulsory nature of admission to the homes and how the system dealt with women who were reluctant to be admitted, a representative from the FMC gave the following explanation.

> The first thing we have to do is talk with the woman to explain clearly to her the need for her to go [to the maternity home]. Since the women who go there don't have problems of hypertension or any life threatening disease, they don't feel like they are sick so they don't understand why it is important for them to be there...

There is another situation, which is that often the woman, who as I mentioned, doesn't feel sick, leaves behind one, two or even three children in her house when she goes to the maternity home. She worries a lot because she wants to be with [the children]. There is another small percentage that worries that while they are away their husbands might be having affairs. So they don't want to be there for fear of being away from their family. What used to happen with much more frequency was that women would escape from the maternity homes. In other words they would leave without authorization, without asking permission… [When this happens] the maternity home has to immediately inform the woman's family doctor, who goes along with the other community organizations to the woman's house to convince her again, to work with her and [make her understand] that it is important for her to be there (author's interview with Arango, October 2004).

A former family doctor elaborated:

The Maternity Homes don't have the best conditions—they are like boarding houses, they're not very comfortable. However, they do have 24-hour access to a doctor and a nurse and there is a car to take them to hospital. Now, what happens? Often women, when they are pregnant, feel vulnerable and don't like being away from their house or separated from their husband and family. And, the majority of these women with low body weight or social problems are of a "low cultural level"[6] so it's hard to make them go to the Maternity Home because they want to stay in their house. They protest saying the conditions and the food in the Maternity Homes are not the best … but the important thing is that there's a doctor present there all the time… They don't understand why they have to be away from their house and many put up a fight; so sometimes as a doctor you have to be tough with them to make them understand that they have to be there, but sometimes once they get there they escape and hide…. The advantage the family doctor has is that, living in the community, he/she knows what your home situation is like…. If a woman has problems at home such as inadequate nutrition, or in other cases more psychological or spiritual problems, then the best thing is to remove that person from the home environment to solve the problem. She might say "This is ridiculous; I can do this at home!" So then it becomes a labor of persuasion made all the more difficult because in the Maternity Home she can't use the bathroom at the time she wants to because there are, say, two bathrooms between 40 women, and she has to eat at a set time and so on. [In the event that a woman continues escaping from the Maternity Home and doesn't want to return] then the other organizations step in—the CDR, the FMC and they try to convince her (author's interview with Diaz, October 2004).

These passages illustrate the tension that can exist between individual and state goals. In this example, what is seen as best for the pregnant women from the perspective of the public health workers, under direction from state authorities to achieve an optimally healthy pregnancy and childbirth in the most efficient way possible, can override other factors (such as personal and family-related emotional considerations) that are important to the individual patient's own conception of her health requirements. As will be discussed later, few avenues exist for patients to dispute medical decisions or actively participate with doctors and social workers in discussion and election of treatment options. This seems to be especially so in matters relating to the preciously-guarded area of maternal-infant health.

Possible Patient Responses to Paternalism: Over-Dependency and Self Medication

The tendency for doctors to exclude patients from medical decision-making may partly explain common Cuban habits of passivity and avoidance when dealing with the health system. A Cuban professor of sociology specializing in the area of public health said she thought Cuba had developed a culture of over-relying on doctors to the point where patients became complacent about their own role. "Cubans recognize the leadership of doctors and consult them for everything, sometimes in excess" (author's interview with Blanco, July 2004, see also Benjamin and Haendel 1991). Another respondent, a social worker at the National Centre for Sexual Education (CENESEX), said Cuba had not managed "to achieve an outcome of people understanding their own responsibility in caring for their health." She compared the experience of the Cuban system to "having a father who deals with all your problems," saying that a consequence of this was that Cubans didn't make much effort on their own part (author's interview with Fernández, July 2004).

One example the respondent gave was that Cubans are not conscientious about attending appointments for *pap smears* or other scheduled consultations. In most cases, it is the doctor who continually knocks on patients' doors and convinces them to come to these consultations. She argued that Cuba needed to make patients more aware of their role in health care if the country's health outcomes were to be deemed sustainable (author's interview with Fernández, July 2004). Indeed, it can be reasonably assumed that informed patients who participate in choosing treatment options are more likely to understand their responsibilities and follow through with treatment than those who are simply told what to do. Other respondents raised the issue of poor contraceptive use as an example that individual responsibility needed to be encouraged. According to the respondents, despite widespread availability of contraceptives and education programs, contraceptive use (a domain that relies on individual responsibility) was still extremely inefficient (author's interviews with Blanco 2004; Sanchez 2004; Valdes 2004).[7]

Paradoxically, there is also evidence of an increasing tendency for patients to circumvent the official system and take medical matters into their own hands. An apparently growing phenomenon of self diagnosis and self medication in Cuba may be a response to the frustrations caused by the combination of the limited decision-making powers in the official system and unreliable availability of medical supplies. The following narrative relates my first-hand experience seeking medical advice while in Cuba conducting fieldwork. The experience provided some personal insights that contributed to an understanding of the process through which many patients find themselves seeking unofficial solutions to health problems.

Several days after cyclone Charley passed through Havana (August 2004) I awoke in the early morning hours with debilitating stomach cramps. I called a friend and with his help I managed to walk down the road in a half-doubled-over state to the local policlinic. Luckily the clinic was just meters away and I remember gaining a new appreciation on that day for the close proximity and easy accessibility of health services in Cuba. On arrival I was led into the doctor's small office. In a dazed state of pain I remember noticing that the lens of the doctor's eyeglasses had a crack in it and the wing of the glasses was patched together with masking tape. The image fitted well with the stereotype of the humble, self-sacrificing Cuban doctor and I pondered to myself that I would probably never see such a thing anywhere else in the world.

Another strong pang in the stomach brought my attention back to business. The doctor took a pen and paper and began asking me questions about my symptoms and scribbling down my responses. He prodded my stomach a few times and then wrote me a prescription for two medicines and told me I should get one at the pharmacy and go to the nurse in the other room for the second one, which was an injection. At this point I remember feeling somewhat unsatisfied with the result. I still didn't know what was wrong with me and I had no idea what the substance was that I had been prescibed. When I asked what it was that I might have contracted, the doctor responded with a scientific term that was incomprehensible to me. Eventually, not feeling very appeased, I stumbled into the nurse's room. She was at a sink washing one of those old, glass, resterilizable syringes (due to blockade-related problems gaining access to disposable syringes, Cuba is one of the only countries that still uses these). Catching sight of the needle, I remember thinking it looked more like something designed for injecting horses than people. Nervously, I gestured towards the syringe and asked the nurse if the one she would inject me with was like that one. She nodded. Already feeling uneasy about not knowing which drug I was to be injected with, this quickly concreted a decision to avoid the needle and go back home instead.

My friend went in search of the other prescription all over town but the response in every pharmacy was "no hay" (there is none). Later in the day a neighbor came around to visit. On hearing that I was sick she started giving her own diagnosis: "Is your stomach rumbling like this (making a noise)? Does it feel like there are things running around in your belly? Did you drink any unboiled water after the cyclone? Yes? Well you have Giardia!" She gave me the name of a medication and told me to buy it at the tourist pharmacy in dollars where they always had supplies. Whether or not I had in fact caught Giardia I still don't know, but I took the medicine and fortunately recovered within a few days (field notes 2004).

According to the Cuban sociologist interviewed, despite the universal access to health care services and their close proximity to the residence of most Cubans, *automedicalisación* (self medication) is extremely common. This is particularly the case for women, who frequently exchanged remedies and medical advice between friends. This ranges from giving advice on herbal home remedies to exchanging prescription pharmaceuticals (author's interview with Blanco, July 2004). Again, Crabb makes a similar observation, describing a culture in Cuba whereby people often seek and provide medical attention or advice between friends. She relates an incident where a neighbor asked Crabb to help sort through a large bag of random pharmaceuticals (most without dosage instructions) that had been sent from the neighbor's family in Miami.

> None of them were medications I had ever heard of, and most of them appeared to be out of date. I tried to caution her against taking them without at least finding out what they were for, but my advice was immediately drowned out by other neighbourhood "experts," who began to offer their own analyses of what the medications [sic]. One woman lifted a bottle out of the pile, "Look. This one says "Gastrosin," she said. "It must be a stomach medicine."
> "Can I take some to my sister?" Another woman asked, pointing to the vial. "She's been having stomach problems." I tried to point out to her that the label actually read, "ganostin," but she felt the distinction was unimportant and took the medicine away and presumably gave it to her sister. When I expressed alarm about this unsupervised sharing of unknown pharmaceuticals to another neighbour later in the evening, she laughed sadly and said Cuba was the only country she had ever seen (she had lived abroad for many years) where people were so casual about informally exchanging medicines (Crabb 2001, 179).

This seems to contrast with the previous interviewees' accounts of Cubans as overly reliant on doctors and unwilling to take personal responsibility for health care. In light of this, and also considering the examples of dependency the interviewees provided (failure to attend scheduled consultations or to respond to education programs promoting sexual health), there is room to speculate that what the interviewees described as Cubans' lack of "responsibility" may be a decreasing responsiveness to demands for public compliance with central health goals. On the other hand, Cubans may be increasingly proactive about taking personal responsibility for self-perceived health needs. As can easily be imagined after reading Crabb's example, relying on these informal means to solve medical problems carries risks of misdiagnosis, incorrect dosage of medications and side effects.[8] While, on the one hand the official medical system in Cuba is highly accessible both economically and geographically, there is also evidence to suggest that internal problems of paternalism can make the system inaccessible in other ways by excluding patient involvement in medical decision-making.

A Chain of Paternalism: Government Pressure on Doctors and its Effects on Doctor-Patient Relations

After centuries of medical paternalism, contemporary medical practice in most of parts of the world has shifted away from the previously
overruling authority of physicians to an emphasis on patient autonomy
and participation (see Chin 2002). The clear consensus in medical ethics
literature is now that health care service delivery should involve patients'
informed consent and that decision-making on health issues is a role that
doctors and patients should share (Sugarman 2003; Thompson 2007).
Ethical considerations aside, numerous studies have also demonstrated
that increased autonomy (participation by informed, competent patients)
and shared decision-making in medical service delivery improves overall
health outcomes, including patients' satisfaction with outcomes (Kravitz
and Melnikow 2001; Kee 1996; Kaplan, Greenfield and Ware 1989).

The Cuban doctors questioned on this subject were clearly aware of
ethical developments relating to shared decision-making. "[Doctors]
should work as a doctor-patient relationship" said one. "In a consultation
they should really give a diagnosis and discuss treatment options with
the patient..., That is the way I work but we know that not all doctors
act in this way." The respondent went on to explain that working under
strict demands from health officials limits the doctors' autonomy, which
in turn affects the way they deal with patients (author's interview with
Valdes, August 2004, also Herrera 2004). In other words, doctors in Cuba
find there is little room for allowing patients a role in decision-making
because ultimately the system holds doctors responsible for outcomes.
Fearing the possible risks involved with giving patients choices, and the
blame for any negative consequences, many doctors prefer to take what
they see as a safer option of basing decisions on their own judgment
rather than encouraging patient participation. That is, doctors have little
room to allow patients to participate in decision-making because their
own autonomy is constrained.

Here in Cuba there is too much of a burden of accountability placed on the doctor.
Even though in many cases the patient is the one to blame for a health problem, the
doctor is always blamed. This is often what causes the Cuban doctor to be paternalistic.
I know that they are going to measure my medical ability based on my results without
considering that maybe I did everything correctly but the patient didn't, so the only
way to protect myself is to be paternalistic with the patient... If [the patient] doesn't
seem very disciplined I am going to impose this and that and make sure that she does
everything possible so that things turn out okay because I know that if I don't, I am
the one they are going to question. So the paternalism comes from a problem of the
system questioning me if anything goes wrong and that to avoid this I am going to

impose [and tell patients] "you have to do this and this and this and that's all there is to it" (author's interview with Valdes, August 2004).

In a discussion with Oppenheimer (1993: 160-161) a Cuban doctor complained that health workers who fail to deliver on government demands are treated as though they have broken the law. "I have to meet the quota, just as if I was working in a potato factory," he explained. Under orders to vaccinate a list of children, even if faced with uncontrollable factors such as where some of the children have moved out of the neighborhood, doctors are punished for having performed their job badly and are issued a reprimand (1993: 161).

Without an understanding of the broader significance attached to the fulfillment of government orders in Cuba, it can be difficult to comprehend why doctors continue submitting to these pressures, even where this detrimentally compromises patients' autonomy. One side-effect of the intensely ideological role of health in promoting the revolutionary project[9] is that it can blur the lines separating health workers' performance in their occupation from their performance as good revolutionaries. Doctors involved in cases of maternal or infant death can face double scrutiny for having let down not only the patients involved, but also the revolution itself. Health sector employees can face harsh consequences when failing to fulfill government demands.

Fidel Castro is inflexible and unforgiving towards those who let him down in his statistical epic with the US. Even his long-term associate, Sergio del Valle, Health Minister for many years, lost his job in a recent high level political reshuffle. His demise may have come about because Castro blamed him for the 1985 infant mortality upturn (Diaz-Briquets 1986: 39-40).

It should also be understood that health workers play a special political role in the Cuban revolution and have historically been expected to live as model revolutionaries (Hirschfeld 2006: 341). Examples of employees in the health sector receiving harsh sanctions for political non-compliance are easy to find. A series of "crackdowns" on dissidents in recent years affected many high-profile health sector employees. In July 2002, amid growing tensions in U.S.-Cuba relations and increasing strength of dissident organizations within Cuba, a drastic reshuffling took place within MINSAP. The Health Minister, along with the majority of his vice ministers and national directors, was fired and new health strategies emerged from the administration that replaced them. These included greater restrictions on foreign collaboration and input (Braa, Titlestad and Sæbø 2004). In the same year, *CubaNet News* published a report that José Luis Blanco, an employee at a Provincial Hygiene Centre, was dismissed from his job when authorities discovered he worked for the independent press in his spare time (Ferro 2002). More recently, in February 2008, Cuban physician Rodolfo Martinez Vigoa complained to the Ministry of Public Health about the poor conditions at the local policlinic in Artemisa and the low salaries of the employees working there. Within weeks of doing so, an organized group of around 300 people arrived at the physician's house yelling insults, calling him a traitor and counterrevolutionary. Following this incident, the Cuban government stripped physician Rodolfo Martinez Vigoa of his medical license (Bureau of Democracy, Human Rights and Labour 2009). These and many other instances suggest that state elites are quick to punish health sector employees for failing to meet policy targets and also for departing from ideological support for the regime. The two are closely intertwined. With the relative political and economic weakness of health sector employees, this can contribute to a situation wherein those who work in the system refrain from addressing or calling attention to systemic problems.

Immobilizing Effects of the Command System

> *Cuba's problem is that everything has to be decided by Fidel. Nothing works, nothing functions, nothing runs without the Commandante's intervention. ...I suspect that in the realm of officialdom, at least while I was witness to it, the system was much more receptive to bureaucratic conformity—that is, to submissiveness— than to work of quality*
> —*Jorge Edwards[10] – Persona Non Grata: A Memoir of Disenchantment with the Cuban Revolution.*

In the conclusion of her dissertation on health policy in Cuba, Feinsilver contends that "the Cuban government's control over all aspects of the economy and society [means] it has a greater chance of success in making positive changes than do other countries where government intervention is considerably less or minimal" (1989b: 261-262).[11] Although it has been argued in the previous chapter that there is some truth in this statement, in another sense the reverse is also true. The political dominance of government elites in setting the health agenda can also have immobilizing effects on subordinate actors in the system in ways that are counterproductive to improving health care quality. Furthermore, the central control of information and decision-making prevents the emergence of "horizontal" cooperative relationships at the local level beyond those focused on complying with state orders. Before returning to explore these issues further, the next section outlines and discusses what the Cuban interviewees mentioned as foremost concerns with Cuban health services.

Some Common Complaints about Health Services

While Cuba's official health statistics support claims that it has built a "world class" or "first world" health system, at the micro-level the system retains many of the problems more typical of developing world settings. A number of problems with the quality of health service delivery are sources of ongoing frustration for patients and health workers alike. Two significant problems interviewees raised in relation to hospitals were (a) frequent disregard for patients' personal privacy and confidentiality and (b) deteriorating conditions in hospitals. These are both factors that detract from the quality of health services but that do not necessarily have a direct influence on aggregate mortality indicators.

Lack of privacy in hospitals

In part, relative lack of regard for privacy and personal space in Cuba can be explained as a cultural factor. As one would expect of a socialist context that celebrates ideals of collectivism and solidarity, the liberal Western emphasis on maintaining clear boundaries separating private and public spheres is noticeably absent in Cuba. "The state has a presence in households through the family doctors and CDR representatives (who knock frequently on doors to check on patients or help a parent with an unruly child)," Rebecca Burwell writes in her dissertation on mothering in Cuba. Observing that many traditionally private practices are carried out in public spaces (including eating, napping, discussing family, health or sexual problems, urinating and even engaging in sexual activity), Burwell argues that Cubans do not prioritise confidentiality and private space in a Western sense due to their cultural emphasis on "togetherness" (2004, 51).

Although the socialist values of solidarity and collectivism may be part of the explanation, it should also be noted that breach of patient privacy in the delivery of health services is common in developing contexts generally, including in many of Cuba's neighboring non-socialist Latin American countries (see for example Levav and González Uzcátegui 2000). In line with Burwell's claims that Cuban culture, influenced by socialist values, does not place great importance on private space and confidentiality, the degree of patient tolerance for the public nature of health care delivery may be greater in a socialist setting. However, the following interview excerpts suggest this is far from an unproblematic, socially accepted norm.

A Cuban sociologist specializing in public health (author's interview with Blanco 2004) argued that, where health care delivery is concerned, the political ideals of solidarity and collectivism officially promoted in Cuba are sometimes adopted in excess, in ways that inappropriately compromise patients' and doctors' privacy, causing frustrations for both parties. Especially where doctors deal with health issues related to the traditionally private realm of sexuality, the respondent argued that there is too little regard for privacy and confidentiality in Cuban hospitals:

> There is a conflict in the community between public and private spaces.... The doctor and the patient in consultation don't always have the privacy they require. This is not just because the nurse (who is part of the medical team) enters the room, but because other doctors and other people are constantly entering. This is a problem in many of the consultations in Cuba. It is a particularly sensitive problem with the area of gynecology/obstetrics because sexuality has always been identified as a person's private realm.... I think this is more of a problem in hospitals than in family doctors' offices. I have been in both and have seen that when visiting the family doctor there is more privacy. This is partly because there are fewer of the medical personnel who invade private consultations in hospitals by constantly entering and leaving the room. Sometimes here we say that Cubans pass the limits of "solidarity"—this ideology we have of being united, of solving problems through solidarity. The problem is that sometimes this gets confused and has a tendency to enter the limits of privacy (author's interview with Blanco, July 2004).

A gynecologist/obstetrician employed at one of Havana's maternity hospitals said he confronted this problem on a regular basis and found it disrupting to his ability to work with patients.

> A lot of people seem to think that because they work in the hospital they can walk in. One enters, another enters, what privacy is there? Many of the women don't say what they want to say because they don't want to say it in front of the other people. Sometimes privacy just doesn't exist here.... Privacy is a right of the patient, not just because it sounds pretty—it is a legally established right! (author's interview with Valdes, August 2004).

Another Cuban interviewee said she had been inside maternity hospitals and described them as "very uncomfortable" due to poor conditions and a lack of privacy. She said that, despite the technical safety of maternal-infant health outcomes, she would prefer not to have a child in Cuba due to the public nature of birthing conditions in hospitals. Based on visits she had made to maternity hospitals, she said women giving birth usually spend their entire labor until the point of the birth "in a large room filled with other laboring women and babies all screaming at once"[12] (author's interview with García, October 2004). To a degree, limited privacy may be an unavoidable compromise associated with providing professional prenatal care and hospital attendance of all births with limited space and resources. However, the comments from interviewees above seem to suggest the problem often derives more from a lack of staff education relating to issues of privacy. Especially in the provision of services related to sexual health, pregnancy or childbirth, respect for personal privacy is likely to be a crucial factor determining the patient's experience of the system and may also affect doctors' ability to communicate effectively with patients. However, issues relating to patients' and health workers' experience of the system are far less visible to outside observers than the outcomes of low morbidity and mortality by which the quality of health services is normally judged.

Deteriorating conditions

Despite Cuba's positive heath indicators and acts of goodwill to its Latin American neighbors in the provision of scholarships and medical aid, one of the most common complaints is of deteriorating conditions of health facilities at home, particularly in hospitals. Partly due to the ongoing lack of hard currency, Cuban hospitals suffer extreme shortages in medical supplies from antibiotics and asthma medication to clean water. Medical staff make do with broken and outdated equipment and patients are often required to bring their own soap and sheets when admitted for surgery (Marquis 2000; Nordlinger 2007).[13] Independent Cuban journalist Raúl Rivero[14] argues that, despite Cuban authorities' desire to provide adequate health services, the collapse of the Soviet bloc, economic crisis and embargo-related shortages have "left the system in ruins." The country has experienced a resurgence of epidemics such as dengue and tuberculosis and increasing hygiene-related problems in hospitals. The author provides the following testimony from a 52-year-old railway worker in Cuba:

> I prefer to cure myself using home remedies, without leaving my room. To enter a hospital is torture. You have to bring your own towels and sheets, soap and food, and then call somebody abroad so that they can send medicine. Physicians are good, but paramedical service is a disaster. They get paid very little. There is a general lack of cleanliness and poor attention. The special clinic for foreigners and government officials is a different story. But I don't fit in there (Rivero 1999).

Material shortages are exacerbated by what is generally seen as inefficiency and corruption. General maintenance of hospital facilities obviously suffers due to inefficiency or absence of maintenance workers and cleaners. Visitors to Cuban hospitals can observe problems such as poor rubbish collection, dirty walls, floors and corridors, broken or uncleaned toilets and windows[15] (see for example Agencias 2007a). These problems clearly worsen the experience of hospitalization for patients and can be a source of frustration for doctors and an interference with their work. A former family doctor speaking of his experience as a dental patient gave the following account:

> I once had to have a molar tooth operated on... When I went on the first day I was really scared. I was afraid of the pain and the anesthetic and so on but I knew I had to have the operation because the tooth was causing me pain. When it was time for me to have the operation though, the tooth no longer hurt because this particular operation can't be done while the tooth is inflamed and painful. So psychologically I didn't want to have the operation anymore because I didn't feel any pain. When I arrived for the operation, I walked in and the first thing they said was "there are no operating clothes." Here [in Cuba] to enter an operating room you have to take off your ordinary clothes and put on sterile hospital clothes.... There the doctor was ready with her instruments to do the operation but there are none of these special green hospital clothes so, no operation. "You'll have to come back next week," [they told me]. Do you think I went back the following week? No I didn't. I never had the tooth operated on. Do you understand? I have my own psychological problems overcoming the fear and getting to the operation—that part is my problem and I overcome it because I know the operation is necessary and I get there and there are no surgical clothes. This is the type of thing that gets annoying here ... it could be that there were no clothes because there was no power or because the person who works there stole the detergent or because they simply didn't turn up to work. Whatever the reason, it is not my fault. I would even prefer to pay for the service and be well-attended[16] than have a service given to me free where I am badly treated ... but you just have to swallow it because we know the state gives it to us free, the state undertakes a lot of effort for it, this is expensive and most people solve their medical problems with it. Well, in my case I never had the operation (author's interview with Diaz, October 2004).

Another issue that has generated criticism in recent years has been that of the drain of resources (especially human resources) out of Cuban health services to expand overseas aid programs despite the above-mentioned problems at home. In particular, growing numbers of doctors sent on overseas missions—especially to Venezuela—have raised concerns regarding increased workloads for doctors in Cuba and the possibly adverse impact on the island's health outcomes. Aside from the "symbolic capital" won through acts of medical diplomacy in Latin America and the world generally (see Feinsilver 2006), Cuba has been sending teams of doctors to Venezuela to work in Chávez' *Misión Barrio*

Adentro health program since 2003 (as of 2004 when interviews for this research were conducted, it had sent 20,000 doctors) in exchange for oil. The government provides financial incentives to doctors who attend missions. Those who leave to work in Venezuela receive significantly higher salaries than they would working in Cuba, but these salaries are still far below international or Venezuelan doctors' salaries (Forero 2007; Weekly Telegraph 2007). Arguably then, the government's ability to keep down the cost of doctors' wages, combined with foreign demand for its human resources, increases its purchasing power abroad.[17]

A representative from MINSAP asserted in an interview that the stream of doctors being sent to Venezuela had caused no adverse impact on health outcomes at home. However, he did concede that a number of adjustments had been made in the health system to compensate for the loss. For example, family doctors who previously only attended one *consultorio* were now often attending three. In other areas, medical interns (students in their final year of study) had been sent to take the place of family doctors in *consultorios* (author's interview with Ramirez, September 2004).[18] It can be logically assumed that these adjustments represent additional pressure and workloads for doctors working on the island, which raises some reasonable concerns about the long-term impact on the quality of health care. Some more recent reports have conveyed growing dissatisfaction amongst patients and health workers in Cuba over declining quality of services at home as a result of the large numbers of doctors leaving on missions (Lakshmanan 2005; Weekly Telegraph 2007; Valera 2009).

The introduction and expansion of "health tourism" as a means for earning foreign currency has also raised concerns that foreign patients who pay for services are now given priority over Cuban patients and receive resources from the public health system. Dr. Hilda Molina, Cuba's first female neurosurgeon, a former deputy to the Cuban National Assembly, and founder of a neurosurgery centre in Havana that became one of the most important scientific institutions on the island, has been particularly vocal on this issue. In 1991 Molina was informed that her centre—which previously treated Cuban citizens—was required, from then on, to treat paying foreigners. She was also asked to release Cuban patients early to make space for foreigners, thereby violating international medical protocols. She protested against these decisions, ultimately resigning from the centre and from her post at the National Assembly (Muñoz 1998; Molina 2005). In a report smuggled out of Cuba, Molina declared that the revolution's central objective of providing quality, free and universally-available medical care was being eroded by the government's moves to turn the health system into a foreign currency earning enterprise. She states in the report that many medical institutions that previously treated Cubans have been forced to focus on foreigners and to fund themselves with revenue raised from selling medical services. As a result, the tourist hospitals have shifted their priority to revenue-raising; regularly advertising services they are not equipped to provide and extorting money from patients on top of fees for medical services. Foreign patients are often deliberately misinformed about their medical conditions and charged unnecessary services, sometimes worsening rather than improving their condition. Medical staff often demand extra payment for better services, have sexual relations with patients in return for gifts or bribes, and have been known to steal patients' personal effects (Molina 2006).

Punishment, Disempowerment and the Resulting Under-Participation of Health Workers

Despite causing concern and dissatisfaction for many health workers and patients, the issues outlined in this section are virtually never raised in the state-run media or publicly debated on the island. Cases of health workers receiving harsh punishments for drawing public attention to problems in the health system are often reported in the foreign press, however. Since 1994, Hilda Molina (mentioned above) made repeated requests to leave Cuba to visit her family in Argentina, and for professional purposes, but was repeatedly denied exit over a period of fifteen years until finally being granted exit in June 2009 (Muñoz 1998; Molina 2005; *The Australian* 2009). According to Molina, immigration officials told her on two separate occasions: "You can't leave Cuba because your brain is the patrimony of the state." In 2004, then Foreign Minister Felipe Pérez Roque accused Molina of being a dissident financed by the U.S government, stating this as the reason she would not be granted permission to leave the island. Molina denied this accusation, claiming that Fidel Castro had not forgiven her for objecting to official orders (Marx 2006).

Another prominent example is the case of Dr. Dessy Mendoza Rivero, whose efforts to expose a rampant dengue epidemic in 1997 ended in his dramatic arrest by Cuban State Security. In the government's attempt to cover up the epidemic, doctors were ordered not to provide patients with a correct diagnosis of the illness. Common explanations for the cover-up are that the government was embarrassed to admit to the breakout because it had earlier declared dengue to be officially eradicated, and that reports of a breakout would have damaged the tourism industry (Faria 2004; Hirschfeld 2007).

Other cases include that of Dr. Oscar Elías Biscet who, in the year after he received a degree in internal medicine, was suspended from his work for protesting against long unpaid hours. He went on to found the Lawton Foundation for Human Rights and was later sentenced to 25 years jail for activities related to campaigning for press freedom and human rights (International Society for Human Rights 2005; Lawnton Foundation for Human Rights 2004). Dr. Marcelo Cano Rodriguez, national coordinator of Cuban Independent Medical Association and several other doctors and dentists[19] affiliated with this association are currently serving long sentences (International Society for Human Rights 2005; NewsMax 2004; World Medical Association 2004), indicating low tolerance for attempts by doctors to strengthen their collective political influence through voluntary associations outside the government's jurisdiction. A 2003 report described an incident where a Cuban doctor working in maternal-infant health vocalized complaints with the system. The following text appeared in the Havana Newspaper on 21 November 2003.

> [A Cuban] gynaecologist rushed into an operating room at National hospital in Havana to perform an emergency Caesarean section and found there were no gloves or sterilized equipment available. In his frustration, [the gynaecologist] loudly excoriated the government's inefficiency (in Campos 2004).

The gynecologist involved lost his job and had his medical license and hospital privileges suspended after hospital authorities informed government officials of the incident (Campos 2004).

In light of these reports, and given the crucial role health plays as a symbol of the regime's success, health sector employees have reason to expect harsh consequences if they speak out about observable problems with the health system. This can have a silencing effect on those who might otherwise draw government attention to or even initiate local action to deal with perceivable problems. As Crabb points out, "the ability of family doctors and mass organizations to identify and respond to pressing social or public health concerns seems largely contingent on whether these problems are acknowledged by those in power" (2001: 172). Many of the health and sanitation hazards that were prioritized as vital "social problems" requiring mass local participation during the early post-revolutionary years—such as poor rubbish and sewage disposal—are still observable today. However, since "officially" Cuba has now overcome and moved on from "underdevelopment," the government no longer prioritizes these problems. As a result, family doctors and local branches of mass organisations are limited in their ability to mobilize community action to deal with such problems because to do so would signify a departure from official priorities and therefore an act of insubordination (2001: 172).

The Cuban government's obsession with the health areas which serve as political symbols often means that other areas do not receive the attention they need. Problems that do not fit with the centrally-determined development plan can be ignored, even if important to the country's overall social and economic progress (Sæbø and Titlestad 2004: 4). Policy-makers apparently refuse to negotiate with or pay heed to the perspectives of subordinate actors when deciding where the country's assets are invested or spent. It has been suggested, for example, that the intense concentration on maternal-infant health may result in other public health issues being ignored or downplayed, such as the needs of the elderly or mortality resulting from suicides and accidents (Diaz-Briquets 1986: 41). Significant expenditures were devoted to reversing the slight upturns in infant mortality that occurred in 1994 and 2000, despite the desperate need for resources in other areas such as improving sanitation and the provision of potable water in rural areas. These areas, of course, indirectly contribute to infant mortality outcomes in the longer term. Due to the declining sanitation and water quality, cases of diseases such as acute diarrhea and tuberculosis[20] increased dramatically throughout the 1990s (Sixto 2002: 335-336).

Another consequence of the tight state control over health priorities is the marginalization or even criminalization of alternative, traditional medicine and health care services such as those provided by midwives and traditional healers. Although the crisis period of the 1990s saw a renewed interest in medical alternatives that led to an endorsement and incorporation of natural "green" medicines, ultimately any practices that are not officially endorsed are actively suppressed (Brotherton 2005: 346).

Evidence also exists that aspects of health service that are important to patients' comfort, but do not directly contribute to positive aggregate outcomes, may be neglected. For example, the previously mentioned problems—that food provided in hospitals tends to be inadequate and of poor quality and that hospital rooms often lack basic provisions such as bed linen, soap and sterile water—persist despite the hundreds of millions of dollars Cuba spends on medical equipment (Feinsilver 1989b: 259-260; Marquis 2000; Kinzer 2010). Sixto points out that during the Special Period beginning in the early 1990s "there has been a sharp decline (15 percent in 1990-94; 3.1 percent in 1997) in the expenditures on the maintenance and construction of basic health sector infrastructure, as well as on hospitals and policlinics." The deteriorating buildings and their facilities worsen the conditions under which health services are delivered (2002: 341).

A strong contrast between health sector employees' substantial contribution to health policy implementation and their limited participation in actual policy-making is also observable in the design and workings of the country's health information system. Despite the highly decentralized distribution of health services, doctors, as well as employees in management, statistics and IT, have little access to disaggregated health data that could be useful in enhancing work practices at the local level. Furthermore, the system is vertically fragmented; information tends to travel upwards towards the central level but is rarely shared horizontally between regional levels (Sæbø and Titlestad 2003; Braa, Titlestad and Sæbø 2004).

One of the side-effects of this dynamic is that it promotes excessive gathering of data, even when the data has no specific purpose.[21] This is partly because the task of collecting data is disconnected from its practical use. In other words, those who collect the data do so to fill a quota in order to satisfy or impress their boss, using the data as a symbol of competence rather than with the aim of informing and enhancing their own work practices. More generally, the health sector's extensive data collection is also a means to signal to the world that monitoring is taken seriously. In effect, this can lead to a focus on quantity rather than quality of data (author's personal e-mail communication with Sæbø, 2007. See also Feldman and March 1981). Earlier studies have identified this as a more generalized problem with the Cuban system. The following comments from Mesa Lago (1969a) describe a report by Pedro Rios summarizing Cuba's general situation in the mid-1960s.

> Cuban statistics are computed for no specific reason, without consideration of either the high cost of the system or the importance of the subject matter to be included. The most common vice is of "mechanicism" because the tasks are routine and monotonous. The important thing is to deliver the figures, giving priority to quantity rather than quality. Those in charge of gathering the information forget that their work concerns real life, which must be accurately represented by the data obtained (1969a: 76).

Excessive data collection takes up resources and compromises efficiency. Furthermore, alongside overprovision of information to higher levels of the system, regional actors are under-sourced with information. As a response to this, some doctors implement their own unofficial systems for recording information that would help them in their own work. When unable to access the information they need, they invent "parallel" systems, "extracting useful information from the multitude of reporting forms, and posting graphs and reports of performance on the hospital walls" (author's personal e-mail communication with Sæbø 2007). It can be assumed that the data collection workload for these doctors would be virtually halved if they were provided with access to the segments of data relevant to their work.[22] As the following case suggests, however, there seems to be reluctance at the national level to change current arrangements that allow only central access to information.

Norwegian Collaboration to Improve Cuba's Participatory Health Information Systems

Some interesting insights into the current participatory arrangements for employees involved in management, statistics and IT in the health system emerge from the recent experiences in Cuba of a team of Norwegian scholars from the University of Oslo. In 2001, the Norwegians undertook a collaborative pilot project with Cuba aimed at improving the island's participatory health information systems; the project also served as action research for several Masters theses. The project was initiated by Cuban interest in the Health Information Systems Program (HISP), initially derived from the Scandinavian work-life tradition, which sought to empower workers and their unions and to improve the functioning of organizations and workplaces by understanding them as networks rather than single operations. The HISP, which has the goal of facilitating effective management and delivery of health services in developing countries by improving local involvement and participation in health information systems, has been exported to a number of countries including South Africa, India, Mozambique and Mongolia (Braa, Titlestad and Sæbø 2004: 53-54). After a Cuban delegation and later the Cuban national director of health statistics visited the University of Oslo expressing interest in the project, a joint agreement was signed to introduce the system to Cuba. During a year of practical work in Cuba attempting to set up the system, the Norwegian parties encountered a number of obstacles mainly derived from the centralized nature of the Cuban health system, which ultimately led to the suspension of the program (2004: 57).

The project focused mainly on increasing horizontal participation, collaboration and information sharing between the main user groups of the country's health information system (health management, health statisticians and IT staff) at all levels of the system (national, provincial, municipal and primary health care organizations). The pilot project showed the potential to involve users, with significant local interest and willingness to participate especially in more remote areas. However, there were ultimately three main obstacles preventing efforts to realize this potential. First, the Cuban system was found to be vertically fragmented, characterized by an hierarchical line of command with very little interdepartmental collaboration (2004: 58-60). Similarly to the former Soviet systems, the statistics offices' main function is to transfer data upwards to the central level, not horizontally to other regional offices. The current information system focuses on "monitoring and measuring fulfillment of centrally defined plans at the central levels, rather than on local use for improved quality of services" (2004: 60).[23]

Second, the project was stifled by a lack of political support at the national level. Given the power balance of the Cuban system, which is heavily weighted towards the national level, any kind of initiative at any other level depends on the approval of central management. Although the national office of statistics (DNE) seemed aware of the value of local participation in terms of improving the health system overall, the unwillingness to deal with the problem was probably due to a recognition that it would bring a shift in the existing power dynamics; more control would be shifted to local levels of the system, thereby compromising the DNE's control. This power dynamic also meant that local participants were reluctant to continue participating for fear that word would reach the national level—the situation was tense given the recent sackings of the health minister and many directors and the tightening of restrictions on foreign involvement (2004: 60).

In November 2002, after three months of local development actions, the DNE management stopped all activities in the two provinces and demanded a new approach with focus solely on the national level. Much efforts [sic] invested by the local levels were neglected by the central decision-makers, and many potentially good development processes were stopped. The DNE management explained that their need to change the development approach was based on a lack of control of local project activities. The DNE did not agree on the need for local participation and to spend so much time out in the two provinces, as this context sensitive approach was completely new to them. They argued that a top-down approach with development solely at the national office had always been a success in Cuba, and that the project should follow this method. There is no tradition for involving local levels in decision-making, and the DNE did not agree that local involvement in the development would lead to a better system. This citation from the DNE management illustrates their view of local-level participatory processes: "The local health managers do not know what good information is and they do not know what data that [sic] is important to them" (2004: 57).

Finally, by contrast with other countries where HISP was introduced, the authors found that employees in the Cuban system rarely spoke out publicly to challenge government orders. The political environment allowed little space for the kind of open debate over competing opinions that is necessary in order for participatory processes to function (2004: 61). This also suggests limited potential for health sector employees to circumvent state power by building relations abroad, a tactic Mann has described as one way for civil society to counter despotic state power (1993: 59).

Evaluation of Existing Institutions for Popular Participation and Registering of Complaints

It should be acknowledged that some avenues exist for registering complaints about the health system and for popular participation generally. Certain individual health facilities occasionally survey patients about the quality of services, but such surveys are neither routine nor standardized. Effectively all legal opinion polling at the national level in Cuba is conducted by the Institute for Research and Orientation of Internal Demand (ICIODI). The Institute usually seeks public opinion regarding goods and services but rarely surveys broader issues such as whether people would prefer more expenditure in other areas than health. The main avenues for providing feedback regarding the health system are the country's mass organizations, local branches of the Communist Party, and People's Power representatives (Feinsilver 1989b). All of these avenues appear to be fairly effective in terms of *involving* the population in state-led health decisions, especially in the implementation process. Less convincing, however, is the official portrayal of these establishments as channels that allow civil society groups to genuinely influence or act independently of the state.

As Raúl Castro has stated, Cuba's leadership defines the country's civil society as its mass organizations[24] (Dominguez 2000; Amaro 1996: 273). The Communist Party's official description of Cuban mass organizations is as follows: "Our society has developed in its midst genuine mass organizations that are independent and autonomous, constituting limitless political and revolutionary energy, and real popular democracy"[25] (Partido Comunista de Cuba 2007). This portrayal of mass organizations as autonomous from the Party has come under frequent scrutiny, particularly from foreign observers. Although some accept the party line (Saney 2005; Dominguez 1977; Bohmer 2004), the more common assessment is that the organizations are tightly interwoven with the Communist Party. The hierarchies of the organizations closely resemble that of the government and it is common for leaders of the Party to hold top positions in the organizations or to switch between the two. Militants of the Party or of its youth branch, the UJC, are usually also required to be members of either/or the CDR or FMC and members of the FMC are obliged to also be members of the CDR. Originally established with the purpose of monitoring and preventing counterrevolutionary activity, CDRs in particular work closely with the Party and have often been described as organs of social control. The Vigilance and Public Order (VOP) component of the organization has a direct collaborative relationship with the Cuban police. CDR executives are required to make daily reports of activities in their block to a sector controller and to keep files on all individuals in their block; and these can contain information regarding citizens' households, neighborhood arguments, rumors and gossip (Amaro 1996: 272-276; Donate-Armada 1996: 287-291).[26]

However, in relation to the health sector, the facilitative role of mass organizations cannot be overlooked. Both the FMC and CDR have public health responsibilities and have played powerful roles in mobilizing popular involvement in health campaigns set by MINSAP. These have already been discussed to some extent in the previous chapter, especially relating to collaboration between family doctors and local CDR and FMC representatives. Importantly, their work has included organizing and training teams of paraprofessional volunteers such as health brigade workers, who make household visits and engage the population in campaigns of mass vaccination, blood donation, health education and other preventive efforts (Dominguez 1977). That mass organizations have been an integral source of state capacity in relation to achieving state health goals is indisputable. That they act as autonomous bodies with the capacity to shape official opinion in advance of its public enunciation is far less likely.

In terms of registering complaints about the health system, a noteworthy establishment is the process of "rendering accounts" (RRC) whereby elected local delegates are required to report their work performance twice a year in meetings with their local community and community members are invited to express their general concerns (Amaro 1996: 271; Constitución de la República de Cuba 1999: 31). An account of how health complaints are registered through these meetings is provided by Arnold August in his study of Cuba's electoral system. According to August, in one of these meetings he attended, citizens complained of shortages in pharmacies and of medical staff having a "detached attitude" and not dealing with medical emergencies because they lacked medical materials and the local representative responded by organizing a public forum to discuss the issues (1999: 387). The author portrays such avenues for participation as legitimate and effective.

When asked what were the processes for lodging complaints about hospital service in Cuba, a Cuban expatriate and former member of the Communist Party gave a far more skeptical view, suggesting that participatory formalities usually exist as symbols of participation that lack substance in terms of their function.

> In all institutions, including hospitals, there exist shall we say, "mechanisms for lodging complaints." If there is a problem the thing to do is usually is to go to the administration of the facility. The amount of attention paid to the matter, the level of person who attends you and the length of time you wait for a response will depend on the implications of the matter, how angry the person is who makes the complaint and how loudly they speak out. Ninety percent of the time the response is an explanation or an excuse but rarely a solution and never compensation. Never is there any written record made of the complaint, or any real process for analyzing causes and solutions. I have heard of serious processes regarding claims of medical negligence only in cases of deaths…I am sure that with the new systems that exist for internationally categorizing the quality and viability of services, surely in the hospitals that attend foreigners or that are associated with universities, there is an obligation to have things working better. But in Cuba this is always done as if preparing for a play in the theatre. In the end nothing is written down that is not convenient and when something goes wrong the blame is always laid on "imperialism" (author's interview with Mendoza, January 2007).

Assessing the effectiveness of RRCs, Cuban researchers Dilla Alfonso and González Núñez (1997) write that there is significant public utilization of this process and it is fairly legitimate in terms of providing public feedback to the government. However they argue that the reverse flow of information (from the government to the community), and the accountability function of the process generally, is fairly weak. Nor have RRCs promoted collective action to deal with issues in the community independently of government authority.

> An inevitable consequence is the regrettable underuse of the population's participation potential. Arguably, the imbalance between its successes as a conduit for raising and addressing demands and the weaker results of the accountability and accord functions may be a reflection of one of the greatest shortcomings of the community process: a paternalistic relation between the government, on one side, and the community and citizens, on the other. Not only does this work to the detriment of

the stated objectives, but, from a strategic perspective, it is also detrimental to the establishment of a society where collective action and social self-management are meant to prevail (Dilla Alfonso and González Núñez 1997; see also Dilla Alfonso and González Núñez 2007: 83-85).

In a 1987 meeting with the provincial committee of the Party in Havana, Fidel Castro addressed the issue of complaints about the quality of services in hospitals (including employee absenteeism, inefficiency, poor service and unavailability of pharmaceuticals). In response to these and as part of a general process termed "rectification of errors,"[27] he announced that monthly meetings would be held in hospitals with the Party secretaries for as many years as it took until "every hospital runs like clockwork" (in Feinsilver 1989b: 261). However, despite responding mainly by increasing Party involvement in hospital supervision (1989b: 261), many of the same problems persist today. At least ostensibly, it would appear that increasing top-down pressure on health workers has not been a particularly successful response. Given the growing recognition that the sustainable development of health systems benefits from citizen participation in health policy decisions (see PAHO 2006), in retrospect this may have been a more effective strategy.

Arguably, Cuba already has an extensive system of popular participation; it is one of the few, if not the only Pan American Health Organization (PAHO) country that has managed to establish a coordinated system of popular participation at the national level (Feinsilver 1993, 80). The establishment of People's Power (*Poder Popular*) Assemblies in 1976 indicated an official awareness that a lack of institutionalized popular participation was a political weakness. While some accept the move as a genuine effort to improve participation, critics tend to argue that *poder popular* has "acted as a rubber stamp upon authoritarian executive decision-making, offering semblance but not the reality of popular control." In other words, the argument is that the institution serves to disguise a lack of popular support for the Communist Party (Lievesley 2005: 10). In the health sphere, the establishment of *poder popular* at the municipal, provincial and national levels in 1976 led to greater administrative decentralization and increased opportunities for non-health workers to participate in health policy-making. "The polyclinic became accountable to the Ministry of Public Health on issues of norms, policies and methodology and to the municipal People's Power Executive Committee in administrative and operational matters" (Feinsilver 1993, 81). Each level of people's power (including its local services) brings together representatives from the corresponding levels of the country's mass social and political organizations such as the CDR and FMC (author's interview with Ramirez, September 2004). Although these structures play an important role in educating and mobilizing the population to participate in the implementation of health policies (a considerable achievement), many observers have been critical of the degree to which they offer real participation in actual policy-making. Feinsilver notes that the extent to which People's Power Assemblies offer a means for popular participation in the health sector is greater in theory than in practice. "[S]ince these services are under the normative and methodological control of the Ministry of Public Health, actual decision-making and planning do not take place in the assemblies but rather in the ministry and at the local level of administration by ministry appointees" (1993, 81-82). Elaborating this point, Ramos (2004b) from Cuba's National School of Public Health argues that, given the available participatory structures in Cuba, participation in problem-solving and decision-making by different sectors and groups in society (generally, but also in relation to health) is technically feasible. However, she outlines numerous obstacles preventing real participation including the centralized nature of the system, paternalism, too much bureaucracy, insufficient or non-existent information systems and the sometimes inadequate interpretation of what social participation means. Similarly, in a discussion of popular participation in Cuba, Hernández and Dilla argue that it is important to distinguish the difference between participation and real power. "To participate is not simply to have access to multiple areas of discussion but to contribute to decision-making in these areas. Participation in discussion and execution is relatively high; in political decisions and their control it is considerably less" (1991, 53).

Discussion

On more than one level, the findings presented in this chapter problematize the assumptions and aspects of the hypothesis with which this project began. In a sense, the Cuban health system can be correctly described as characterized by cooperative relationships and wide-ranging popular participation. However, the fact that multiple sectors and institutions cooperate and are unified in striving towards the same health goals in Cuba, and that health policies are carried out with extensive public involvement and compliance, is often misleadingly portrayed and interpreted as evidence of an integrated and egalitarian system of collective decision-making. Wide-reaching popular participation in the *implementation* of health policies is evident in Cuba, and in this sense

the "state" can be construed as "embedded." However, central decision-makers maintain considerable autonomy over which decisions are
made, which areas of health are prioritized and how the state's "obligation to protect and improve the health of the Cuban population" is
interpreted.[28]

The social relations of the Cuban health system can therefore be
described as predominantly paternalistic; population health improvement is defined and imposed by central elites, who have demonstrated
on many occasions an unwillingness to accept outsiders' (other social
groups, individuals or institutions) attempts to infiltrate this power by
influencing, deviating from, or failing to comply with central decisions.
Part of maintaining this control has been the government's effectiveness
in fragmenting and obstructing the formation of oppositional groups.[29]
Legal restrictions governing association inhibit the growth of horizontal
ties in the community that would strengthen the representation of different social groups and their influence on policy-making. The consequences
have been severe for health workers who have in the past attempted to
form professional associations without government endorsement, for
example. The government's hostile reaction to the Norwegian collaborative project is also illustrative—efforts to improve regional access
to health information were thwarted with the justification that "local
health managers do not know what good information is [nor what data]
is important to them" (Braa, Titlestad and Sæbø 2004: 57).

Central control is further consolidated whenever attempts to permeate
it are shut down. Punishments for non-compliance serve as warnings that
deter future attempts to challenge this control. In the context of arguing
that "the state" is more than the state apparatus but is also "a set of social
relations that establishes a certain order, and ultimately backs it with
centralized coercive guarantee," O'Donnell (1993) describes this process
through which existing power relations reinforce themselves.

> [Under both capitalist and bureaucratic socialist systems] when decisions are made
> at the political center (the "orders given") those decisions usually "give order," in
> the sense that those commands are regularly obeyed. This acquiescence affirms
> and reproduces the existing social order. Social relations, including those of daily
> preconscious acquiescence to political authority, can be based, as Weber argued, on
> tradition, fear of punishment, pragmatic calculation, habituation, legitimacy, and/or
> the effectiveness of the law (1993).

The paternalistic relations generating health policy at the national
level in Cuba reproduce themselves in the interactions between institutions at various levels of the system's hierarchy. In turn, this contributes

to tendencies towards medical paternalism[30] at the point where patients come into contact with the system.

This brings us to the major challenge these findings present to the assumptions underlying the project's initial hypothesis. The assumption of Cuba's exceptional health achievements was based largely on its statistical outcomes—reduced mortality and morbidity, the doctor-patient ratio, increased life expectancy and so on. Beyond the improvements in such health indicators, the research process brought to light a range of persistent problems with health services in Cuba that national-level health statistics do not reflect, many associated with the paternalistic nature of the system. These include the lack of patient autonomy which is often a product of health workers' limited autonomy and the intense political pressure under which they work.[31] Not only is it common for patients to be excluded from medical decisions, but varying degrees of coercion appear to be adopted in order to achieve patient compliance with policies to improve aggregate outcomes, even where this compromises other considerations such as the patient's emotional or psychological well-being, thereby negating some aspects of the government's declared project of providing quality health care. The coercion is sometimes mild, such as recommending an abortion to a pregnant woman who has fetal abnormalities; but more extreme in others such as that of the young girl who was sterilized without her consent. Furthermore, a number of persistent and unaddressed problems with health services—including deteriorating conditions in hospitals and lack of regard for ethical considerations—are antithetical to the government's proclaimed goal of providing quality health services to the population. The politicized nature of health, combined with the central control over decision-making, can prevent patients and health workers from speaking out about these problems.

The obvious argument mitigating the above-mentioned problems is that they are all inevitable and ethically justifiable consequences of a society that values the health of the overall community over individual considerations.[32] Central control of health policy decision-making may be an ideal arrangement for improving collective outcomes, especially given resource shortages. From this perspective, relinquishing decision-making powers at the local level may be a small price to pay for ensuring overall health improvements. However, much of the evidence presented in this chapter suggests that the choice between collective and individual considerations is not as simple a trade-off as is sometimes portrayed. Besides detracting from individual patients' and health workers' experience of the system, the absence of provisions to increase local decision-making power can in many ways undercut the system's collective potential and the sustainability of health achievements. For example, the intense politicization of health and the restrictions on acting outside government orders can paralyze health employees who might otherwise publicize or even mobilize local collective initiatives to deal with public health problems in the local community such as rubbish disposal, cleaning and repairing of health facilities, and so on. In some cases it is also possible that health authorities do not receive accurate information about problems in the system due to health workers' and patients' fears about lodging complaints. Therefore, authorities may even be unaware at times of the sources of dissatisfaction with the system at the local level, and hence unable to respond appropriately or to gauge public support for public policies and arrangements.

Furthermore, some of the observations emerging from the Norwegian researchers' experiences with the HISP project suggest that central control of all information can be more a source of incapacity and inefficiency than the reverse. Local health workers do not have access to relevant health data and are not free to define their information needs or to share information horizontally with other local institutions. Instead, information is collected with the sole purpose of reporting upwards; the result being collection of useless information and time spent constructing informal systems to make up for the lack of local information. Development of local autonomy over defining information needs, as well as access to and the ability to share health information horizontally would most likely improve rather than compromise the country's health achievements; provided that standards were maintained to ensure the necessary information was still reported to the national level (author's personal e-mail communication with Sæbø 2007).

Arguably though, increasing the political influence at the local level could undermine the dominant position of state elites that currently provides the leverage to achieve multi-institutional and general public compliance with central health goals. Health workers' limited political influence (due to their inability to form associations or trade unions, lobby the government or work professionally beyond the public sector)[33] has been a factor allowing the government to keep wages low, thereby increasing its capacity to offer free medical care to the population and improving its "purchasing power" when it trades human resources overseas. Freedom to form professional non-government alliances could change this by increasing health workers' capacity to collectively bargain for improved wages and conditions. Further, avenues for more open public debate about problems with the health system could undermine the government's efforts to maintain a positive health reputation internationally. The current power dynamic works to suppress attempts to publicly draw attention to the health system's weak points, thereby allowing the government to control the image of the system promoted at home and internationally. Maintaining the health system's positive image is in some ways important to the survival of the regime—it secures international support and also more tangible benefits such as much-needed oil to supply other sectors of the economy.[34]

But at what long-term cost are current power arrangements being maintained? So far the country's health results have been sustained due to a long lasting leadership by a government that prioritizes key health improvements. In turn, the government's legitimacy and longevity have relied considerably on its positive record of health improvement. However, existing paternalistic arrangements have involved an over-reliance on central decision-makers (especially Fidel Castro) for direction, initiative and definition of collective health priorities. This could be a problem in the event of a change in regime priorities. How this unfolds under Raúl Castro's government, especially after Fidel Castro dies, is yet to be seen. Arguably there had already been some shifting of priorities under Fidel Castro from the provision of free, quality health care for the Cuban population to the use of medicine to raise revenue (through health tourism and the exchange of doctors for Venezuelan oil). That decision-making arrangements are not especially embedded in mechanisms of popular endorsement and participation is worrying for the long-term survival of the country's public health institutions. As argued in Chapter 3, institution-building aimed at integrating the widespread public participation into the implementation of national health plans has been the basis for some important collective health advancements. These arrangements, I have shown, are aspects of social capital; they are social structures which have raised the threshold for what can be collectively achieved. Social capital as it has been conceptualized for this project refers to collective investments in durable social arrangements (collective institutions). However, social institutions are only durable if they are collectively acknowledged and continue to inform public behavior and therefore reproduce themselves through ongoing social exchange. The examples of exclusion, passivity and avoidance outlined here arguably detract from the extent to which social capital has really been built in the Cuban health sector.

The paternalistic decision-making arrangements in Cuba, aside from compromising patients' and health workers' experience of the health system (an aspect of its quality), may therefore be the greatest threat to the long-term sustainability of the country's statistical outcomes and its public health system as a legitimate challenge to a privatized system.[35] The provision of free health care to the population and improvements in health indicators *are* state achievements and are justifiably envied by other developing countries. However, the paternalistic means by which these results are achieved, while efficient in terms of achieving compliance with little negotiation, could eventually work to undermine these achievements by failing to deal with problems in the system that, even if not directly affecting health statistics, are sources of public frustration and resentment. Furthermore, an increasing prioritization of the country's health image over its quality runs the risk of eventually undercutting the system's reputation both at home and abroad. Improved avenues for open debate and public influence over policy-making could pull the government into line, ensuring it continues to prioritize health care for *Cubans*. As briefly visited earlier, persistent problems in the formal system can also drive patients to circumvent the system and resolve the issues via informal arrangements, which I argue presents long term concerns for the system's sustainability. This subject is the focus of the following chapter.

Appendix to Chapter 4
The Medical Profession and the State

"Professional dominance" has long characterised medical practice. However there have been perennial counter-tendencies towards "proletarianisation" or "de-professionalisation." Professions have traditionally been seen as occupations with organised autonomy or self-direction in the division of labour. In medicine, this is usually sustained by "special status," a persuasive professional culture (emphasising trustworthiness, ethical behaviour, distinctive skills and authority). Public support and recognition of this authority requires the creation of institutions able to protect against external attempts to intervene, direct, or compete with its dominance (Friedson 1970a in Wolinsky 1993: 11). Whatever else may be observed about the Cuban health system, there are bound to be differences from and similarities to these general processes there.

Some theorists have argued that the medical profession in the West has been subject to processes of de-professionalization or proletarianization. That is, its dominance, prestige and authority have been undermined by various transformations in the management and organization of health care (Lewis, Marjoribanks and Pirotta 2003: 44). Mary Haug, one of the main proponents of the de-professionalization theory, has argued that technological advances, including automated retrieval systems such as those used to assess medical symptoms, have weakened the experts' control over knowledge. She adds that increased levels of public education have demystified medical knowledge, leading more patients to question physicians' decisions and judgment. Further, increasing medical specialization has led doctors to depend on one another more than ever before, and this has decreased their individual autonomy. Finally, the emergence of numerous allied health workers, the growth of consumer help groups and the increasing reliance on "lay" referral systems have created alternatives to physicians' knowledge (Wolinsky 1993: 13-14; Haug 1988).

"Proletarianization" constitutes another challenge to professional dominance. Drawing on aspects of Marxian social theory, the proletarianization thesis contends that, in capitalist societies, physicians along with all workers inevitably lose control over their work and are reduced to serving the interests of capital accumulation (Wolinsky 1993: 15). It has been argued that the increasing bureaucratisation of the medical workplace, among other factors, has placed external constraints on areas of the profession that were once self-regulated, bringing about the decline of the "golden age of doctoring" (McKinlay and Marceau 2002).

A key determinant of the medical profession's capacity to achieve and maintain dominance and autonomy is its ability to organize politically. This includes its relationship with the state and the structures of civil society. In particular, the degree to which the profession adopts a "corporatist mode of interest representation" influences its political position and its capacity to oversee policy (Frenk and Duran-Arenas 1993: 36). In a broad sense, corporatism since the 1970s has been seen as "a system of interest representation characterized by hierarchical and noncompetitive occupational or functional associations, which represent their members' interests through direct negotiations with the state" (1993: 37). Physicians' collective control of their environment varies significantly from one context to another in line with their capacity for corporatist organization, depending on arrangements of state power and organization within civil society. In the United States, for example, the collective strength of physicians' associations is linked to their organization along corporatist lines as well as relatively weak state intervention. In Scandinavian countries such as Sweden, the profession's power is more moderate because the groups in civil society have a greater capacity to themselves assert power through the state. In the former Soviet Union, where the state predominantly controlled and organized civil society groups (including the medical profession and other groups with which it interacts), physicians' power was relatively weak (1993: 37-38). Resonances with the Soviet system can be discerned in Cuba as my research shows.

Although this book discusses the positions of Cuban doctors, including their collective organization, autonomy and relationships with the state and with patients and other groups, its unit of analysis is the contemporary Cuban health system overall, rather than the medical profession specifically. While a detailed examination of the condition of the Cuban medical profession in relation to global historical transformations does offer interesting and worthwhile avenues for future research, it is not within this book's scope.

Notes

1. A report in Time magazine drew attention to this point in the Soviet context. Despite the Soviet state's highly publicised priority on childbearing, the female former Soviet citizens interviewed for the article told of undignified way in which they were treated in Soviet maternity hospitals. The women described the hospitals as unsanitary and uncomfortable and the treatment degrading. One interviewee's description was that women in labour were treated "like cattle" (Smolowe 1988).
2. What the respondent most likely meant when he said the patient "came through the usual system in her local area" was that the patient entered the system via the formal channels rather than with a private, informal referral from a friend or socio who could have ensured better treatment. This subject is explored more thoroughly in Chapter 6.
3. "Anonymous interview" is where the respondent did not want to be identified by name, job title, or affiliation with an institution.
4. Cuba's educational levels are high, however.
5. I had a video camera during the visit to the *hogar materno* and filmed some images of those employees on duty and women in the rooms who gave their consent to be filmed. One pregnant woman agreed to give a short interview on camera explaining why she was in the home. She said she had been identified as a high risk pregnancy because she had previously experienced a number of miscarriages. She had other young children at home. Her family was allowed to visit her in the *hogar*. She mentioned that she had requested a pass to leave the home to visit her family but wasn't granted one. She did not go into further detail, possibly because several of the *hogar's* employees and a room full of other pregnant women were present and watching her speak.

6. This is a direct translation of *"bajo nivel cultural."* I heard the term used to describe people on several occasions and it was usually accompanied by a somewhat judgmental tone. The closest formal term in English is probably 'low socio-economic background.'

7. It can be assumed that inefficient contraceptive use, although partly a result of general patient complacency, would also be a result of other factors such as cultural norms of machismo.

8. The next chapter contains a more detailed discussion of informal health service delivery practices and their broader impact.

9. As detailed in the previous chapter

10. Left-wing diplomat, author and intellectual sent by Chile's Allende government to Cuba as ambassador in 1970 and later declared persona non grata by Castro. Edwards' book (based on his experiences in Cuba) won the Cervantes prize (Spanish equivalent to a Nobel Prize for literature).

11. Developmental statists also argue that the state's control over other social groups increases its capacity to achieve the goals it pursues.

12. The respondent also discussed the issue of fathers usually not being permitted to attend births in Cuba. Despite the country's supposed advancement in gender relations, men have only recently gained permission to accompany their wives in childbirth, and only in some maternity hospitals. The respondent said she thought this was due to a combination of reasons: first, not all fathers want to attend their child's birth; second, since birthing spaces are so public it would be logistically problematic to have men present where so many women were giving birth at once; third, fathers might argue with health workers if they saw the conditions in the hospital.

13. In January 2010 it was reported in the Cuban and foreign press that 26 patients died within one week at Havana's largest psychiatric hospital during a spell of cold weather. According to a statement from the Cuban government, the deaths were "linked to the prolonged low temperatures... and to risk factors peculiar to mentally ill patients and to natural biological deterioration" and that an investigation had identified a number of deficiencies at the hospital. Human rights activists argued that the patients died from hypothermia resulting from "criminal negligence" and deteriorating conditions at the hospital including broken windows and other problems (BBC News 2010).

14. Rivero is one of Cuba's best known independent journalists. He left the Cuban state-owned press in 1988 after growing increasingly disillusioned with the country's political system. In 2003 he was sentenced to 20 years jail, but was released in 2004. He subsequently left Cuba and moved to Spain and has since been awarded a UNESCO/Guillermo Cano World Press Freedom Prize (Words Without Borders 2007).

15. I observed these problems during all of my to public Cuban hospitals; the tourist hospital Cira Garcia was extremely clean and well-maintained by comparison.

16. It is unclear here whether the patient meant that he favored a private system or was referring to existing informal arrangements of paying doctors in the public system with favors, gifts or money in exchange for preferential treatment (discussed in the next chapter). Either way, although free medical services are an invaluable provision that most Cubans recognize—a provision that ensures even the poorest sections of the population are able to receive treatment—these secondary problems with facilities create frustrations that undermine patients' appreciation of the free services, even where the quality of medical care from doctors is good.

17. The exchanges of doctors for Venezuelan oil have met with a fair share of problems. Despite the grateful welcome from poorest of Venezuelan's citizens who are now

receiving free treatment, there has been a backlash from some Venezuelan doctors who argue that Cuban doctors are taking their jobs and aim to 'indoctrinate' or "Cubanize" the country. Chávez argues that most Venezuelan doctors refuse to work in the poor areas where the Cuban clinics are being set up (BBC News 2005; Robles 2003). Some Cuban doctors have used the missions as opportunities to leave Cuba (to date, as many as 500 doctors have defected from Venezuela). Some of those who defected have made complaints against Cuban doctors' working conditions and low salaries. One doctor publicly declared that, aside from delivering health services in Venezuela, doctors were also forced to campaign for Chávez (Forero 2007; Newman 2000). More recently, in February 2010, seven Cuban doctors and a Cuban nurse filed charges against Cuba, Venezuela and the state-run oil company Petróleos de Venezuela, claiming to have been forced to work as "modern slaves" (El Universal 2010).

18.   In a 2006 British Medical Journal report, a Cuban doctor living in Miami after defecting from Venezuela (Otto Sanchez) claimed that one in five family doctor offices had been forced to close due to lack of personnel and supplies (Carrillo de Albornoz 2006).

19.   Dr. Marcelo Cano Rodríguez, Dr. José Luis García Paneque, Dr. Luis Milán Fernández, and dentists Alfredo Manuel Pulido and Ricardo Enrique Silva Gual.

20.   Cases of acute diarrhea increased from 5,707 to 10,242 in 1965-1993 and decreased again somewhat to 7,703 by 2000. Cases of tuberculosis increased from 4.7 in 1991 to 14.1 in 1994, declining again to 10.1 in 2000 (Sixto 2002: 338).

21.   To give some idea of the excessiveness of data collection in Cuba, the country gathers over 10,000 data elements as opposed to South Africa's 250 and Botswana's 1,800. A "data element" is, for example, "Malaria, less than one year" or "Hospital beds" (author's personal e-mail communication with Sæbø 2007).

22.   Worker autonomy, or the ability for workers to control their work situation, is also known to increase workers' motivation and job performance generally (Brey 1999).

23.   This is compatible with, and probably goes some way to explain why Cuba's statistical outcomes are positive when service deterioration can be observed at the local level, as discussed in earlier sections of this chapter.

24.   The country's mass organisations are: Committee for the Defense of the Revolution (CDR), Federation of Cuban Women (FMC), Central Organisation of Cuban Workers or Central Trade Union (CTC), National Association of Small Farmers (ANAP), and the Mid-Level Students' Federation (FEEM). There also exist mass political organisations; the Union of Young Communists (UJC) (the youth branch of the Communist Party) and the Jose Marti Organisation of Young Pioneers (OPJM) (Partido Comunista de Cuba 2007). With its motto: "Pioneers of Communism: We will be like Che!" the OPJM introduces children and adolescents to revolutionary values.

25.   Cuban law does not provide space in which NGOs can operate (Pax Christi Netherlands 1999). Raul Castro has suggested that NGOs in Cuba are often counterrevolutionary organisations sponsored by the "enemy," masquerading as interested in research or civil society (Amaro 1996: 273).

26.   A more detailed, nuanced discussion of the links between mass organizations and the party is not within the scope of this project but can be found in other works including (see, for example, Donate-Armada 1996; Amaro 1996).

27.   This Rectification campaign began in 1986 and was largely a response to the government's recognition of a decreasing public confidence in the regime and the need to address some of the system's problems including its economic inefficiency and over-bureaucratization (Lievesley 2005: 10).

28. Following from the final point, the Council of Ministers also has considerable autonomy in defining the parameters within which the government fulfills the health obligations on which much of its legitimacy is based. In other words, if improving population health is defined narrowly in terms of progress in key health indicators such as mortality rates and life expectancy and these are achieved, it has claims to success regardless of any compromises entailed in the process.

29. Stepan (1985: 317) ascribes this effectiveness in atomizing potentially opposing groups to Latin American bureaucratic authoritarian regimes of the 1970s, such as in Brazil, Chile, and Argentina.

30. Medical paternalism by definition refers to medical decisions made for the patient by the doctor based on what the doctor considers best for the patient. In the Cuban context this is not exactly the case in many instances. Doctors may sometimes be placed under pressure to override their professional opinion regarding the individual patients' best interests to comply instead with overarching demands to prioritize broader public health goals. Ultimately, however the patient's autonomy, and possibly wellbeing too, are constrained.

31. As has been discussed here, there are limitations on doctors' professional autonomy in Cuba, especially given the extent of politicization in Cuban society. Nonetheless, the medical profession worldwide is also subject to considerable historical transformation. In broad terms the profession's dominance, autonomy and legitimacy are affected by varying degrees of proletarianization, de-professionalization, and corporatisation in different contexts. Some explanation of these concepts is included in Appendix to Chapter 4.

32. This has been identified as an essential difference in ethical approach between Cuba (where collective priorities are emphasized) and other liberal nations such as the United States where individual autonomy is highly prioritised (Zaglul 2002).

33. Doctors educated after the revolution cannot practice privately in Cuba. Those who want to leave the country to work overseas (aside from those leaving on government-sponsored missions) must serve in their practice for five years before obtaining an exit visa .

34. According to one report, the increase in exports of medical services including doctors was a significant factor contributing to Cuba's expected 10 percent GDP growth for 2007 (Agencias 2007b).

35. The efforts to establish participatory arrangements in Cuba suggest that the Party leaders recognise that the appearance of pluralised decisions, even if not genuine, is important to its legitimacy (at home and abroad) and that the inclusion of many different groups in decisions is important.

5

Underground Health Care Arrangements as Temporary Solutions and Long Term Challenges to the Formal System

Introduction

I have argued that the underdevelopment of effective formal processes for including health workers and the population generally in decision-making can lead to unaddressed problems in the health sector. In turn, these persistent problems can contribute to a tendency for circumvention and avoidance of formal institutional arrangements. This chapter explores this phenomenon in more detail.

Although numerous authors have devoted attention to the subject of Cuba's burgeoning second economy, it is usually overlooked in studies of the country's health system. Rarely have reports on health in Cuba included any mention of the informal practices of exchange operating beneath official health care delivery arrangements. Although most Cubans receive their medical care through state facilities, there appears to be a widening but commonly-overlooked practice amongst patients and health workers of circumventing "official procedures" and instead resolving medical problems via informal arrangements. This usually involves the exchange of favors for preferential medical treatment through networks of friends or *socios*.

An examination of informal practices in the health sector was not one of the goals of this project at its outset. The research plan was not designed with this subject in mind, mainly because the issue is seldom mentioned in the background literature. It was only inadvertently through personal observations, informal discussions and some interviewees' comments on the subject that the pervasiveness of informal exchange practices in the health sector became apparent (to me). The claims of this chapter are therefore fairly modest. The intention is mainly to draw attention to some of these informal practices and their causes and to reflect on the quality and sustainability of the public health system. In doing this, I consider informal health practices in light of other authors' broader insights regarding the second economy in Cuba (and other socialist settings).

Expanding underground practices in the health system erode social capital and the collective achievements of the public health system. Although networks of informal exchange temporarily "prop up" the formal system by providing alternative solutions to problems the formal system fails to resolve, over the longer term they perpetuate these problems and degrade the legitimacy of public health policies on both practical and ideological levels, thereby undermining state capacity.

Brief Overview of Approaches to the Underground Economy

As a concept, the "informal economy" or "informal sector" is relatively recent. The modernisation approaches to development prevailing throughout the 1950s to 1960s regarded informal economic activity as exclusively a problem of the underdeveloped world that would disappear once these societies became "modern"—a term normally signifying Western values and institutions including market-oriented economies (Henken 2005: 363). A number of pioneering studies discredited this approach. A study by anthropologist Keith Hart in the early 1970s, along with studies in Kenya by the International Labor Organisation (ILO) in the same period, introduced the term "informal sector" and challenged the stereotype of informal activity as necessarily linked to "backward" traditions typical of poor, marginalized communities. Studies by Alejandro Portes and other authors have contributed to the recognition that informal economic activity is an international phenomenon occurring in both market-oriented and centrally planned economies, and in both the developing and developed world. It has therefore been increasingly understood as an inherent feature of both capitalist and socialist economies, rather than an anomaly (Henken 2005; Ritter 2005; Portes, Castells and Benton 1989; Hart 1971).

Various terms including "informal economy," "underground economy," "black market economy," and "illegal economy" have been adopted by different authors, not always with consistency. However, some useful categorizations have been made that bring more clarity. Portes and Haller differentiate between the "formal economy" (encompassing legal economic activity which occurs "within the regulatory regime of the state"), the "informal economy" (legal goods or services traded "outside the regulatory and fiscal regime of the state") and the "criminal economy" (involving trade of illegal goods or services) (2005: 405). A separation of terms can also differentiate between underground economic activity in capitalist contexts (the "informal economy") and that occurring in socialist, centrally-planned settings (the "second economy") (Henken 2005; Stark 1989). Drawing on the concept introduced by Grossman (1977), Perez-Lopez uses the term "second economy" in the Cuban context to encompass all activities that fall outside of the centrally planned "first economy." This includes cases where "(1) the activity is for private gain; or (2) it is in some substantial respect knowingly illegal." The second economy therefore encompasses a wide spectrum of activities ranging from illegal or shadow practices, to legalized small-scale private enterprises that are nonetheless officially discouraged (1995: 77).

Two important and essentially contrasting approaches to the informal economy in the recent literature have been identified as "neo-liberal" and "structuralist" theories (Henken 2005: 363-366). The neo-liberal approach emerged in the late 1980s mainly following from work by Hernando de Soto, who characterized the informal sector as a popular revolution against the over-regulation imposed by mercantilist patrimonial states—informal activity according to de Soto is a struggle by masses of micro-entrepreneurs against a state-led economy that locks them out of formal arrangements and therefore restricts their capitalist potential (2005: 364-365). In *The Mystery of Capital,* de Soto argues that the poor who are dispossessed through exclusion from the formal system "are not the problem but the solution." He proposes regulatory changes that would allow informal groups to access the formal arrangements, importantly including property systems that integrate informal participants, allowing them to convert their resources into capital (2000: 241).

Contrasting with this approach, structuralists (including Portes and collaborating authors) have argued that formal and informal economies are closely linked. Under this approach "these relations (and workers) are actively "informalized" by capital under the logic of peripheral capitalist accumulation" (Henken 2005: 365). For Portes and Shauffler, informal markets provide a subsidy to the overall capitalist system: they reduce labour costs (official firms regularly hire workers "off the books") and allow workers to obtain more with low wages, thereby making it possible for capital to pay labor below the cost of living (1993: 49). Rather than decreasing in advanced capitalist contexts, informal activity has been shown to persist and even increase with the development of capitalism, with many employers contracting informal labor as a matter of routine—a measure that allowed cost-cutting and avoidance of the regulations governing wage labor (Lozano 1989: 639; Portes, Castells and Benton 1989).

These debates about informality have largely focused on capitalist settings. Most of the studies of informal economies in Latin America have excluded consideration of the Cuban case. This is understandable given that, despite its similarities to other Latin nations in terms of history, language and culture, Cuba's political and economic arrangements are fundamentally different from its neighboring capitalist nations, having more in common with other centrally planned economies (Henken 2005: 362). However, building on these developments, some authors have devised more appropriate models for explaining informality in the very different sociopolitical context of socialist systems.

Following earlier insights that informal economies are integrally linked to capitalist systems, David Stark's landmark publication *Bending the Bars of the Iron Cage* observes that the second economy is not a leftover relic of pre-socialist times as previously assumed but an integral facet of modern state socialism. However he goes on to argue that, despite there being important parallels between capitalism's informal economy and socialism's second economy, the two are neither "functional equivalents [n]or structural counterparts" (1989: 639).

An informal economy is the product of efforts to circumvent accountability to the explicit rationalizations of regulatory bureaucratization. It operates according to principles disparate from those of the rules of internal labor markets but congruent with the market principles that coordinate the formal economy. In the centrally planned economies of state socialism where informalization responds to the contradictions of redistributive bureaucratization, the embryonic market relations of the second economy are incongruent with the bureaucratic principles that coordinate the formal economy, and in fact, stimulate the institutionalization of transactive market relations and the expansion of property rights inside the socialist enterprise. As a sphere of activity relatively autonomous from the state, the second economy is a source of fundamental change remaking the economic institutions of socialism (1989: 637).

Comparing different theoretical approaches to informality and considering their relevance to the Cuban case, Henken argues that the second economy in the socialist system is a unique instance that in some ways reconciles the otherwise opposing approaches of neo-liberals following de Soto and structuralists such as Portes. He points out that both these approaches "focus on the power dynamic that exists between informal underground workers on the one hand and the state/capital nexus on the other" (2005: 366). On the one hand, comparable with de Soto's description of informals, the private informal entrepreneurs in the socialist systems of former Soviet Union, Eastern Europe and in Cuba today represent a rebellion against the paternalistic central control over the formal economy. At the same time, Portes' observations that capitalist enterprises regularly rely upon and exploit the informal sector is interestingly comparable to the socialist state's reliance upon the second economy to compensate for its inefficiencies and shortcomings (2005: 366). Just as informal economies allow capitalist enterprises to operate at costs below those that would be possible in the formal system, socialism's second economy allows the formal socialist arrangements to continue despite their flaws and contradictions. A flexible second economy "provides state socialism with a very convenient, if potentially corrosive, subsidy"(2005: 366-367). It compensates for the shortcomings of the formal system but at the same time has an antagonistic relationship to formal arrangements and constantly generates pressure to transform them.

Cuba's Second Economy

> Now I spend my time day dreaming, or going to
> the Malecón[1] and selling dresses I no longer need
> to the street hustlers, the jineteras, in exchange for
> dollars, or exchanging sugar for sweet potatoes,
> sweet potatoes for beans, beans for onions, onions
> for rice, rice for powdered milk, powdered milk for
> detergent, detergent for aspirin, aspirin for sugar...
> —Zoé Valdés – Yocandra in the Paradise of Nada:
> A Novel of Cuba.

At Havana University in November 2005, Fidel Castro gave a speech in which he discussed with unusual openness the problem of widespread corruption and black market activity in Cuba and the threat this represented to the survival of the country's socialist system.

As you know, we are presently waging a war against corruption, against the re-routing of resources, against thievery.... I am going to say something, just to see if it will raise the sense of honor of the construction workers because when they want to be heroic, they are.... I recall, we were building an important biotechnological centre in Bejucal. There was a little cemetery close by. I was making my rounds, and one day I passed by the cemetery. There I saw a colossal market where the construction crew, both the foremen and many of the workers, had put up a market selling cement, steel rods, wood, paint, you name it, all kinds of construction materials. You know that construction has always been a very serious problem. We have resources now; sometimes there have been shortages, but now we have the possibility of improving the situation of construction materials. However, it's tragic the dilemma with the workers, the weaknesses of the foremen, and of others in leading positions...

Is it that revolutions are doomed to fall apart, or that men cause revolutions to fall apart? Can either man or society prevent revolutions from collapsing? I could immediately add to this another question: Do you believe that this revolutionary socialist process can fall apart, or not? (Exclamations of: "No!!") Have you ever given that some thought? Have you ever deeply reflected about it? Were you aware of all these inequalities that I have been talking about? Were you aware of certain generalized habits? Did you know that there are people who earn forty or fifty times the amount one of those doctors over there in the mountains of Guatemala (part of the "Henry Reeve" Contingent) earns in one month? It could be in other faraway reaches of Africa, or at an altitude of thousands of metres, in the Himalayas, saving lives and earning 5% or 10% of what one of those dirty little crooks earns, selling gasoline to the new rich, diverting resources from the ports in trucks and by the ton-load, stealing in the dollar shops, stealing in a five-star hotel by exchanging a bottle of rum for another of lesser quality and pocketing the dollars for which he sells the drinks (Castro 2005).

As Heinz Dieterich points out, this was a momentous speech coming from a President who for the past fifty years had publicly declared the revolution glorious and invincible. Following Castro's speech, the then Cuban Minister for Foreign Affairs Felipe Pérez Roque publicly reiterated the message in December 2005 stating: "we must pay great attention to Fidel's call at the University, to that phrase never pronounced publicly before in the history of the Revolution: the Revolution can be reversed, and not by the enemy that has done everything to bring about that reversal, but by our own mistakes" (Dieterich 2006). While this was not the first time Fidel Castro had reproached Cubans involved in illegal private enterprise (see for example Perez-Lopez 1995: 88), his warning of the possibility that Cuba's socialist system could "fall apart" was unusual. Speeches by Cuban officials in previous decades have tended to be intensely defensive and protective of the country's socialist system and its public image.

To place Castro's comments in further context, they partly responded to significant losses Cuba suffered in its fuel redistribution program when black marketeers were found to have been diverting truckloads of fuel from the ports to sell at private outlets. As a result, around half of the country's revenue from fuel found its way into private hands. As Castro's descriptions suggest, this was no isolated incident. Especially in light of these acknowledgements from Fidel Castro and his Ministers that the problem embodies a significant threat, the second economy has been recognized as a great enough force that any study of Cuba should consider it.[2] Indeed Portes and Borocz have commented that the second economy is such a pervasive facet of state socialism today that "any inquiry into the actual economic, social, political and even cultural processes of the supposedly "centrally planned economies" is bound to be misspecified unless it takes into consideration the socialist informal sector" (in Henken 2000: 321).

The existence of a second economy in Cuba is no secret: Tourists and journalists, even those who have only visited the island for short periods, have often reported observing widespread illegal economic practices (Ritter 2005: 343). Despite frequent mentions in journalists' reports, however, the subject of Cuba's second economy remains under-researched in the academic literature. In one of the few existing thorough academic analyses of the subject, *Cuba's Second Economy,* Perez-Lopez observes that this lack of attention is mostly due to the difficulty of researching the area. Those directly involved in the underground economy are unlikely to divulge information on the topic due to obvious concerns with concealing their participation. The lack of information available in relation to the informal economy is also a logical result of the activity being outside the official reporting system. Further, researchers of Cuba's *official* economy face obstacles and challenges related to access to the island, reliability of information and so on; factors which further complicate the prospect of studying the informal economy (1995: 77-78).

The magnitude of Cuba's second economy is therefore difficult to ascertain but a glimpse can be gleaned from newspaper reports. A report that appeared in the weekly Cuban publication *Bohemia,* for example, states that "between January and October 2003 the police found 181 illegal workshops, 525 clandestine factories and 315 spaces being used as warehouses" (Habel 2004). A 2004 *CubaNet News* article reports that in three of Havana's 15 municipalities, 150 underground cigar-making enterprises were raided and shut down. According to a 2004 article in *Juventud Rebelde,* in the province of Guantanamo where much of the population uses wood and charcoal for cooking, there were 400 wood sellers and 500 charcoal producers/sellers (all private and illegal). Ritter estimates there to be far more in other more forested provinces (2005: 347).

In March 2008, a month after Raúl assumed presidency, Cuba's National Office of Statistics released for the first time a report on prices and inflation in the private sector—"Survey of Prices in the Informal Sector." The report studied government sanctioned markets, *cuentapropistas* (government sanctioned small businesses), as well as some illicit activity including covert sale of food, medicines, and other products stolen from state factories and warehouses. According to the report, the cost of goods and services purchased from private sources rose 4% from February 2007–February 2008, with the most common goods and services obtained from private sources declared to be rice, cheese pizzas, eggs, pork, manicures, vegetable oil, lard and the informal exchange of local pesos to convertible pesos to buy goods in the more expensive stores. Further, the report found that approximately 78% of Havana's workforce is employed, 3% cannot find work, and 19% prefer not to work. Of these almost one in five who prefer not to work, the most common reasons given for not working were "they don't pay me well," "my parents support me,"[3] or "the business (black market) provides for me." These findings provide not only further evidence of the pervasiveness of the informal sector in Cuba, but their release would seem to signify a more open acknowledgement by Cuban authorities of its existence and significance (Rodriguez 2008).

The types of informal activities common in Cuba can be best understood when accompanied by some explanation of the factors that produce them. Ritter (2005) identifies six main factors: historical roots, central planning and the rationing system, common property, the dual monetary system, limitations on micro-enterprise and economic necessity. Disregard for authority in Cuba may be a trend with pre-revolutionary roots dating back to the colonial era, when Cubans regularly broke bilateral trade agreements with Spain, conducting illegal trade with the French, British, and North Americans and with pirates. Examples of enterprises that evaded state regulations have also been identified as operating throughout the 1950s. Those already working "in the shadows" easily went on to continue these practices after the revolution (2005: 348-349).

The rationing system introduced in 1961 was a centrally designed policy for redistributing food and ensuring minimum requirements of basic food and hygiene products were supplied to the population. One of the side effects of rationing was the development of an extensive system of bartering (*trueque*) as a way to deal with consistently long queues for scarce consumer goods. This is still one of the most common activities for private gain in Cuba. Generally, supplies in Cuba are only available erratically and tend to disappear quickly as soon as they arrive in stores; this is particularly the case for rationed goods sold at subsidized prices. The appearance of any consumer goods (particularly rations) is invariably met with large queues. Since there is rarely any prior warning about when and where supplies are to appear, basic household shopping requires constant vigilance and a lot of time. This causes problems for those of the population who work day jobs and are not present when supplies arrive, and it is not uncommon for some individuals (*coleros*) to devote themselves to watching stores and waiting in lines to obtain goods to then resell or exchange with others. Cubans will rarely turn down an opportunity to obtain their full share of rations, even if they do not intend to consume them—rations can always be exchanged later with neighbours or friends for other scarce items (Perez-Lopez 1995: 81-83; Rosendahl 1997: 40; Rundle 2001).

Bartering is tolerated by the Cuban government, provided it occurs on a small scale within households and does not involve money (1995:81). However, the boundaries separating legality from illegality are unclear. Whereas the term "black market" in most contexts conjures up images of illicit goods, in Cuba many items sold on the black market are legal, including foodstuffs (such as unused rations), homemade clothes and handicrafts, construction materials and car parts. The illegality of informal economic activity usually derives from the avoidance of state regulations surrounding production and distribution, rather than the nature of the product or service involved (see also Ledeneva 1998: 49).

One of the most common sources of black market goods is the misappropriation of state property (Perez-Lopez 1995: 98-99). As the previous excerpt from Castro's speech suggests, the theft and diversion of resources from factories or warehouses for private sale is widespread. This problem affects most sectors; employees in state food outlets often skim ingredients to sell on the side, pharmaceuticals are often diverted on the way from factories to pharmacies and resold on the street, fuel station employees siphon off petrol to resell to private car owners/taxi drivers, port workers steal merchandise from shipping containers carrying foreign imports, and so on (Perez-Lopez 2006: 10).

Anecdotal evidence from a discussion with an Australian woman (Brown 2006) who spent three years living in Cuba during the period 2005-2008 provided another example. Brown detailed the informal activity of her Cuban boyfriend, a shop worker in Old Havana. Like many shop workers, Juan's main source of income was illegal. Whereas most state salaries in Cuba amount to the equivalent of around US$5-20 per month, Juan's earnings were between US$100 and US$400 per day. The state-run kiosk where he worked sold soft drinks and other food and beverage items. Juan was paid a state salary to order and sell X amount of goods, and the profits from those goods were handed over to the state so as to maintain the appearance of legitimacy. Unofficially, however, Juan also purchased his own order of goods to sell at the same prices through the kiosk. Since the goods Juan bought with his own money were always the same brands and items as those he bought for the state, the two allotments were indistinguishable to the customer. With the general shortage of goods in Cuban stores, there was never any difficulty in selling the stock. Juan kept separate books to record items sold for the state and items sold for his private business. When state inspectors visited the store, he would produce the "official" book for inspection. If inspectors ever became suspicious, Juan always had more than enough money with which to bribe them.

> They are really cracking down on things now. They have been calling meetings with all the people who work in stores and telling them "we know what you do [how you make your money] but we have to start thinking about the country." They have these social workers put in everywhere now, pumping petrol in the fuel stations and watching over everything. Some of them can be swayed too though. [Juan] said he had one of the worst inspections ever the other week. Two women came into the shop and went through everything with a fine-toothed comb but luckily he had made sure everything in order (author's interview with Brown, April 2006).

One Cuban expatriate commented that whenever a Cuban is hired in a new job, the first question friends and family will ask is "¿Y que se resuelve?" This implies: what can you steal from your workplace that will help you get by? (author's interview with Perez, May 2006). Observing the pervasiveness and normalization of theft from the state, Ritter argues that the practices are part of a "tragedy of commons," where property is not respected because nobody and everybody owns it (2005: 349-350). The more convincing explanation is the problem of necessity resulting from insufficient wages and conditions of shortage that force Cubans to adopt endless strategies in order to make ends meet.

Following the collapse of the Soviet Union, when Cuba lost the majority of its markets over a short space of time, the country entered into a period of extreme economic crisis and desperate scarcity known as the "special period."[4] The conditions of this period (some have described the crisis as having a more severe economic impact than the Great Depression of the 1930s) forced a drastic increase in underground activity. Despite the government maintaining free health care, education and rationing policies (Anderson 2002) (albeit limited to scarce goods available), many of the rations were trimmed back and most Cubans had to find new, usually illegal, ways to survive (Perez-Lopez 1997: 15). The introduction of tourism and legalization of the U.S. dollar (now fully replaced with the convertible peso) were a means for attracting foreign currency to the island, but gave way to a host of new inequalities between those with and without access to dollars, and this further encouraged a second economy.

Those who can obtain dollars (sometimes legally from overseas relatives or earned in the tourism sector) have access to consumer goods and privileges unavailable to Cubans surviving exclusively with *moneda nacional* (domestic currency). While ongoing rationing helps many Cubans survive, the list of subsidized goods on ration books is not comprehensive[5]—others need to be purchased in stores. Many goods are increasingly available only in the dollar/convertible peso stores (originally intended for tourists but now also frequented by Cubans[6]), which drives up the cost of living (Sánchez 2007; Habel 2004). The disjunction between salaries and living costs has seen a parallel increase in corruption levels and black-marketeering as many state-employed Cubans find unofficial ways to acquire dollars. Since the cost of subsidized items sold in *moneda nacional* is drastically lower (Ritter estimates about 260 times lower) than the same goods sold in "new" currency, the intermittently available subsidized goods are often acquired and then resold later at higher prices, as is the case with stolen state property (2005: 350).

Partly as a means for negotiating with and legitimizing a burgeoning black market and for dealing with increasing idleness and underemployment, the government legalized some forms of self-employment in 1993, including certain agricultural producers and small business owners (*cuentapropistas*) such as hairdressers, landlords, dressmakers, plumbers, craftspeople and taxi drivers. However, these enterprises were tightly restricted. Professionals with university degrees were not permitted to engage in self employment. In order to maintain single, nationalized health and education systems, doctors, dentists, academics and other services associated with these sectors were excluded from self employment. Tough registration guidelines, high taxes and heavy regulation of business earnings and transactions governed the self-employed (Perez-Lopez 1997: 18-19). The number of legal small businesses was increased in the years that followed but later intermittent crackdowns and readjustments have scaled back these reforms (although there has been regular shifting of policies in a cycle of increasing, then reducing, scope for self-employment).[7] This has included regular crackdowns on profiteering, increasing restrictions and scaling back of licenses. For example, in 2004 the government reduced the number of licenses available for 40 types of self-employment (Perez-Stable 2007). In turn, these changes provide greater incentives to sidestep the official system and, despite severe penalties and heavy policing, many *cuentapropistas* operate illegally or at least partly outside official guidelines (see also Salloum 1996). First-hand experiences during my fieldwork trips were consistent with this. Life in Cuba inevitably involved frequent encounters with the pervasive underground economy.

The house where I first lived during my period of fieldwork in Havana was legal—at least that's what I thought when I moved in. Before long I realized that, although the landlord (Josefina) was indeed officially registered to rent her house to foreigners, the way she maintained and operated her licence was another story. Although Josefina assured me before I moved into the house that I would be living alone, it didn't take long for me to notice that her cousin from the provinces actually lived permanently in the second room. I learned through conversations on the street that private landlords were legally required to live in the houses they rented out (rules governing the activities of cuentapropistas *seemed to change constantly). I thought this rule was strange considering Josefina lived in her (illegally owned) second house around the corner. One day Josefina turned up unannounced at the house wearing her nightgown and with her hair ruffled. She seemed flustered and told me the authorities were on the way to perform a house inspection and that I should leave the talking to her. It wasn't hard to decipher that turning up in pajamas was part of her way of maintaining the appearance that she actually lived in the house. On another occasion, a sudden increase in my monthly rent came with an explanation from Josefina that she needed to pay rental for a phone extension from the neighbor. After a brief conversation with the neighbor I realized, first, that renting out phone extensions in dollars was illegal and second, that Josefina was actually pocketing most of the "phone rental money" herself.*

When I finally decided to move house I was faced with a new challenge. The absence of any formal, centralized system for coordinating private rentals meant that finding another place to live was a task to be confronted by foot. In the end I think I must have walked through every street in Havana and visited almost every existing casa particular.[8] *As a foreigner, it was illegal for me to stay with friends or to change address without following strict bureaucratic immigration procedures. I was to advise immigration of my place of residence at all times and could only stay in state hotels or expensive official houses that paid monthly state taxes. Navigating the underground real estate system, although exhausting, was a learning experience. Whenever I visited one house that was already occupied, the landlord would enthusiastically produce a contact book and start dialing other landlords: "Oye, I have a foreigner here, is your place vacant?" Presumably, referring tenants meant either receiving a percentage of the rent as a reward, or having the favor returned in the future.*

This in itself attracted a host of opportunists on the lookout for foreigners to refer to the private landlords. Street hustlers regularly approached tourists on the way from the airport offering to guide them to a nice casa particular. *Others, although not landlords themselves, operated from home as underground rental agents dealing mostly with students on temporary residence visas as well as local Cubans. One of these operators explained to me that the latest strategy deployed by foreign students was to live in illegal rental properties (with cheaper rent) while simultaneously paying a small fee to an "official" landlord in order to have the landlord vouch that the student was living there. The official landlord would provide a rent receipt to the student, who would produce this receipt to immigration as proof of residence in an official, tax-paying house. And so the story went. Eventually, after more than a week of constant walking, a reasonably priced and legal house appeared (field notes 2004).*

This anecdote illustrates a struggle involving the government's efforts to harness private activities and the response from "private businesses" of inventing equally complicated methods for avoiding the government's regulations. It also provides examples of some of the unfavorable business practices that take place in the raw capitalist world of the second economy, where no formal regulations exist to protect the interests of parties involved. The chapter returns to these themes later. The following section describes some of the specific ways in which the second economy affects the health sector. Many of the informal practices can be linked to the problems of limited participation outlined in the previous chapter. Further, in line with theories about socialism's second economy, the relationship between the formal and informal health "systems" are inter-reliant and at the same time mutually undermining.

Informal Practices in the Health System

As with the second economy generally, the extent of informal activity in the health sector is difficult to gauge accurately. Considering the prioritization of health in Cuba continuing through the crisis period of the 1990s, it may be that informal activity is less significant here, given the relatively easy access to health services compared with other sectors that have suffered more desperate shortages. Nonetheless, some problems linked to the overall expansion of the second economy also affect the health sector. Along with the majority of the workforce, doctors are state-employed and paid in the domestic currency.

> No Cuban health professional in the present day, nor from any of the generations born after the triumph of the revolution, graduates or decides to pursue a career in medicine for reasons of personal material gain because you know this is not what you will get. I, for example, have fifteen years of experience since I graduated, I work and teach in medicine and I have international experience. When I have been in other countries and told people that I earn twenty dollars a month they can't believe it, they simply laugh at me[9] (author's interview with Herrera, September 2004).

Given that employment as a health professional is not normally associated with economic advantage in Cuba, it is probably reasonable to assume that those who gravitate towards medical careers do so for humanitarian reasons or professional fulfillment rather than remuneration. This may have contributed to Cuban doctors' generally positive reputation for dedication, compassion and self-sacrifice (Aidi 2001; Schweimler 2001; Obaid-Chinoy 2005). However, this does not mean Cuban doctors are immune to the economic difficulties that most state-employed Cubans face.

With the dramatic increase of living costs in Cuba since the intro-duction of the U.S. dollar, even accounting for rations, free education and other state-provided services, Cuban doctors struggle to make ends meet on their peso salary. As is the case with a large proportion of state employees, stories of hospital staff "moonlighting as taxi drivers" (The Economist 1999b) or inventing some other unofficial source of income are not uncommon (Ritter 2005: 346; Sixto 2002: 341). Non-medical workers in hospitals, such as cleaning and culinary staff, appear to be particularly dispirited by the low salaries and demonstrate this through absence from and inefficiency in their jobs. Further, as similarly oc-curs in many other Cuban workplaces, hospital employees have been known to steal meat and other foodstuffs the state provides for patients and take these home to eat or sell (field notes, report of an expatriate experience in a Cuban hospital, 2004. See also Feinsilver 1989b: 259; De Vibe 2004: 56).[10] The following passage from an interview with a former family doctor details the gradual evolution and escalation of this illegal activity:

> The people who work there [in the hospitals] have their own problems at home. Here [in Cuba] in any given workplace where they deal with anything saleable, any product, the employees always try to take something home for themselves because here wage earners don't earn anything. So everybody tries to steal something. If you are a mechanic, you steal a spanner; if you work with food of course you steal some rice. So, what happens? People keep taking and taking. Normally small things don't get noticed much but slowly greed makes you steal more and more. If before you stole a bit of rice, one day you want to take a chicken that might be to eat for yourself because in your house there is no chicken, and soon you are stealing one that you need to eat and another one to sell. So you keep going like that until one day people go and report you to the boss.... There was always a lot of stealing going on in pharmacies. Apparently they have put in a new system and they say it is better at controlling the problem; but, look, just today I went out to by an antihistamine because I have this allergic reaction [showing hand] and I couldn't find any. I don't understand why there wasn't a single antihistamine. So my opinion is that nothing has changed [with this new system] because in the pharmacy there is none but at any given moment you can find a person in the street selling the antihistamine at 10 pesos, the same one the state sells you at three or four pesos in the pharmacy. Where did this medication come from? It came from the factory here in Cuba and it just happened to get sidetracked on the way to the pharmacy (author's interview with Diaz, October 2004).

In other words, any area of the health sector that deals with saleable resources (such as pharmaceuticals, food, cleaning products, bandages and so on) would appear to suffer problems with theft of state property. Although not the only explanation for material shortages in health facilities, this syphoning-off of already scarce resources detracts from the quality of service patients receive in the formal system. The following narrative from a Cuban woman born in Havana shortly before the revolution indicates that, even if doctors perform their work well, some citizens feel deep dissatisfaction with other aspects of health care.

> In Cuba, health care is free. But, when you go to the family doctor, the clinics or the hospitals, there are generally no medications, no disinfectants, no cotton, and, sometimes, no needles. If you need to be admitted to the hospital, you have to bring your own sheets, a towel, and a fan because there is no air conditioner, or it is broken. For the most part, you have to find a way to get the medications you need if they are not available, which is often the case, even the most basic drugs, such as aspirin. But, yes, healthcare is free.... In this country, the government goes on and on about how "nobody is without access to health care from the most advanced to most basic." But, really, if it were not for the people *luchando* (struggling) you would really see what our health care system actually provides. We are the ones, *el pueblo* (the people), that make the sacrifices so Fidel can give his grandiose speeches about how wonderful our health care system is! (Interview excerpt from Brotherton 2005).

As mentioned, this research project did not set out with the intention of exploring informal health care delivery practices. Rather, the significance of the subject became increasingly evident when some of the interviewees' comments (combined with personal observations), suggested that the channels through which health care is delivered in Cuba may be quite different from the official portrayal of the system. While most descriptions of health care in Cuba paint a neat picture of a highly organized system wherein family doctors, each attending a small population defined by a local geographical area, are the first checkpoint for patients (Eckstein 1994; MINSAP 2004), anecdotal evidence from some of the interviews for this project suggest this is not an entirely accurate representation of the channels through which all health services are delivered.

One Cuban interviewee said she thought the number of people who visited the family doctor in their residential area was much lower than superficial appearances suggest. She said she believed most Cubans preferred to consult doctors they knew personally or had been referred to by a friend, rather than visit their ascribed local family doctor (author's interview with García, October 2004). This in itself does not seem particularly problematic. When questioned on this issue of patients seeking medical attention outside their health area, a representative at the Ministry of Public Health (MINSAP) said Cubans were permitted to visit the doctor of their choice rather than the local family doctor but that there were no official statistics to show what percentage of the population took up this option (author's interview with Ramirez, October 2004). That patients are able to consult a doctor of choice is surely a good thing in terms of patient autonomy and satisfaction with the system.

However, the respondent (García) went on to say that patients' choice of doctor can be based not only on personal preference but informal exchange arrangements. Within the health system, this type of exchange has become such a norm that there is even vocabulary (*"tiñosa"*— literally meaning "vulture") to describe a person who receives prioritized attention on the basis of being the doctor's *socio*. The interviewee said it was commonplace to queue in a doctor's waiting room for hours, only to see a *tiñosa* arrive, skip the queue and be admitted immediately for a consultation (author's interview with García, October 2004). Another interviewee gave the following account.

> Doctors here have very bad salaries; so often they rely on patients to resolve their everyday problems. If a patient of mine brings me coffee in the morning or if my briefcase breaks and he fixes it for me, well, this creates a closer bond of friendship or affinity with that patient. If one day I can do something to repay the patient I will. It's not like he's paying me money to do something. Its just normal things like if I have to refer him to another doctor I will personally take him to see a colleague who will look after him rather than just writing him a normal referral paper. It's true that sometimes other patients might get annoyed and say I am treating him better than them but that's the way things work here. Let's say I'm working in a hospital and a friend of mine comes in. I will let him go first in the line or I will make sure a more experienced doctor operates on him rather than the resident.... It's unethical, but just imagine, when I have to go to where he works for some reason, he will return the favor and help me out. This is not just the case with doctors but in any place where you go to do something and there is a friend involved... If you work in a factory that sells chairs and you give me a chair or you are a dressmaker and you make something for me, at some stage I will repay the favor.... So who gets annoyed about this? Those who are not friends of the doctor! Why? Because they've been there waiting in the queue since six in the morning because they need to see a doctor and, when the consultations start at ten, somebody else who hasn't been waiting gets to take the first appointment just because he's friends with the doctor! Another example: If there's a particular medicine that has disappeared from the pharmacies, I'm going to go out and make a special effort to find it for you if you're my friend. These are the kinds of things that annoy most of the population when it comes to dealing with doctors (author's interview with Diaz, October 2004).

This testimony draws attention to one of the defining characteristics of informal practices in Cuba; that is an intricate social web of personal connections (*sociolismo*). In other words, an unofficial bartering system operates beneath the formal system involving personal relationships of trust and affinity built up around the mutual exchange of goods and services. In her dissertation, Crabb describes a "parallel system of informal health services." According to Crabb's fieldwork observations, many Cubans choose to side-step their local family doctor and the "formal" system and seek medical consultation instead with doctors who are also friends, relatives or "*gente de confianza*" (2001).

> In my neighborhood in Sueño, for instance, no one I knew who fell ill during my entire seven months of residence ever consulted his or her "official" family doctor. Instead they chose to solicit medical advice from friends, neighbors and/or family members (2001: 176-178).

Crabb offers a number of explanations for this tendency. First, she found there was a common perception among Cubans that family doctors lacked expertise compared with specialists; many patients would therefore attempt to contact specialists, rather than follow the conventional protocol of making the family doctor "first port of call." Further, she explains the reliance on informal networks as originating partly from "the historical importance of kinship and patron-client relations in Cuba." These practices are perpetuated by "the political and bureaucratized nature of medical practice under socialism" and are most prevalent in areas plagued by resource shortages (2001: 177-180). In other words, a cultural norm of holding greater trust the opinion of friends or *socios* is part of the explanation; but problems of shortage, bureaucracy and a highly politicized health system increase reliance on informal practices as a matter of necessity.

Individuals finding themselves faced with the obstacles like waiting in day-long queues and searching all over town for unavailable pharmaceuticals take matters into their own hands and seek alternative ways to resolve the problem. Sometimes, this can effectively mean opting out of the official "free" system to "buy" medical services with gifts, favors or money. When personal networks are accessed to obtain goods or solve problems, there is usually an automatic assumption that the recipient owes a favor in return (Crabb 2001: 179-182). In the words of one Cuban expatriate, "everything operates on a system of exchange where each person builds up a whole web of possible future necessities" (author's interview with Perez, August 2005). In other words, favors are not always immediately returned but a person who provides some unofficial service can then count on preferential treatment from the recipient at some stage in the future when he or she needs it (most often in the recipient's workplace).

> In Cuba, even though things like medical attention are "officially" free, the reality is that if you want to get any kind of service you either come with a personal reference or you have something material to offer. The first thing they're going to ask you when you arrive is "who sent you?" If no personal contact sent you, then you

can forget it unless you clearly have something to offer. Everything is about appearances. That's how you get what you need because it's all about them seeing you as a potential material opportunity. If you turn up to the hospital, for example, dressed badly, you're not going to get very far. Now, if you turn up dressed well, wearing perfume and giving the appearance that you have money then doors will open for you. But you will have to give something in return. For example, not so long ago I needed to get some X-rays done. Luckily I knew the brother of the radiologist and he sent me so I got an appointment to see her right away. Anyway, when I meet the radiologist she says to me "Wait 'til you see the perfect X-rays I'm going to take for you!" And then she adds, "I tell you what though, I'm dying of hunger right now! Any idea if they're selling pizzas around here?" So of course that is my cue. I get on my motorbike and go in search of pizza and I make sure it is the best pizza my money can buy (author's interview with Perez, August 2005).

This type of practice can be construed in different ways. On the one hand, even if exchange of money for services does not take place, it can be argued that an underground economy based on the exchange of favors and goods for services exists beneath the official façade of cost-free health care. If this is the case, then it can be assumed that there is variation in the quality of medical attention patients receive, depending on their capacity to pay—an outcome that works against the country's aim to provide equally accessible and free medical care to its population. Cuban officials rejected this controversial suggestion. When questioned on the issue of doctors receiving gifts and favors from patients, representatives from Cuban government institutions said the practice was not an example of corruption but of "solidarity" between the Cuban people. A spokesperson for Cuba's Commission for Social Attention and Prevention, for example, said it was normal for people to give gifts to doctors, teachers and work colleagues as "social recognition of their work."

It is legal [to give gifts] but it depends on the gift. If, for example, I am your doctor and you are a woman who earns dollars and you think it would help me to give me ten dollars, nobody can prohibit you from giving it. The doctor takes it. What the doctor can't do is demand payment for the service … maybe the doctor will tell you "I'm having a hard time because I don't have any soap in my house to wash myself" and you happen to have five dollars in your wallet.[11] You say "look, I'm going to give you two so you can buy three bars of soap." That's not prohibited … We are not such a closed society that we don't allow people to have normal social, human relations. This is a society that has a great deal of solidarity (author's interview with Espinoza, October 2004).

It may well be that many instances of gift-giving to doctors are simply patients' way of expressing gratitude for free services, not means for securing preferential treatment. Given the mixed accounts, the most accurate assessment may be that both scenarios occur; that gift-giving serves different purposes in different situations, sometimes being an expression of "solidarity" and at other times as a means for influencing doctors to provide preferential treatment. Both are "normal, social, human relations" depending upon the context in which they take place. It is likely that gift and favor-giving for instrumental purposes increases in situations of scarcity or where individuals face problems they are unable to solve in the official system.

The relative disempowerment of patients under formal arrangements, especially regarding medical decisions, persists alongside the growing economic power of some sections of the community, namely those who have access to foreign currency via tourism, remittances[12] or black market activity. These increasingly wealthy patients have the economic means to afford private favors to secure greater autonomy over medical decisions and prioritized access to public resources (Brotherton 2005: 352-353). Given the material difficulties doctors face living on inadequate wages, the situation lends itself to reciprocity.

Beyond gift-giving, some accounts from non-government respondents indicate that the line between accepting gifts and charging for services is more blurred than the officials acknowledge. The respondent (Perez) who told of the incident involving the radiologist also recounted another experience that demonstrated this. He said he remembered once taking his aunt, who was suffering from a toothache, to the local policlinic in the middle of the night. On arrival he was told his aunt could not be attended to because on that night the policlinic had no running water. The next day he returned and was told the services the policlinic offered did not include tooth extraction. At this point he told the two staff members working at the policlinic that if they helped his aunt he would "show them his appreciation." They immediately said they would make an exception for his case and performed the tooth extraction. To show his appreciation, Perez offered a sum of money but the staff refused, saying one of their colleagues had previously been sanctioned for accepting money. "This money is not for *you* specifically," Perez explained, "it is for your grandson, to buy him a present." Satisfied with this subterfuge, the staff accepted the money. "I don't blame them" the respondent went on to say. "These people are there working night shift with nothing to eat and earning a salary of eight dollars a month" (author's interview with Perez, August 2005).

Similar occurrences have been observed in other socialist health systems. The Cuban interviewees' accounts bear remarkable resemblance to Konstantin Simis' (1982) description of corrupt practices within the former Soviet Union's hospitals. According to Simis, Soviet doctors earned low salaries that did not cover the cost of living. As a result, doctors resorted to accepting gifts, services and sometimes money from patients in order to get by, and in exchange they gave preferential medical treatment.

> Of course a woman about to go into labor will be taken to her local maternity home without any bribery, but if she wants to give birth in a hospital known for its high standards of service and its qualified staff, or if she wants specific midwives and anesthetists to perform the delivery, then a bribe will be required. ... All medical services are provided completely without charge to all Soviet citizens.... [However,] money or gifts can ensure more attentive care and more time being spent on one patient than on another. Almost all people—even the very poorest—seek to do this whenever they use the services of the local polyclinic doctors.... It is relatively rare for doctors to be offered money in such relationships: most often, thanks for better care is expressed by small gifts and services (1982: 222-223).

In the case of Cuba, how should these informal practices be interpreted, especially in light of the country's positive health outcomes? One possible explanation is that these informal practices "prop up" the formal systems, maintaining its current arrangements because its problems are "filled in" by informal arrangements. Centeno and Portes note that in underdeveloped nations the informal economy sometimes acts as a "cushion" that "can make all the difference between relative tranquility and political instability" (2003: 14) Correspondingly, Ericson describes the second economy, particularly its "shadow" aspect as playing "an essential role in the first economy as a 'pressure valve,' a release 'fixing' command by maintaining micro-balance and covering 'holes' in economic life, left by the mistakes or oversight of the planners" (2006: 12). In other words, the overly-bureaucratic, inefficient or otherwise frustrating aspects of a system can be eased by avoiding formal procedures, and this avoidance temporarily prevents political crises that might otherwise emerge.

In the Cuban health system, the possibility of cutting through the frustrations (such as long waiting lines and unavailable pharmaceuticals) of the formal system may mitigate the discontent of patients and health workers. Patients faced with long waiting lines, unavailable pharmaceuticals and so on, may be placated by the option of calling on a doctor who is a personal contact in order to resolve the problem more quickly or ensure what they consider to be a better service. To some degree then, the informal system could be considered an "alternative" health system. However, this is not entirely accurate in the sense that a private system constitutes an alternative, since the informal system in Cuba is not *independent* of but entirely dependent upon the formal system. Services accessed through informal channels are often still delivered physically within the public system, using public resources. Hence, those who receive services informally are not avoiding the official system entirely. There appears to be no official backlash against the trend of patients consulting with doctors outside their allocated health area (author's interviews with Ramirez 2004; Espinoza and Raiz 2004) and the "payoffs" doctors receive are fairly invisible due to the fact that they are tied up in social relations, often involving favors repaid at a later (or earlier) date (author's interview with Perez, August 2005).

Further, gifts and favors may act as a material incentive encouraging health workers to spend a larger proportion of their time delivering health services (albeit through informal channels) rather than moonlighting as workers in other sectors to supplement their state salaries. In this way, the informal system of exchange in the health sector, despite being outside the prescribed official guidelines of health care delivery, may actually facilitate the government's health goals. Cuban authorities apparently turn a blind eye to gift-giving and rationalize it in revolutionary terms as an act of "solidarity" or appreciation by the patient for the doctor's work. Some authors have described this kind of tolerance as common in cases where governments are indirectly benefiting from unsanctioned activity (Centeno and Portes 2003; Stark 1989).

Even where more tangible payoffs are involved, officials appear to construe these as compassionate acts of appreciation by the patient after receiving treatment, with no connection to the quality of the service received. Hence, except for cases where patients pay money (which is formally forbidden), or where state property is stolen (such as medical supplies from factories and pharmacies), there would seem to be little effort required to hide informal practices from officials, as opposed to Cubans operating clandestine factories, for example. Certainly, services received through friends or *socios* can usually still be delivered and recorded through state facilities, without revealing the underlying exchange of favors (that is, the fact that the patient skipped the queue or received preferential treatment). Unlike the case of black market exchanges then, many shadow activities in the health system may not result in information being withheld from authorities. Since most health services are physically delivered within the public health system, MINSAP retains the ability to track and monitor the population's health. In the terms set out by Mann then, despite the shadow system, the state maintains a fair degree of its "penetrative" power (the ability to reach in and interact directly with the population) and "extractive" power (ability to reach into and extract resources—in this case, information—from the population).[13] This in itself may one reason why the state has continued to meet its statistical health objectives so far, despite unofficial activity.

Further, as as a number of Cuban interviewees acknowledged, the success of the Cuban health system relies to a large degree on human capital (Rivera 2004; author's interviews with Blanco 2004; Castillo 2004; Herrera 2004). Cuba's ability to offer a comprehensive universal health system while simultaneously shipping in thousands of foreign patients for treatment in Cuban facilities and exporting thousands of doctors on overseas missions is facilitated by keeping the cost of human labor (that is, doctors' salaries) low. However, this may be a source of aggravation for many doctors, who are aware of the relatively high sacrifices and low remuneration they receive. Receiving favors from patients in exchange for prioritized medical treatment serves as the equivalent of an "extra income" which may moderate the frustrations doctors otherwise experience, which could induce them to abandon the profession or more vigorously protest their lack of remuneration.[14]

Comparing the role of socialism's second economy with capitalism's informal economy, Stark observes that informal activity under capitalism serves as a means for firms to carry out income-generating activities *outside* of the internal bureaucratic regulations built up around labor-capital relations. These regulations emerge from a history of negotiation inside the firm between labor and employers regarding the conditions of employment. Workplace health and safety guidelines, minimum wages, accident compensation and so on are the result of workers' collective bargaining with employers achieved through affiliations with trade unions, state agencies and personnel departments. The institutionalized rules governing profit-making activity usually serve to *protect* workers from the market. The circumvention of formal regulations then is often "a means to lower the costs of labor and reduce its bargaining power." Informal workers are usually worse off than the formally employed (1989: 641-645).

By contrast, under state socialism the state employs workers, sets wage levels and allocates the funds with which wages are paid. Whereas under capitalism the informal activity is a means for employers to reduce the cost of labor, the second economy under socialism is usually a means through which workers can negotiate a greater financial return on their labour. Workers in the second economy normally have an advantage over exclusively formal workers, because they have greater income and "interest representation." In this way the second economy is in some ways the equivalent of the trade union (1989: 645-651). Henken elaborates this point: "Though not institutionalized and legally protected as is the trade union, the second economy functions to protect workers from arbitrary abuse by the 'dominant class' (state firms and the party) and provide them with the supplemental wages they are denied in the first economy" (2005: 367). So, in this way the second economy allows the state to maintain wages at a level many have argued is below the cost of living.

However, while supporting and maintaining formal arrangements in these ways, informal practices also work against the legitimacy and goals of the formal system. For example, the act of circumventing formal channels by queue-jumping naturally contributes to frustrations for those following official procedures. This in turn increases incentives to avoid the official system. Similarly, buying stolen state supplies of pharmaceuticals on the black market indirectly contributes to shortages in pharmacies that necessitated the black market purchase in the first place. When materials are pilfered from the state to perform medical operations "under the table," another patient is likely to miss out on an operation (Ledeneva 1998: 88; Hirschfeld 2006).

> [T]heft damages the enterprises and institutions in which it occurs, as their capacity to provide the goods and services they are intended to provide to the general public is impaired. Second, theft worsens income distribution in that those who do not have access to it have lower effective incomes than those who do, but at the same time their access to lower priced state sources of goods and services is reduced ... those with privileged access gain at the expense of the broader society (Ritter 2005: 353).

One would logically expect some form of crisis as the end point of this cycle. A number of authors have examined it, drawing attention to the social transformations attached to thriving informal systems that temporarily support and ultimately subvert the official system by undermining its legitimacy (Wallace 2006; Ericson 2006; Ledeneva 1998; Grossman 1977). Referring to the Soviet Union, Ericson remarks that the second economy "both shored up the operational foundations of the 'first economy' and undermined its long-term viability, corroding its ideological and systemic foundations" (2006: 15). The following section examines this cycle in further detail.

Cuban *Blat*? Social Dimensions of the Underground and Ideological Subversion

In her book *Russia's Economy of Favours*, Ledeneva (1998) casts a new light on the subject of informal exchange in socialist contexts using the concept of *"blat,"* which refers to the system of social networks used to procure goods and services. In contrast with what most authors have characterized as an essentially economic phenomenon, Ledeneva emphasizes the social dimension of the second economy as a vital component to understanding the informal sector in socialist societies. In her detailed study of *blat*, Ledeneva describes how material shortages and social constraints under the Soviet system led to the development of an "economy of favors" that became an integral part of everyday life. The difficulties involved with obtaining consumer goods and services, even with money, meant that often the only viable option was to call on personal contacts. Her descriptions of *blat* in the Soviet Union bear close resemblance to the social networks at play in Cuba, particularly evident in the preceding description of the health system. A common Soviet folk expression, "do not have 100 rubles, do have 100 friends" (1998: 104), reflects this practice. In other words, under the Soviet system networks of friends came to be more valuable than money. This point is evident in the following account from a Soviet dentist, which closely echoes the Cuban interviewees' stories.

> I do dentistry and never make money out of it. But I make my contacts, I know that my patients will help me, if I need something. I keep these contacts but this does not mean that a long-term relationship cannot be developed from them. If my request gets refused the relationship breaks, but if the contact is good and reliable, we may become friends (Interview excerpt from Ledeneva 1998: 145).

Ledeneva's description of *blat* practices underpins a central argument of her book; that *"blat* subverted the Soviet economic system at the same time as it sustained it" (1998: 182). Her discussion follows on from earlier theories about the Soviet system's "tendency to subvert itself" (1998: 74-75). In other words, even where the philosophy of the official world is one of egalitarianism and non-materialism, where everyday problems are increasingly resolved via an unofficial system where buying power is what counts, then acquisitive tendencies and materialistic values increase. So, although the "second economy" places pressure on the "first economy" in a practical sense, it also challenges the socialist project at a deeper level by undermining its ideological foundations. These insights are worrying in relation to the Cuban health system and its defining principles, particularly the establishment of health as a free and universally-available human right. Practices of exchanging preferential medical treatment for material favors work to establish a norm that good-quality health care is not a citizen entitlement but something that must be bought.

The misuse of state resources also works to undermine state legitimacy. Widespread and routine misappropriation of state property can normalize a sense of alienation towards state property and from the state itself. In his description of the Soviet system, Simis (1982) argues that using state resources to make a living "on the side" became so commonplace that citizens no longer recognized the behaviors as improper or criminal.

> [T]he mass of the population does not look upon theft from the state as real theft, as stealing someone else's property.... This demonstrates the complete alienation of the Soviet citizen from the state, his total indifference and even hostility toward it. Without such feelings, factory thefts on such a scale would be impossible (1982: 253-254).

Similarly, Amaro explains that personal appropriation of state goods in Cuba is often so subtle that "it is difficult to draw the line between corruption and proper behavior on the part of civil servants" (1996). According to Perez-Lopez, stealing from one's employer in Cuba "is widely accepted and there is no stigma attached to it." Most of the population considers theft from the state to be normal, not a crime (1995: 99). The practice of evading the official system can become invisible and normalized if repeated over a long enough period by a large proportion of the population.

Also apparent in the literature but rarely addressed directly is the issue of the necessary adoption of double standards required to survive in an inherently conflicted system of formal/informal duality. This dynamic brings social transformations of its own. Participating in the second economy, although virtually unavoidable in Cuba, necessarily involves the conscious concealment of one's activities from authorities while maintaining an appearance of supporting "The Revolution." At the individual level then, everyday life requires the constant fabrication of stories and adoption of double standards in order to maintain the appearance of a good revolutionary and simultaneously engage in unsanctioned practices to get by. One needs only to perceive the countless code words built up around the business exchanges in Cuba, as evidence of the covertness adopted when any private "business" transactions take place. A "monja" (nun) has come to mean five pesos, a "pescado" (fish) ten pesos and a "bomba" (bomb) one dollar. One Cuban interviewee explained how the code words "agua" (water) or "tumba" (knock it over) are often used to warn that authorities are near when informal business is taking place in public. Petrol, a frequently-traded commodity on the black market, is known as "jama" (food), any person with whom one is connected through informal business is a *"punto"* (point) and an informal business arrangement is a *"jugada"* (play)[15] (author's interview with Perez, May 2006). Commenting on the situation in Cuba in the early 1990s, a foreign journalist gave the following account:

> Every day, almost every Cuban I know does something illegal just to get by. They may buy black market coffee or shoes for their kids, call in sick at work so they can have time to shop for food, swipe supplies from the office to use at home, or get their toilet fixed by a plumber working illegally. They might be members of the Communist Party or staunch supporters of the revolution, but they break the law as a matter of course. And since everyone sees everyone doing it, it becomes part of the game. But deep down it creates a kind of double standard that flies in the face of the mores this revolution stands for. In some ways, Cuba has created a nation of hypocrites and liars (Benjamin in Perez-Lopez 1995: 114).

Although a seemingly cynical description, other authors draw similar conclusions. Eilat and Sinnes remark that the persistence of shadow economic activity in transition countries "can contribute to the deterioration of morals in the society" (2002). Ritter observes that stealing from the state in Cuba "breeds attitudes and cultures of lawlessness that damage trust and the ethical foundations of the economy and society" (2005: 354). Observing the general mistrust and resentment towards authority and legality that pervasive informal activity can produce, one Cuban independent journalist comments: "Society has been taken over by the Robin Hood syndrome: the rogues who steal something from their workplace every day, those who *resuelven*, are seen with sympathy. Their crime, their sin, their actions, are not perceived by the community as a fault, but rather as a form of struggling for survival" (Rivero 1999). Furthermore, since authorities are aware that necessity forces most people to break the law in order to survive, they sometimes take advantage of this as vehicle to arbitrarily punish citizens. As one Cuban woman commented: "Regardless of who you are, if they want to find a pretext for disciplining you for political non-compliance, all they have to do is investigate the means by which you are surviving" (author's interview with Mendoza, December 2006). Aside from causing resentment, this also renders many citizens fearful of reclaiming their rights in the formal system due to feelings of guilt and criminality (Rivero 1999). This may be another explanation for authorities' lenience of informal activity in many instances. Aside from having a "cushioning" effect on the frustrations of the citizenry, a general tolerance for illegal practices—and intolerance where convenient—could be interpreted as part of an architecture of social control, motivating compliance by guilt and vulnerability to sanction, and providing instruments for persecuting troublesome individuals.

According to Ledeneva, "structural (both economic and cultural) forces or constraints of the Soviet over-controlling centre resulted in flourishing *blat*: life became impossible *unless* the rules were broken" (1998: 46). She incorporates numerous Soviet cartoons that reflect the pervasiveness of *blat*. One in particular (printed in 1952) suggests that inventing stories had become normalized part of everyday life. The cartoon depicts a man in a business suit putting on his coat to leave home while scolding his child: "You naughty boy telling lies like that. You're grounded! Don't you dare go out anywhere! And if I get a call from the ministry, tell them I'm not back from the business trip yet. And tell mummy I've gone to a meeting at the ministry. Have you got that?" (1998: 80). One Cuban woman expressed her concern about the social impact of a similar culture in Cuba.

> I worry about the current generation of Cubans who are in this climate of lies because they have nothing to trust or believe in. Children in Cuba grow up seeing, for example, a father who stands up in meetings at work and delivers all the revolutionary talk and then on the same day brings home things he's stolen from work. If they can't even trust what their parents say, who can they trust? All their lives, they have seen everybody around them saying one thing and doing another, so they learn to behave in the same way (author's interview with Mendoza, December 2006).

Concerns raised in the 1992 Congress of the Communist Party about illegal economic practices "contaminating" the Party, particularly its youth wing, the Union of Young Communists, suggest the party is also aware of social transformations brought by informality. The social consequences of widespread and enduring underground activity (including the disintegration of moral values such as trust, transparency and honesty) are easy to overlook due to their relatively intangible nature. Consequently, researchers tend to pay little attention to these factors and to focus instead on more measurable short-term economic consequences of underground activity and corruption, such as loss of government property or revenue and the ensuing impact on official GDP growth. Considering the antagonistic relationship between the first and second economy in more social terms might be a way to gain some new insights into factors that perpetuate cycles of informality.

Where To from Here?

As discussed earlier, the neo-liberal response to informality proposed by authors such as de Soto has tended to propose the complete removal of state interventions in the economy, seeing this as a means for allowing the micro-entrepreneurs of the second economy to flourish into effective capitalists. Rejecting this general conclusion, Portes and Schauffler argue that such a shift would not achieve de Soto's goal of incorporating informals into formal arrangements, but would rather result in the "informalization of the entire economy." The entire workforce would come to operate under the same raw market conditions as the informal sector, with no protective regulations ensuring standards of work conditions, wages, accident insurance and unemployment compensation (Portes and Schauffler 1993: 55; Centeno and Portes 2003: 25). Aside from other well-documented problems associated with neoliberal reforms—such as increased inequalities and deteriorating standards of health and education—another point to consider is that capitalist economies and liberal democratic institutions also rely on underlying social factors such as generalised trust, honesty and transparency (Newton 1997; Schwab 2003; Surowiecki 2002; Klein 2003) as well as collectively-provided infrastructures or evolved "systems" of law, education, health and so on. As outlined in the previous section, many of the secondary social consequences ensuing from the antagonistic relationship between the formal and informal sectors not only ideologically undermine the formal socialist system, but also erode ethical values such as trust and honesty. The competence and effectiveness of any modern bureaucracy is surely diminished when avoiding and defrauding the official system becomes customary. Since institutions are obviously shaped and influenced by the behavior and accepted norms of those who work and operate within them, the task of re-establishing legitimate, transparent and efficient official institutions is complicated where practices of dishonesty, theft and illegality have become normalized. As Stark has observed, the expansion and contraction of the second economy and its qualitative transformation do not correspond in any linear fashion with the tightening and loosening of legal regulations. "[L]egalization in itself cannot make a shadow economy into a legitimate private sector where a distrusting populace fears re-expropriation and where even legal and formally registered activities have an official status as less than legitimate" (Stark 1989: 651).

Applied to the health system, the equivalent of the general neo-liberal solution to informality would be privatization. That a privatized health system would improve current arrangements is doubtful; rather the result would more likely be worse inequalities of access to services. The establishment of universally free health care in Cuba is an achievement allowing most of the population to deal with their medical problems. Even a mixed system could lead to greater inequalities of service quality, with better doctors moving to the private system where wealthier patients could afford to pay for the services. As has been outlined in previous chapters, the single nationalized health system has many advantages in terms of coordination of institutions, epidemiological surveillance and prevention, optimizing public access to limited medical equipment and so on that have contributed to the country's positive overall health outcomes.

The Cuban government's general response to the second economy over the years has been one of punishment and increased regulation applied in cyclical crackdowns.[16] These periodic campaigns are usually only effective for a short period of time before another is required (Ritter 2005: 354). Typical of these crackdowns are punitive measures such as shutting down illegal productions, firing staff from their state jobs and replacing them with new employees and closer supervision. For example, in recent years many pharmaceutical factory employees found stealing and reselling medicines have lost their jobs. Authorities have increased monitoring of private family-run businesses, farmers' markets, food outlets and other areas that handle saleable goods. Havana port operations have been taken over by the military in an effort to monitor truck drivers and port workers (Whitney 2006; Perez-Lopez 2006: 10). The examples outlined in the previous chapter demonstrate that attempts by health professionals to form non-government associations that would increase their bargaining power have also been severely punished. However, that these punitive measures are regularly repeated suggests they have not been especially effective in terms of addressing the underlying causes of informality.

Centeno and Portes describe the relationship between the state and the informal economy as "by definition, one of inevitable conflict." Whereas a state seeks to exercise authority over a territory, the goal of actors in the informal economy is to evade or undermine this authority (2003: 7). While informal economic activity takes many forms and variations, it exists only in relation to the existing formal system. The varying nature of informal economic activity can be simplified and explained as essentially the result of this ongoing interplay between the state and civil society (2003: 13). In a study of the relationship between public spheres and informal economies in the context of Latin America, Centeno and Portes identify a number of paradoxes involved. Observing Michael Mann's (1993: 59) distinction between different types of state power, the authors differentiate between those polities with a high regulatory intent and limited success in implementation, and polities that can effectively enforce their decisions and authority. Many of the polities with a high regulatory intent, in fact come to be trapped in a vicious cycle wherein efforts to re-establish control over the informal economy result in more complex avoidance methods in civil society, which in turn weakens state authority, leading to a burgeoning of informal activity and so on. Countries with a high level of central control such as Cuba, they argue, enter into a similar self-perpetuating circle wherein state efforts to control all aspects of entrepreneurship in civil society flounder. Rather than encouraging cooperation, these efforts instead result in further attempts by civil society to avoid the state, while in the meantime concealing and withholding information the state depends upon for effective planning. Figures 1 and 2 demonstrate this cycle.

Effective states then, are those that have managed to break this cycle by achieving a relationship of cooperative negotiation with groups in civil society; in other words, what Mann has called "collective power" or "power through" society (1993: 59). No simple formula exists for the practical achievement of this cooperative negotiation. However the obvious starting point is to address the causes of informality rather than increasing the regulatory load that only gives way to new avoidance strategies that seek to deal with these underlying problems.

Since informal economic activity in Cuba varies in character across different sectors of the economy depending on the particular circumstances and conditions to which they respond, reforms aimed at formalizing would have to take this into account. This chapter has not sought to provide the solution to Cuban informality, although some authors have offered ideas to this respect (Henken 2005; Ritter 2005). Specifically

Figure 1
The Process of Informalization under "Frustrated" States

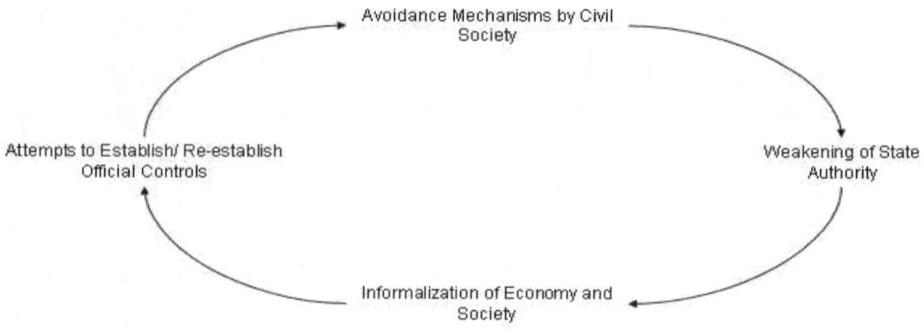

Avoidance Mechanisms by Civil Society

Attempts to Establish/ Re-establish Official Controls

Weakening of State Authority

Informalization of Economy and Society

Figure 2
The Circular Character of Informalization under Totalitarian States

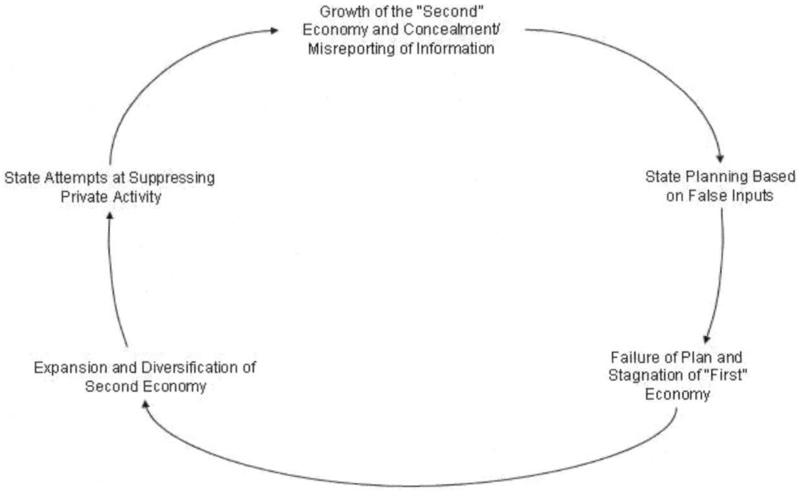

Source: Centeno and Portes. 2003. pp. 31.

in the health sector, a number of persistent problems with the formal system have been shown to encourage informal solutions. These include: health sector employees' insufficient wages and inability to negotiate the value and conditions of their labor; the intensely politicized nature of health resulting from its legitimizing role for the regime, which creates an environment where criticism of the health system is equated with political dissidence; an over-emphasis on health indicators and under-emphasis on patients' experience of the system, contributing to deteriorating conditions in health services; limitations on patients' and health workers' capacity to participate both in medical decisions and heath policy-making.

These shortcomings, which I have argued derive from inadequate investment in structural arrangements for incorporating public engagement with decision-making, should not obscure the aspects of the system which *are* inclusive and integrated, and which have served as foundations for health improvements. Notably, these include the increased accessibility of medical services through the establishment of free health care, the expansion of heath facilities and collaborative arrangements for implementing national health goals. Importantly, reforms aimed at responding to underground activity should seek to maintain these facilitative establishments, because of their contribution to social capital and to the improvement of the population's health.

Based on the findings of this research, I would argue that one of the more obvious ways to stimulate renewed cooperative "negotiation" between central decision-makers and civil society in the health sector would be to focus on the improvement of participatory channels at all levels of the system, not just in implementation of health policy but in actual responsibility and decision-making. Some possible changes in this direction might be to establish regular formal procedures allowing patients to register anonymous complaints, a system for reviewing and appropriately responding to these complaints, procedures for informed consent and the right to refuse treatment,[17] improve regional access to health data, increase health worker responsibility in terms of defining the public health needs of their local community and their own professional needs, anonymous national polling to gauge public support for health funding allocation and satisfaction with particular aspects of health service. However, comprehensive and specific policy recommendations for practically achieving this really require more systematic research into the character, causes and magnitude of informal activity in the health sector than was possible within the scope of this book. Many useful ideas for improvements to the system are likely to be sourced from patients and health workers themselves. Although central planning at a national level has played an important role in Cuba's ability to improve its health outcomes (see Chapter 3), patients and health workers have a uniquely grounded perspective regarding the realities of the system and thus may offer a uniquely pragmatic set of improvements, fully cognizant of the capacities and day-to-day limitations of current arrangements. Unfortunately, national health policy-making in Cuba usually lacks consultation and negotiation with, and active participation by, these subordinate actors. Clearly, this runs the risk of the legitimacy of public policy being undermined, and the sustainability of public institutions being cast in doubt.

Notes

1.   The famous boulevard that runs along Havana's seafront (footnote added).
2.   Dieterich (2006) observes that most of the international left-wing community ignored Castro's speech.
3.   Of course, many who are state employed also engage in informal business activities.
4.   Since most reports of the special period describe the crisis in political and economic terms, I only became properly aware of the extent of human suffering this caused after hearing the many anecdotes Cuban friends have recounted. Among these

are stories of surviving with virtually no food and living on mainly a mixture of sugar and water for weeks or months on end; riding miles from Havana into the provinces on pushbike in hope of finding a potato or some vegetable to eat; trying to raise small children with virtually no food, clean water, transport, clothes or any other provisions; tearing up every book in the house to light a fire in order to cook; neighbors collaborating to clandestinely raise a pig in a bathtub to eat; and blackouts lasting days or weeks. Although these are limited and scattered examples they give some idea of the real human impact of conditions that were not short-lived, but continued for most of the 1990s.

5. In 2004, rationed goods included "rice, sugar, beans occasionally, cooking oil occasionally, eggs occasionally, meat very occasionally, milk for children, pasta, bathing and washing soap occasionally, matches, and tooth paste occasionally" (Ritter 2005: 351). Supporting evidence of the discrepancy between state salaries and living costs is supplied by Ritter (2005: 350).

6. This is one way for the government to absorb remittances from abroad sent to Cubans on the island.

7. For example, in the case of *paladares* (private restaurants), legal self-employment was introduced, then abolished, then resurrected (Scarpaci 1995).

8. Private houses for rent.

9. State salaries in Cuba should be considered in context of free or subsidized services such as education, health and rations. It is worth noting that the UNDP, in its 2003 and 2004 Human Development Reports, made significant upward revisions of its estimates of per capita GDP for Cuba based on a new method of calculation. The revisions appear to have included estimates of some of these shared services.

10. This may be one of the causes underlying the reported nutrition problems among patients in Cuban hospitals. One multinational study of Latin America observed 1905 patients in 12 Cuban hospitals and found high levels of malnutrition amongst hospital patients. These increased progressively with longer stays in the institutions. The study recommended improved policies for patient nutrition in hospitals (Penié 2005).

11. US$5 seems a trivial sum but it equates to the weekly salary of a doctor.

12. Foreign currency sent from abroad into the hands of individual Cubans on the island increased drastically through the special period from US$50 million in 1990 to US$750 million in 2000 (Brotherton 2005: 352).

13. Although its "negotiated" power is of course significantly less, as argued in the previous chapter.

14. Since the existence of the underground economy (and therefore the ability for some to personally profit from it) depends on official regulations, ironically many who engage in corrupt practices are in favour of the official system because it indirectly benefits them. One Cuban woman described this as "socialism of the stomach," saying that those who materially profit from the system will often support it, even if the real source of their profits is the system's corruption (author's personal communication with Mendoza, January 2007).

15. In his detailed work on the "hidden transcripts" underlying the relations between the powerless and the powerful, Scott (1990: 36) identifies language as one common tool of deception deployed in the face of authority.

16. In the context of observing a general regulative volatility in Cuba, some authors have also commented that the central government's policy adjustments tend to follow "a pattern of reform counter-reform" fluctuating between moderate economic liberty and tight central control (De Vibe 2004: 55-56). Johns observes that drastic policy shifts can occur "with little notice and no public dialogue" (2003: 56).

17. The implementation of procedures of this kind might be a step towards re-negotiating the boundary between the state's political obligation to improve national level health outcomes and patient rights to more autonomy in medical decision-making.

6

Conclusion

This project began as an investigation of a case that has almost always been represented as an unambiguous success story. This success story—Cuba's positive health performance—is widely applauded but under-explained. Many observers have remained puzzled over the question of how a country with poor economic performance, which has rejected conventionally accepted liberal development model, has nevertheless managed to perform so well in health. Therefore, the general goal of the research was to gain new insights into this case. What seemed most surprising about the Cuban health outcomes is that they were achieved under conditions of extreme material shortage. It seemed logical therefore to speculate that non-material factors might have been important. As a concept that has explicitly sought to demonstrate that societies' wealth and developmental capacities rely on more than material resources, social capital was an appropriate conceptual tool for examining the case.

However, despite the voluminous literature on social capital over the past two decades, a lack of theoretical reflection and definitional clarity has seen the concept indiscriminately adopted to describe all social interactions. Since Bourdieu and Coleman first (re)introduced the concept, discussions have digressed from an appreciation of why social capital is capital. More recent conceptions have therefore often fallen short of explaining precise causal connections between social arrangements and societies' development outcomes. Hence, part of the preliminary work for this project was a theory building exercise (Chapter 2) aimed at extracting from the literature some theoretical inferences regarding the types of social arrangements which might be important to societies' collective outcomes. It was established that social capital, like all capital, is the product of previous investments of social energy aimed at constructing a capacity for producing desired outcomes. Social capital is collectively produced and collectively owned; it increases with greater participation/ownership (Bourdieu 1986: 250); once built, it raises the threshold for what its members can collectively (and individually) achieve; in order to be reproduced, though, it relies on ongoing collective recognition and acknowledgement.

Cuba's health outcomes are usually explained as the results of deliberate public health policies. If the country produced and sustained its outcomes through purposeful political decisions, then its effectiveness in executing these decisions seemed as important to consider as the decisions themselves. For this project, it was decided that, in order to understand Cuba's apparent success, the research needed to do more than describe the various health policies the country had adopted. An approach that would reveal something about the manner in which policy is designed and implemented seemed critical. This position was especially influenced by the revised understandings of state power emerging from recent statist literature. In particular, neo-statists have argued that a one-dimensional conception of state power has led the dominant discourses of our time to underestimate the potential of deliberative political processes. Drawing upon the social capital and state capacity literatures, it was theorized that public institution-building aimed at sustaining useful cooperative relationships between diverse actors in the health sector and integrating public contributions into health policy might partly explain the apparently effective collective decision-making in the Cuban health sector. In particular, this included the idea that infrastructural state capacity (including state embeddedness, or the interpenetration between the central organs of the state and other social structures) might have been important. One of the central aims of the research was therefore to examine the extent to which different actors associated with the health system are integrated into policy design and implementation.

Summary of Research Findings

As detailed in Chapter 3, a coordinated national effort by all institutions in the health sector (with additional collaboration from other sectors) was found to be one important explanation for Cuba's capacity to transcend its limiting circumstances of crisis and poverty to some extent in the improvement of health outcomes. The network of formalized collaborations that comprise the Cuban health system bring together various institutions and sections of the community on a regular and ongoing basis in the pursuit of clear health objectives (defined in written health programs). These arrangements were examined here in relation to the PAMI but it can be assumed that they are similarly relevant to other prioritized health programs. The combined efforts of groups with diverse functions working together to avert health risk factors associated with pregnancy and birth is an important part of the explanation for the country's low incidences of maternal and infant morbidity and death.

Regular communication and collaboration between family doctors and specialists at policlinics and hospitals, between all directors of the country's hospitals, between mass organizations and health institutions, between the director of public health and directors of other sectors, and so on improves information-sharing, resource optimization, monitoring and surveillance. At the local level, close working relationships between family doctors and local FMC representatives combine doctors' medical knowledge with the FMC workers' awareness of patients' social situations. FMC workers support family doctors—especially with difficult cases—and contribute to decisions regarding patients' medical needs. The family doctor therefore, through regular contact with patients and communication with local mass organizations, develops knowledge of multiple factors that influence patients' health, including biological, psychological and social factors (see Feinsilver 1993: 29). Mass organizations, which have wide public membership, have also served as arrangements for mobilizing community involvement in public health campaigns (aimed at improving public education, vaccination and so on). Every institution pertaining to the health sector, as well as sectors outside of health, is directed (and has in turn become conditioned) to direct prioritized attention to pregnant women, mothers and infants. That groups with diverse technical capabilities have over a sustained period concentrated on improving this health area has reduced the multi-factoral causes of maternal-infant death. That this has been sustained over a long period can be linked to investment in formal structures which support such collaboration, and these investments are reasonably interpretable as aspects of social capital.

Formal procedures for sustaining regular contact between doctors and patients have also been important since these build trust between the two parties, improves doctors' knowledge of medical cases and their capacity to predict and prevent health risks. The regular doctor-patient contact is maintained through the institution of family doctor clinics in local communities, the establishment of clearly defined health programs, the procedures doctors are taught for overseeing these programs and procedures for regular public health monitoring and screening. The incorporation of pregnancy cases into the system is automatic; scheduled appointments with specialists, home visits from public health workers and doctors and adjusted food ration books are arranged as a matter of routine. Established mechanisms such as these, which guarantee automatic health care to all pregnant women and infants as a right of citizenship can not be overlooked as important to the country's maternal-infant health outcomes. It can be assumed that this similarly applies in the cases of other prioritized health programs.

The collaborative arrangements in the health sector are part of the explanation of how it was technically possible for Cuba to implement the health policies set out in the PAMI, despite resource shortages. Lasting arrangements which incorporate different groups into the national health policy implementation process have provided the basis for sustaining popular mobilization or "civic engagement" in the pursuit of public health goals. These findings illustrate various positive roles assumed by public institutions. Particularly important has been the establishment of formal channels for incorporating diverse groups in the health policy implementation process, thereby raising the threshold for what is practically achievable in the health field.

These findings are significant enough to suggest that discussions of social capital could benefit from more attention paid to the role of public institutions as structures which can encourage a permanent civic engagement with public policy. Other authors have also recently suggested this may be the missing link in the nexus between social capital and improved outcomes. Research by Freitag, for example, found that politico-institutional structures play an important role in generating civic engagement and associational life. The author also recommends that "a top down perspective needs to supplement the more usual bottom-up approach championed by Putnam" (2006: 124. See also Skocpol 1996; Evans 1997b). Moreover, the findings presented here illustrate an element of purposeful collective investment in the construction of social capital. These contributions have been made in the context of a prevailing lack of attention to the question of how social capital emerges (Freitag 2006: 123). Furthermore, the institutional capacities outlined in Chapter 3 are aspects of what the neo-statists have described as "penetrative" state power; the interaction between the state and the populace. The mobilization of social energy in line with state goals can also be seen as "extractive" state power; that is, state elites are able to draw upon resources from the community with (relatively) little resistance.

However, this project has been as much a story about the social dynamics involved in the construction of Cuba's public health goals as the way in which those goals are technically delivered. In other words, important to this study was also the question of how the improvement of maternal-infant health (defined mainly as the improvement in mortality indicators), among other health achievements, came to be a common and relatively undisputed focus of collective effort. Chapter 3 answered this question to some extent, attributing the sustained attention to maternal-infant health to a longstanding and politically dominant government, which has for various reasons (humanitarian, symbolic and political) prioritized key health improvements.

Given the political priority of health in Cuba, the puzzle of how the country achieved and sustained its health outcomes is in essence a question about the sources of state capacity. That is, understanding Cuba's ability to arrive at collective decisions and effectively honor those decisions was central to this inquiry. Neo-statist literature has proposed the argument that the effectiveness of collective decision-making increases with state embeddedness (not incompatible with the conception of social capital developed in Chapter 2). As mentioned, one of the aims of this project was therefore to evaluate the extent to which diverse sections of Cuban society contribute to health policy design. This was seen as equally important as policy implementation because presumably the former influences the legitimacy and effectiveness of the latter. So, whereas Chapter 3 revealed the "top-down" mechanisms that have mobilized participation in health policy implementation in Cuba (an aspect of state embeddedness that appears fairly well developed), Chapter 4 examined the extent of negotiation with social groups in the process of arriving at national public health decisions.

The research found that, by contrast with the well developed arrangements for mobilizing collective action towards effective policy implementation, the formal avenues for genuine community involvement in decisions regarding health policies and priorities are noticeably insubstantial. Rather, an official monopoly of public health planning and decision-making persists and negotiation with public health workers, patients and the community generally is limited. Historical examples demonstrate the obstruction and severe punishment of attempts to influence or infiltrate this central control. The perpetuation of this power dynamic is partly attributable to (and also a cause of) the politicized nature of health in Cuba. That health achievements have played a powerful legitimizing role for the Cuban revolution may to some degree explain the reluctance of the state elite to negotiate decision-making on a more participatory basis. The Castro government's fulfillment of its populist promise of public health improvement is important to its claims to popular endorsement. Its capacity to construct the terms of this promise and its delivery (that is, to define health improvement) is a clear political advantage in this context.

The decision-making arrangements of the Cuban health sector have been described here as largely paternalistic. Although population health improvement has been legally established as a state obligation, there is little space for public debate over what the detailed responsibilities entail. Political pressures obliging health workers and citizens to comply with the government's health targets (aimed at improvements in national-level statistics), on the one hand, have usually achieved compliance. On the other hand, limited avenues for employees to debate and contribute to health policy decisions and implementation plans can compromise local level concerns which are important to the quality and sustainability of actual outcomes. Health sector employees have little professional autonomy and virtually no collective bargaining establishments for negotiating terms and conditions of employment. Nor do they always have access to the information they need, nor the ability to share information horizontally. Rather, inter-institutional collaboration is largely passive participation focused on formally satisfying official directives; debate, fine-tuning and "bottom-up" influence on the design of those orders is noticeably constrained. This under-utilization of the technical knowledge and participative potential of the sector's workforce (and the community generally) is lamentable, especially considering that the framework for more meaningful participation exists. The collaborative structures already assembled in the Cuban health sector technically allow for more *active* popular involvement in policy-making.

At the point where services are delivered, health workers' limited autonomy reproduces itself in their relationships with patients. Political pressure to deliver positive results and fear of reprisal can lead doctors to exclude patients from medical decision-making and can encourage coercive measures for convincing patients to comply with medical decisions and procedures. Most Cubans seem to be aware of the intensely politicized health system and the possible ramifications of open criticism. This can discourage health workers from taking initiatives to deal with perceivable health problems in the community that are not on the government's agenda. It can also deter both health workers and patients from protesting problems with the system or constructively criticizing state decisions. Therefore, certain problems with the services persist, including deteriorating conditions of facilities, medical paternalism, inadequate salaries, interventionist policies and long queues. In the absence of formal, legal procedures for responding to these problems, patients and workers circumvent the formal system and find underground solutions. I have argued in Chapter 5 that "shadow" activity in the health system, while it serves to temporarily overcome unresolved problems in the formal system, ultimately perpetuates those problems and erodes the legitimacy of formal arrangements.

The discovery of underground health care delivery practices in the Cuban health system was not anticipated at the outset of this research. Nor had I encountered any mention of this phenomenon in the literature on health in Cuba.[1] Given that little systematic investigation of this subject in relation to the Cuban health sector has been carried out and my methodological design provided only anecdotal evidence, I have drawn upon the broader literature on second economies as an additional means for analyzing the findings. I have argued that although the reasons for the emergence of underground activities are complex and multi-factoral, causal connections can be drawn between the lack of public participation discussed in Chapter 4 and the expansion of informal practices.

Drastic changes in Cuba's economic and social circumstances, especially the transformations brought by the special period, have created new social dynamics and problems in the health sector. Surviving on a state peso salary has become increasingly difficult with expanding living costs brought by the dual currency and a growing black market. Health sector employees, like all state employees, face these difficulties and their inability to protest or negotiate state salaries often leaves no other option than to find alternative sources of income. At the same time, general wealth disparities have increased, with some sections of the community gaining access to foreign currency via tourism, remittances or combinations of legal and illegal activity in the second economy. The growing economic power of some Cubans, by contrast with health professionals' relatively impoverished situations, lends itself to private relationships of convenience, allowing both parties to bypass official arrangements but through this process also changing the relationships between doctors and patients generally and threatening to contaminate even the system's positive aspects. For health workers, favors, gifts and sometimes money in exchange for preferential treatment can supplement insufficient incomes. For patients, making private arrangements with doctors who are *socios* can provide access to otherwise unavailable medicines and supplies. Private informal agreements can also guarantee individuals faster and better quality services in hospitals and clinics where deteriorating facilities, long queues and a lack of privacy and autonomy persist. In this way, shadow practices serve to fill in problems that patients and health workers encounter in the formal system.

Not everybody benefits from informal exchange, however. The poorer sections of the community with little to offer in exchange for preferential treatment and those with no personal connections in the health system are forced to endure deteriorating health care. So, while informal arrangements alleviate frustrations for some, they perpetuate or worsen the situation for others. Each patient who jumps the queue at a hospital or doctor's office increases the waiting line for others who enter via formal channels. Medicines and supplies stolen for resale increase scarcities in the formal system, intensify demand for black market supplies and drive up the overall price of health care. Through this cycle, patients' expectations and perceptions of the health system also change; it can be assumed that expanding informal networks of exchange lead citizens increasingly to expect inferior services unless they pay with gifts, money or favors. A cycle of informality perpetuates the deterioration of facilities and shortages of medicine and supplies in the formal system. At the same time, health workers' political powerlessness prevents them from calling public attention or demanding solutions to these problems. Hence, informal practices, while in some ways compensating for persistent problems, also give way to practical and ideological transformations which erode public health arrangements. These issues that were raised in Chapters 4 and 5 are sufficiently important to detract from the investments that comprise Cuba's health system. They suggest that *social capital is being lost* through processes which are not properly endorsed by the public, which do not achieve the objectives they set themselves and therefore do not constitute permanent accomplishments.

Contributions and Implications for Future Research

As it turned out, the theoretical framework adopted for this project helped to produce important findings regarding the Cuban health system and its outcomes which other researchers have usually overlooked. Some of these findings were anticipated in a general sense and others were entirely unexpected. However, the unexpected findings, far from detracting from the usefulness of the theoretical framework, in fact reinforced its relevance and usefulness. Rather, what the unexpected findings challenged were the prevailing assumptions regarding Cuba's health outcomes. Given that the existing literature on the Cuban health system under Fidel Castro is heavily imbued with glowing descriptions of the country's health achievements, it was surprising to discover a number of areas where the system is not performing so well.

Reflecting now on the literature which first informed this project, it seems that most accounts of Cuba's health system over-rely on narrow quantitative measures (key national health statistics). These statistics reveal a dimension of the country's health outcomes but fail to capture other important aspects of the system's quality, including many of those detailed in this research project. Foreign observers' reports of health care in Cuba usually work on the assumption that the statistics speak for themselves and rarely engage in critical evaluation of whether the statistics mask a more complex reality. As the findings of this research suggest, numerical data reveal a dimension of a system's quality but can lead to evaluations which are reductionist and misleading, obscuring qualitative aspects of the phenomenon (see also Greenhalgh and Taylor 1997). It is worth considering that "quantitative measurements rest on qualitative assumptions about which constructs are worth measuring and how constructs are conceptualized" (Bowen 1996). These constructs are also open to manipulation by dominant groups.[2]

Some studies have included useful descriptions of Cuba's various public health policies, offering these as explanations for the country's statistical outcomes. Seldom examined though are the social arrangements—the distributions of power and the nature of exchanges— between different social groups associated with the sector, which are necessarily implicated in the production of certain public health policies and their outcomes. This project has gone some way towards uncovering these dimensions of the Cuban system. Its findings demonstrate that these are important considerations if we are to properly understand the quality, effects and long-term sustainability of Cuba's public policy outcomes.

The purpose of this project was not to dismiss the many impressive public health advancements Cuba has managed. Even considering the problems outlined in Chapters 4 and 5, it is remarkable that a country facing crisis and underdevelopment has managed to provide access to health services and facilities for all of its population. The formal health care system still ensures free access medical services within walking distance of most Cubans' homes. As detailed in Chapter 3, pregnant women and infants, along with other vulnerable medical groups, receive prioritized attention and have access to a range of guaranteed provisions unimaginable to poor citizens of other developing countries, contributing to low incidences of mortality and morbidity. These achievements, among others, demonstrate a considerable collective capacity to attain certain outcomes in the face of limited material circumstances. I have argued that institutionalized arrangements which integrate the population into the health system (even before they are diagnosed with illness) and which incorporate different sections of the community into the *policy implementation* process are an important part of this capacity. These social structures have therefore been identified as aspects of social capital.

However, social capital (as an institutional capacity) relies on ongoing collective endorsement and participation. Inadequate investment in processes for integrating public involvement in *collective decision-making* (an aspect of what neo-statists have called "negotiated" state power) has produced consequences which work against the construction of a collective institutional capacity. Due to a lack of public debate and general participation in the process of articulating collective interests (regarding how public health improvement is defined) public health policy has not always responded to the needs of the patients and health workers involved. This seems to have led some to abandon the collective system in favor of informal private arrangements. As already elaborated, institutions inform and are informed through ongoing social exchange and rely on collective acknowledgement. The way in which institutions are informed is as important as the normalizing influence they have on those they inform. Resilient public institutions therefore, while embodying a degree of invariability which makes them useful, also need to retain the flexibility to expand and evolve beyond the original purpose for which they were created, and adapt to changing external circumstances and democratic preferences. Importantly, this is what makes them capital.

Reflecting on the different conceptions of social capital discussed in Chapter 2, it is interesting to note that the world of underground exchange in Cuba abounds with examples "reciprocity," "networks," "social connectedness" and other buzz words regularly proffered as examples of social capital. In fact, as the discussion of *blat* (profit through illicit connections) revealed, underground markets can rely almost entirely on informal social relationships to the extent that individuals come to see social contacts as more valuable than money. With the expansion of *blat* in the health sector, securing necessary resources and quality services relies increasingly on being "well connected" and individuals who are active in underground activity are likely to register high levels of social connectedness. However, *blat* in the Cuban health sector relies on private embezzlement of public facilities and material and human resources. It therefore leads to the deterioration of the collectively owned systems and the outcomes of those who use them. The increasing reliance on informal networks to circumvent formal arrangements can breed lawlessness and disregard for formality which can corrupt formal institutions and worsen outcomes for those who follow the rules. Survival in a fragmented formal/informal system can also normalize dishonest and duplicitous behavior, deteriorating ethical social behaviors such as trust and transparency which are necessary foundations of effective governance. These findings serve to further illustrate the futility of assuming that societies registering high levels of aggregated, individual-level social connections will be effectively governed. Not all social connections improve general social cohesion or a society's capacity for collective decision-making. As this case demonstrates, in some contexts the expansion of social networks can be a response to *ineffective* governance. As a measure taken without consideration for historical, political and social context, individual-level social connectedness therefore has limited usefulness as an indication of societal outcomes. The findings of this research (theoretical and empirical) suggest that a useful conception of social capital should capture the degree to which collective decision-making power is dispersed amongst a society's diverse social groups and something sustainable (and productive) has been provided for future generations.

The findings of this research also allow for some interesting reflections on debates about state capacity, particularly the question of what types of state-society relations improve state autonomy in developing contexts. Debates about state-led development have usually focused on the relationships between the state and industrial sectors and their consequences for economic development. However, in the Cuban context where social development (in areas such as health and education) has been a state priority, similar questions about state autonomy can be considered. To recap on the dominant poles of the debate in the statist literature, the developmental statists have tended to argue that state autonomy (the ability of the state to achieve its goals) is increased where the state retains the power to act independently of other social groups to ensure its priorities are maintained. On the other hand, neo-statists have argued that state autonomy and capacity increases with greater embeddedness or integration with non-state actors. For neo-statists the isolation of states from social groups is a state weakness, whereas state strength increases with the evolution of complex institutional linkages between state elites and civil society. What Mann calls "infrastructural power" is achieved through the increasing "interpenetration" between the state and civil society, or the dispersion of state power between diverse social groups.

Such debates are especially interesting in the light of this project's research findings. On the one hand, the autonomy of Cuban state elites over other social groups (combined with the longevity of the Castro government) has ensured a sustained prioritization of clear health goals over a long period and a significant degree of public compliance and mobilization in the implementation of these goals. On the other hand, this research also found that the paternalistic central control over health decision-making means that health policies are not always tailored to respond to public needs. In other words, what central decision-makers consider important for public health improvement does not always correspond with the perceptions of health workers and patients. This, I have argued, is a weakness of the Cuban public health system because it prevents institutional arrangements from evolving in response to new public health problems brought by changing societal circumstances. Problems which adversely affect those who use the system but which do not directly detract from policy-makers' priorities (especially the improvement of national health indices) can persist because insufficient avenues exist for incorporating public evaluation of the system into the policy-making process. There is evidence to suggest that this has contributed to the growth of private arrangements for circumventing the formal system, which to some extent undermine the legitimacy of formal arrangements and therefore state capacity.

I have argued that these findings support neo-statists' arguments that negotiation with social groups is the key to state capacity, even in developing contexts. Further, functionally-important avenues for allowing genuine public participation in policy-making are needed if the system and the country's public health achievements (including national health indices) are to survive over the long term. A factor in "state strength" is surely the state's ability to produce lasting outcomes endorsed by citizens that are not easily torn down by competing forces (market forces, competing political interests and so on). This book contends that state decisions that are the product of a general democratic will face fewer competing forces and would therefore have a greater likelihood of sustainability and permanence, than coerced decisions. Further, I have argued that the resilience of the public system (its chances of surviving a regime change or a shift in political priorities) decreases where central authorities retain non-negotiable control over resources and decision-making power. Some would argue that political priorities have already shifted to some degree with increasing focus on Cuba's health image as a means for earning symbolic and economic capital from abroad. The expansion of health facilities in Cuba for foreign customers, the ongoing exportation of Cuban doctors and the Cuban health care model to Venezuela and elsewhere; and the growing market for Cuban pharmaceuticals have caused some concern that the health sector's resources are being directed away from the priority of providing quality health services for Cubans. If this is the case, the inability of social groups to intervene and "keep the state in line" could over time lead to a decline in health care quality and, in turn, to a deterioration of Cuba's health indices and health reputation.

Admittedly though, other interpretations of the findings are possible. For example, it is arguable that increased negotiation with civil society groups could allow increasingly powerful economic groups to pressure for changes which would dismantle the egalitarian arrangements of the public system. As discussed in Chapter 5, there is reason to believe that achievements that have been possible under the public system would deteriorate with part or full privatization of health services. As detailed in Chapter 3, public provisions ensuring resource sharing and optimization, equal access to facilities, the protection of vulnerable groups and so on (achievements in themselves) have been the basis for important public health advancements. However, increasing underground activity also presents a threat to these arrangements. It should be acknowledged of course, that it is difficult to arrive at any firm conclusions regarding the pervasiveness of this informal exchange. The anecdotal evidence emerging from this research and other authors' observations suggests the phenomenon is significant enough that many Cubans are aware of it and that it has detracted from strong aspects of the formal system. Given the restrictions on public opinion polling in Cuba, more information regarding characteristics and the magnitude of shadow health care arrangements could indirectly provide indications of public support for and the long-term sustainability of public health policies and arrangements. A thorough assessment of this kind was beyond the scope of this project but its findings suggest the subject is worth further investigation. There is also room for Cuba's informal health care practices to be assessed in broader global context than this project's research design allowed. Considering Cuba's experiences in light of findings in other countries regarding issues such as patient compliance, "lay referral systems" self help in relation to health care and so on could bring valuable new insights regarding the meanings and implications of the findings in Cuba.

Finally, the research findings allow for some reflections on institution-building in non-wealthy contexts. Social capital and state capacity are concepts which have usually been discussed in relation to wealthy countries. This has been partly because it is somewhat counter-intuitive to devote public resources to efforts whose ostensible objectives are social, political and cultural. Affluence gives rich societies a certain license to attend to "non-material" needs (Boreham, Dow and Leet 1999: Chapter 6). However as proponents of social capital and state capacity have successfully demonstrated, there are undeniable positive feedback effects for *economic* capacity from improvements in political capacities. Therefore, it is at least plausible that the assumption that a central role for collective decision-making can only be effective as a progression from the material affluence generated by market arrangements is mistaken. In Cuba, purposeful political decisions have produced some important health achievements despite extremely low levels of material affluence. As I have argued, the relative effectiveness of these political decisions in the area of health is attributable to institutionalized state-society linkages which incorporate cooperative efforts from diverse sections of the community into the policy implementation process. It would seem that in a context of shortage and crisis, building effective, sustainable institutions which incorporate public contributions to policy-making is just as likely to yield positive outcomes, even if it is more problematic and complex than in wealthy contexts. However, to prevent a further decline in compliance with state health policies and of support for public institutions in Cuba, the problems I have highlighted cannot remain unaddressed. In the decades ahead, Cuban authorities must realize that, in order to sustain popular support for public institutions over the longer term, and to shore-up the country's positive health record, further institutional reforms aimed at incorporating genuine public participation into the collective decision-making process will be necessary.

Notes

1. After returning from fieldwork, I established that other contributions to this subject in the literature on health in Cuba were scant with only a few authors drawing attention to it (in particular, Hirschfeld 2007, 2006; Crabb 2001; Brotherton 2005).
2. Arguably, Cuban authorities, aware of the political role of health in Cuba, have had a powerful influence on the construction of health improvement and are able to draw attention to certain health statistics (as evident in the frequent mentions of infant mortality indicators in Fidel Castro's speeches).

References

Agencias. 2007a. "Amigos de Jóvenes Españoles Accidentados en Cuba Critican la Falta de Médicos en los Hospitales." *Cuba Encuentro: Agencias*, 5 March.

Agencias. 2007b. "La Habana Prevé un Crecimiento Económico del 10% en 2007." *Cuba Encuentro: Agencias*, 30 April.

Ahrne, G. 1996. "Civil Society and Civil Organizations." *Organization* 3(1):109-120.

Aidi, H. 2001. "Havana Healing: Castro's Minority Scholarship Plan." Afro Cuba Web. URL: <http://www.afrocubaweb.com/infomed/havanahealing.htm>.

Aitsiselmi, A. 2001. "Medical Research in Cuba: Strengthening International Cooperation." Pugwash Online. URL: <http://www.pugwash.org/reports/ees/ees8e.htm>.

Almeida, M. 2004. *Interview 7, 2 August*. Havana.

Amaro, N. 1996. "Decentralization, Local Government and Citizen Participation in Cuba." *Cuba in Transition* 6:262-282.

Anderson, T. 2002. "Island Socialism: Cuban Crisis and Structural Adjustment." *Journal of Australan Political Economy* 49:57-83.

Anderson, T. 2005. "Social Organisation and Infectious Disease: The Mexican and Cuban Health Systems Compared (Working Paper)." *Sydney University*.

Anderson T. 2006 "The Structuring of Health Systems and the Control of Infectious Disease: Looking at Mexico and Cuba," *Pan American Journal of Public Health* 19(6): 423-31.

Anderson, T. 2007. "Why Cuba is a Democracy and the US is Not." Online Opinion. URL: <http://www.onlineopinion.com.au/view.asp?article=5609>.

Arango, C. 2004. *Interview 21, 7 October*. Havana.

August, A. 1999. *Democracy in Cuba and the 1997-98 Elections*. Havana: Editorial José Marti.

Australian Productivity Commission. 2003. *Social Capital: Reviewing the Concept and its Policy Implications*. Canberra.

Baum, F. 1999. "Social Capital: Is it Good for your Health? Issues for a Public Health Agenda." *Journal of Epidemiology and Community Health* 53(4):195-196.

Baum, F.E. and A.M. Ziersch. 2003. "Glossary: Social Capital." *Journal of Epidemiology and Community Health* 57(5):320-323.

BBC News. 2005. "Venezuela Medics March over Jobs." *BBC News,* 15 July. URL: <http://news.bbc.co.uk/>

BBC News. 2010. "Cuba Investigates Psychiatric Hospital Deaths." *BBC News.* 16 January. URL: <http://news.bbc.co.uk/>

Benjamin, M. and M. Haendel. 1991. "Cuba: A Healthy Revolution?" *Links* 8(3):3-6.

Bergstrom, S. 1994. "Maternal Health: A Priority in Reproductive Health." In *Health and Disease in Developing Countries*. London: Macmillan.

Berkman, L.F. et al. 2004. "Social Integration and Mortality: A Prospective Study of French Employees of Electricity of France–Gas of France." *American Journal of Epidemiology* 159:167-174.

Birch, S. and L. Norlander. 2007. "The Cuban Paradox." *American Journal of Nursing* 107(3):75 - 79.

Blanco, S. 2004. *Interview 3, 20 July*. Havana.

Blum, W. 2005. "The US, Cuba and Democracy." Znet. URL: <http://www.zmag.org/content/showarticle.cfm?ItemID=7491>.

Bohmer, P. 2004. "Present and Future: The Cuban Revolution." CounterPunch. URL: <http://www.counterpunch.org/bohmer09092004.html>.

Boreham, P., G. Dow and M. Leet. 1999. *Room to Manoeuvre: Political Aspects of Full Employment*. Melbourne: Melbourne University Press.

Bourdieu, P. 1986. "The Forms of Capital." In *Handbook of Theory and Research for the Sociology of Education*, ed. J.G. Richardson. New York: Greenwood Press.

Bowen, K. 1996. "The Sin of Omission-Punishable by Death to Internal Validity: An Argument for Integration of Qualitative and Quantitative Research Methods to Strengthen Internal Validity." URL: <http://www.socialresearchmethods.net/Gallery/Bowen/hss691.htm>.

Braa, J., O.H. Titlestad and J. Sæbø. 2004. "Participatory Health Information Systems Development in Cuba—the Challenge of Addressing Multiple Levels in a Centralized Setting." Paper presented to Proceedings of the Eighth Conference on Participatory Design: Artful Integration: Interweaving Media, Materials and Practices- Volume 1, Toronto.

Bravo, E.M. 1998. *Development within Underdevelopment: New Trends in Cuban Medicine*. Havana: Editorial José Martí.

Brey, P. 1999. "Worker Autonomy and the Drama of Digital Networks in Organizations." *Journal of Business Ethics* 22(1): 15-25.

Brotherton, P.S. 2005. "Macroeconomic Change and the Biopolitics of Health in Cuba's Special Period." *Journal of Latin American Anthropology* 10(2): 339-369.

Brown, S. 2006. *Interview Y1*. Brisbane.

Bureau of Democracy, Human Rights, and Labor. 2009. *2008 Human Rights Report on Cuba: Country Reports on Human Rights Practices*. 25 February 2009.

Burges, I., A. Edwards and J. Skinner. 2003. "Football Culture in an Australian School Setting: The Construction of Masculine Identity." *Sport, Education and Society* 8(2):199–212.

Burlamanqui, L.C., Célia, A.; Chang, H.J. (Eds), ed. 2000. *Institutions and the Role of the State*. Cheltenham: Edward Elgar.

Burwell, R.C. 2004. *(Re)producing the Nation: Mothering and Making Ends Meet in Cuba*. Ph.D thesis, Loyola University Chicago.

Cabezas Cruz, E. 2006. "Evolución de la Mortalidad Materna en Cuba." *Revista Cubana de Salud Pública* 32(1).

Cacioppo, J.T. and L.C. Hawkley. 2003. "Social Isolation and Health, with an Emphasis on Underlying Mechanisms." *Perspectives in Biology and Medicine* 46(3):39-52.

Campos, J.H. 2004. "The Impact of the U.S. Embargo on Health Care in Cuba: A Clinician's Perspective." *Transnational Law & Contemporary Problems* 14(2):517.

Carr, K. 1999. "Cuban Biotechnology Treads a Lonely Path." *Nature* 398:22-23.

Carrillo de Albornoz, S. 2006. "On a Mission: How Cuba Uses Its Doctors Abroad." *British Medical Journal*. September 30, 333(7570): 678.

Carranza Valdes, J. and J. Valdes Paz. 2004. "Institutional Development and Social Policy in Cuba: "The Special Period."" *Journal of International Affairs* 58(1):175.

Castillo, E. 2004. *Interview 11, 20 September*. Havana.

Castro, F. 2004. "Speech by Fidel Castro Ruz for International Labour Day." Plaza de la Revolucion, Havana URL: <http://www.cadenagramonte.cubaweb.cu/noticias/discurso_fidel010504.asp>.

Castro, F. 2005. "Speech delivered by Dr. Fidel Castro Ruz, President of the Republic of Cuba, at the Commemoration of the 60th Anniversary of his admission to University of Havana, in the Aula Magna of the University of Havana." Havana URL: <http://www.walterlippmann.com/fc-11-17-2005.html>.

Castro, F. [1953] 2001. "History Will Absolve Me." Castro Internet Archive. URL: <http://www.marxists.org/>.

CEDISAP. 2001. *El Sistema de Salud Pública en Cuba.* Havana: Ministerio de Salud Pública (MINSAP).

Centeno, M.A. and A. Portes. 2003. *The Informal Economy in the Shadow of the State (Working Paper).* Princeton University. URL: <http://www.princeton.edu/~cenmiga/works/informal%20economy%20in%20the%20shadow%20of%20the%20state%20final.doc>.

Charen, M. 2003. *Useful Idiots: How Liberals Got It Wrong in the Cold War and Still Blame America First.* Washington: Regnery.

Chelala, C. 1998. "Cuba Shows Health Gains Despite Embargo." *British Medical Journal*, 14 February (316):493.

Chen, L.C. and L.G. Hiebert. 1994. *From Socialism to Private Markets: Vietnam's Health in Rapid Transition (Working Paper).* URL: <http://www.hawaii.edu/hivandaids/From_Socialism_To_Private_Markets__Vietnam_s_Health_In_Rapid_Transition.pdf>.

Chin, J.J. 2002. "Doctor-Patient Relationship: From Medical Paternalism to Enhanced Autonomy." *Singapore Medical Journal* 43(3):152-155.

Chomsky, A. 2000. "The Threat of a Good Example: Health and Revolution in Cuba." In *Dying for Growth: Global Inequality and Health of the Poor*, eds J. Yong Kim, et al. Munroe, Maine: Common Courage Press.

Climan, L. 2001. "A Pat on the Back for Cuba." *Dollars and Sense* July:5.

Cohen, S. 2004. "Social Relationships and Health." *American Psychologist* November: 676-684.

Cole, K. 1998. *Cuba: From Revolution to Development.* London: Pinter.

Coleman, J.S. 1988. "Social Capital in the Creation of Human Capital." *The American Journal of Sociology* 94(Supplement: Organizations and Institutions: Sociological and Economic Approaches to the Analysis of Social Structure.): 95-120.

Constitución de la República de Cuba. 1999. Havana: Ministerio de Justicia.

Contacto Magazine. 2007. "Editorial: US/Cuba: No Comments on Human Rights and Democracy." URL: <http://www.contactomagazine.com/uscubarelations06.htm>.

Cornwell, R. 2006. "The Big Question: Has Cuba Benefited or Suffered under Fidel Castro's 47-year rule?" *The Independent*, 03 August.

Coughlin, J. 2005. "Global Community Health Education: Perspectivas Cubanas." *Nursing Education Perspectives.* 26(3):146.

Coulthard, M., A. Walker and A. Morgan. 2001. *Assessing People's Perceptions of their Neighbourhood and Community Involvement (Part 1).* London: Health Development Agency.

Cox, E. 2002. "Australia: Making the Lucky Country." In *Democracies in Flux: The Evolution of Social Capital in Contemporary Society*, ed. R. Putnam. Oxford: Oxford University Press.

Crabb, M.K. 2001. *Socialism, Health and Medicine in Cuba: A Critical Re-Appraisal.* Ph.D thesis, Emory University.

Cullen, M. and H. Whiteford. 2001. "The Interrelations of Social Capital with Health and Mental Health: Discussion Paper." *Commonwealth of Australia National Mental Health Strategy.* URL: <http://www.health.gov.au/>.

Danielson, R. 1981. "Medicine in the Community: The Ideology and Substance of Community Medicine in Socialist Cuba." *Social Science and Medicine* 15C:239–247.

De Brouwere, V. and W. Van Lerberghe, eds. 2001. *Safe Motherhood Strategies: A Review of the Evidence*. London: Centre for Sexual & Reproductive Health.

De Soto, H. 2000. *The Mystery of Capital: Why Capitalism Triumphs in the West and Fails Everywhere Else*. London: Black Swan.

De Vibe, P. 2004. *In the Shadow of the Commander: Reformulating a South African Health Information System in the Cuban Health Sector*. Masters thesis, University of Oslo.

De Vos, P. 2005. "No One Left Abandoned": Cuba's National Health System since the 1959 Revolution.' *International Journal of Health Services* 35(1):189-207.

Delgado, M. and J. Suárez. 2004. *Interview 8, 10 August*. Havana.

Diaz, C. 2004. *Interview 18, 1 October*. Havana.

Diaz-Briquets, S. 1986. "How to Figure out Cuba: Development, Ideology and Mortality." *Caribbean Review* 15(2): 8-42.

Dieterich, H. 2006. "Cuba: Three Premises to Save the Revolution When Fidel Dies." Havana: Rebelion. URL: <http://www.walterlippmann.com/docs365.html>.

Dilla Alfonso, H. and G. González Núñez. 1997. "Participation and Development in Cuban Municipalities." Ottawa: International Development Research Centre (IDRC). URL: <http://www.idrc.ca/fr/ev-54437-201-1-DO_TOPIC.html>.

Dilla Alfonso, H. and G. González Núñez. 2007. "Successes and Failures of a Decentralizing Experience." in Brenner, P, M.R. Jiménez, J.M. Kirk, and W.M. LeoGrande *A Contemporary Cuba Reader: Reinventing the Revolution*. Rowman & Littlefield.

Dominguez, A. 1977. "Stimulating Community Involvement through Mass Organizations in Cuba: The Women's Role." *International Journal of Health Education* 20(1): 57-60.

Dominguez, J.I. 2000. "An Increasingly Civil Cuba (Book Review)." *Foreign Policy* September: 100.

Donate-Armada, M. 1996. "Sociedad Civil, Control Social y Estructura del Poder en Cuba." *Cuba in Transition* 6: 283-299.

Dorschner, J. 2007. "Wellness, Longevity Take Varied Paths in U.S., Cuba." *Miami Herald*, 28 January.

Dotres Martinez, C. 2001. "The Cuban Paradox." MINSAP. URL: <http://www.londonlinks.ac.uk/Archive/Essex/TheCubanParadox.pdf>.

Dresang, L. et al. 2005. "Family Medicine in Cuba: Community-Oriented Primary Care and Complementary and Alternative Medicine." *The Journal of the American Board of Family Practice*. 18(4):297-303.

Duffy, D.M. 1997. "An Assessment of Health Policy Reform in Russia." *Policy Studies Journal* 25(4):535-556.

Durkheim, E. [1933] 1964. *The Division of Labour in Society*. New York: Free Press.

Eberstadt, N. 1988. 'Literacy and Health: The Cuban "Model"' In *The Poverty of Communism*, ed. N. Eberstadt. London: Transaction Publishers.

Eckstein, S.E. 1994. *Back from the Future: Cuba under Castro*. Princeton, NJ: Princeton University Press.

ECLAC. 2004. "Cuba Able to Maintain Social Progress during "Special" Period." United Nations Economic Commission for Latin America and the Caribbean. URL: <http://www.eclac.org/>.

Edwards, B. and M.W. Foley. 1998a. "Civil Society and Social Capital Beyond Putnam." *American Behavioral Scientist* 42(1):124-139.

Edwards, B. and M.W. Foley. 1998b. "Beyond Tocqueville: Civil Society and Social Capital in Comparative Perspective." *American Behavioral Scientist* 42(1):5-20.

Edwards, J. 2004. *Persona Non Grata: A Memoir of Disenchantment with the Cuban Revolution*. New York: Nation Books.

Edwards, R. 2006. "Social Capital, a Sloan Work and Family Encyclopedia Entry." London: Sloan Work and Family Research Network. URL: <http://wfnetwork. bc.edu/encyclopedia_entry.php?id=257&area=All>.

Eilat, Y. and C. Zinnes. 2002. 'The Shadow Economy in Transition Countries: Friend or Foe? A Policy Perspective" *World Development* 30(7): 1233-1254.

El Universal. 2010. "Seven Cuban Doctors Sue Cuba and Venezuela over "Modern Slavery." *El Universal, Caracas*. February 22. <http://english.eluniversal.com>

Ericson, R.E. 2006. "Command Versus 'Shadow': The Conflicted Soul of the Soviet Economy." *Comparative Economic Studies* 48(1):50.

Escambray Digital. 2007. "UNDP Highlights Human Growth in Cuba." *Escambray Digital: Newspaper of Sancti Spiritus province, Cuba.*, 22 March.

Espinoza, J. and A. Raiz. 2004. *Interview 22, 7 October.*

Evans, P. 1992. 'The State as Problem and Solution: Predation, Embedded Autonomy and Structural Change." In *The Politics of Economic Adjustment: International Constraints, Distributive Conflicts and the State*, eds S. Haggard and R.R. Kaufman. Princeton, NJ: Princeton University Press.

Evans, P. 1995. *Embedded Autonomy: States and Industrial Transformation.* Princeton, NJ: Princeton University Press.

Evans, P. 1997a. "Government Action, Social Capital and Development: Reviewing the Evidence on Synergy." In *State-Society Synergy: Government and Social Capital in Development*, ed. P. Evans. Berkley: Institute for International Studies.

Evans, P., D. Rueschemeyer and T. Skocpol. 1985. *Bringing the State Back In.* New York: Cambridge University Press.

Evans, P.E., ed. 1997b. *State-Society Synergy: Government and Social Capital in Development.* London: International and Area Studies.

Evenson, D. 2005. "The Right to Health Care and the Law." *Medicc Review* 7(9):8-9.

Fang, J. et al. 1998. "Residential Segregation and Mortality in New York City." *Social Science & Medicine* 47(4):469-476.

Faria, M.A. 2004. "Socialized (Free) Medical Care in Cuba Part I: A Poor State of Health!' *Surgical Neurology* 62(2):183-185.

Feinsilver, J.M. 1989a. "Cuba as a 'World Medical Power': The Politics of Symbolism." *Latin American Research Review* 24(2):1-37.

Feinsilver, J.M. 1989b. *Symbolic Politics and Health Policy: Cuba as a "World Medical Power."* Ph.D thesis, Yale University.

Feinsilver, J.M. 1993. *Healing the Masses: Cuban Health Politics at Home and Abroad.* Berkeley: University of California Press.

Feinsilver, J.M. 2006. "The Cuban Threat: Medical Diplomacy." Scoop. URL: <http://www.scoop.co.nz/stories/WO0611/S00005.htm>.

Feldman, M. and J. March. 1981. "Information in Organizations as Signal and Symbol." *Administrative Science Quarterly* 26(2):171-186.

Fernández, D.J. 1990. "Fiction and Nonfiction: Problems in the Study of Cuban Foreign Policy." *Latin American Research Review* 25(3): 237-249.

Fernández, S. 2004. *Interview 4, 20 July.*

Ferro, R. 2002. "Despiden a un Trabajador por ser Reportero Independiente." *CubaNet News*, 9 December.

Field, C. 2007. *Salud.* URL: <http://www.saludthefilm.net/ns/index.html>.

Field notes. 2004. *Elizabeth Kath Fieldwork Summary for Cuba March-October.*

Fine, B. 2001. *Social Capital versus Social Theory: Political Economy and Social Science at the Turn of the Millennium.* London: Routledge.

Fonseca, G.L. 2006a. "The German Historical School." New York: New School for Social Research Economics Department. URL: <http://cepa.newschool.edu/het/schools/historic.htm>.

Fonseca, G.L. 2006b. "The New Institutionalist Schools." New York: New School for Social Research Economics Department. URL: <http://cepa.newschool.edu/het/schools/newinst.htm>.

Forero, J. 2007. "Cubans on Medical Aid Mission Flee Venezuela, but Find Limbo." *Washington Post*, Tuesday 20 February.

Freitag, M. 2006. "Bowling the State Back In: Political Institutions and the Creation of Social Capital." *European Journal of Political Research* 45(1): 123-152.

Frenk, J. and L. Duran-Arenas. 1993. 'The Medical Profession and the State." In *The Changing Medical Profession*, eds F.W. Hafferty and J.B. McKinlay. Oxford: Oxford University Press.

Fukuyama, F. 1995. *Trust: The Social Virtues and the Creation of Prosperity.* London: Hamish Hamilton.

Fukuyama, F. 1999. "Social Capital and Civil Society." International Monetary Fund. URL: <http://www.imf.org/external/pubs/ft/seminar/1999/reforms/fukuyama.htm>.

Fukuyama, F. 2001. "Social Capital, Civil Society and Development." *Third World Quarterly* 22(1): 7-20.

García, M. 2004. *Interview 19, 4 October*. Havana.

Gerring, J. 2004. 'What Is a Case Study?' *American Political Science Review* 98(2): 341-354.

Giddens, A. 1971. *Capitalism and Modern Social Theory: An Analysis of the Writings of Marx, Durkheim and Max Weber.* Cambridge: Cambridge University Press.

González, S. 2004. *Interview 12, 21 September*. Havana.

Grattan, M., 2010. "Cuba Does It Better," *The Age* March 15 URL: http://www.theage.com.au

Greenhalgh, T. and R. Taylor. 1997. "How to Read a Paper: Papers that Go Beyond Numbers (Qualitative Research)." *British Medical Journal* 315:740-743.

Grossman, G. 1977. "The 'Second Economy' of the USSR." *Problems of Communism* 26(5): 25-40.

Habel, J. 2004. "Cuba: What Will Happen after Castro?" *Le Monde Diplomatique*. URL: <http://mondediplo.com/2004/06/13cuba>.

Hart, K. 1971. "Small Scale Entrepreneurs in Ghana and Development Planning." *Journal of Development Studies* 6(4): 104-120.

Haug, M.R. 1988. "A Re-Examination of the Hypothesis of Physician Deprofessionalization." *The Milbank Quarterly* 66(Supplement 2: The Changing Character of the Medical Profession): 48-56.

Hay, C. 2006. "(What's Marxist About) Marxist State Theory?" In *The State: Theories and Issues*, eds C. Hay, M. Lister and D. Marsh. London: Palgrave.

Hay, C. and M. Lister. 2006. "Theories of the State." In *The State: Theories and Issues*, eds C. Hay, M. Lister and D. Marsh. London: Palgrave.

Heller, P. 1997. "Social Capital as a Product of Class Mobilization and State Intervention: Industrial Workers in Kerala, India." In *State-Society Synergy: Government and Social Capital in Development*, ed. P. Evans. Berkeley: Institute for International Studies.

Henken, T. 2000. "Last Resort or Bridge to the Future? Tourism and Workers in Cuba's Second Economy." *Cuba in Transition* 10: 321-336.

Henken, T. 2005. "Entrepreneurship, Informality, and the Second Economy: Cuba's Underground Economy in Comparative Perspective." *Cuba in Transition* 14: 360-375.

Hennigan, T. 2007. "Chávez and Bush Battle for Latin American Hearts." *The Australian*, 13 March.

Hernández, R. and H. Dilla. 1991. "Democracy and Socialism: Political Culture and Popular Participation in Cuba." *Latin American Perspectives* 18(2): 38-54.

Herrera, I. 2004. *Interview 15, 22 September*. Havana.

Hirschfeld, K. 2006. "Sociolismo and the Underground Clinic: The Informal Economy and Health Services in Cuba." *Cuba in Transition* 16: 335-350.

Hirschfeld, K. 2007. *Health, Politics and Revolution in Cuba since 1898*. New Brunswick and London: Transaction Publishers.

Hollander, P. 1981. *Political Pilgrims: Travels of Western Intellectuals to the Soviet Union, China, and Cuba 1928-1978*. Oxford: Oxford University Press.

Hollerbach, P.E., S. Diaz-Briquets, and K.H. Hill. 1984. "Fertility Determinants in Cuba." *International Family Planning Perspectives* 10(1): 12-20.

Holveck, J.C, et al. "Prevention, Control, and Elimination of Neglected Diseases in the Americas: Pathways to Integrated, Inter-Programmatic, Inter-Sectoral Action for Health and Development." *BMC Public Health*. 7(6): 1471-2458.

Huber, E. and J.D. Stephens. 2001. *Development and Crisis of the Welfare State: Parties and Policies in Global Markets*. Chicago: University of Chicago Press.

Human Rights Watch. 2007. "Cuba's Repressive Machinery: Human Rights Forty Years after the Revolution." URL: <http://www.hrw.org/reports/1999/cuba/>.

Iatridis, D.S. 1990. "Cuba's Health Care Policy: Prevention and Active Community Participation." *Social Work* 35(1): 29-35.

International Society for Human Rights. 2005. "ISHR Demands the Immediate Release of Cuban Doctors." Frankfurt URL: <http://www.ishr.org/press/pr2005/1205/051207cuba(1).htm>.

Janes, C.R. and A.O. Chuluundorj. 2004. "Free Markets and Dead Mothers: The Social Ecology of Maternal Mortality in Post-Socialist Mongolia." *Medical Anthropology Quarterly Washington* 18(2): 230-257.

Jessop, B. 1990. *State Theory: Putting Capitalist States in their Place*. Cambridge: Polity Press.

Jessop, B. 2002. *The Future of the Capitalist State*. Cambridge: Polity Press.

Jessop, B. and N.-L. Sum, eds. 2006. *Beyond the Regulation Approach: Putting Capitalist Economies in their Place*. Cheltenham: Edward Elgar.

Jiménez, A. 2004. *Interview 14, 22 September*. Havana.

Johns, M. 2003. "Foreign Investment in Cuba: Assessing the Legal Landscape." *Boletín Mexicano de Derecho Comparado* 106(Enero-Abril): 35-64.

Kaplan, S., S. Greenfield and J.J. Ware. 1989. "Assessing the Effects of Physician-Patient Interactions on the Outcomes of Chronic Disease." *Med Care* 27(7): 679.

Kawachi, I., B.P. Kennedy and K. Loochner. 1997. "Long Live Community: Social Capital as Public Health." *The American Prospect* November/December(35): 56.

Kawachi, I. et al. 1997. "Social Capital, Income Inequality, and Mortality." *American Journal of Public Health* 87(9): 1409-1411.

Kee, F. 1996. "'Patients' Prerogatives and Perceptions of Benefit." *British Medical Journal* 312(7036): 958.

Kennedy, B.P., I. Kawachi and E. Brainerd. 1998. 'The Role of Social Capital in the Russian Mortality Crisis." *World Development* 26(11): 2029.

Kennelly, B., E. O'Shea and E. Garvey. 2003. "Social Capital, Life Expectancy and Mortality: A Cross-national Examination." *Social Science & Medicine* 56(12): 2367.

Keon, W.J. 2009. "Cuba's System of Maternal Health and Early Childhood Development: Lessons for Canada." *Canadian Medical Association Journal*. 180(3): 314-316.

Kinzer, S. 2010. "Caribbean Communism v Capitalism." *Guardian Unlimited*. 22 January.

Klein, S. 2003. "The Natural Roots of Capitalism and its Virtues and Values." *Journal of Business Ethics* 45(4): 387.

Knack, S. 1997. "Does Social Capital Have An Economic Payoff? A Cross-Country Investigation." *Quarterly Journal of Economics* 112(4): 1251-1288.

Kravitz, R.L. and J. Melnikow. 2001. "Engaging Patients in Medical Decision Making: The End is Worthwhile, but the Means need to be More Practical." *British Medical Journal* 323(7313): 584.

Krygier, M. 1997. *Between Fear and Hope: Hybrid Thoughts on Public Values.* Sydney: ABC Books.

Lakshmanan, I.A.R. 2005. "Help for Venezuela Strains Cuban Health Care." *The Boston Globe*, Friday 26 August.

Lawnton Foundation for Human Rights. 2004. "Dr. Oscar Elías Biscet." Miami URL: <http://www.lawtonfoundation.com/information/index.php>.

Ledeneva, A.V. 1998. *Russia's Economy of Favours.* Cambridge: Cambridge University Press.

Leonard Castillo, A., M. Ermeso Rivera and M. Sosa Marín. 1985. *Programa Nacional de Atencion Materno Infantil.* La Habana.

Levav, I. and R. González Uzcátegui. 2000. "Rights of Persons with Mental Illness in Central America." *Acta Psychiatrica Scandinavica* 101(399): 83-86.

Levy, J.D., ed. 2006. *The State after Statism: New State Activities in the Age of Liberalization.* Cambridge: Harvard University Press.

Lewis, J.M., T. Marjoribanks and M. Pirotta. 2003. "Changing Professions: General Practitioners' Perceptions of Autonomy on the Frontline." *Journal of Sociology* 39(1): 44-62.

Lewis, O., R.M. Lewis, and S.M. Rigdon. 1977. *Four Men: Living the Revolution.* Urbana: University of Illinois Press.

Lievesley, G. 2005. "The Latin American Left: The Difficult Relationship between Electoral Ambition and Popular Empowerment." *Contemporary Politics* 11(1): 3-18.

Loose, C. 2006. "The Cuban Solution." *Washington Post*, Sunday, 23 July.

Lozano, B. 1989. *The Invisible Work Force: Transforming American Business with Outside and Home-Based Workers.* New York: Free Press.

Lundasen, S. 2005. "Socio-economic and Voluntary Associations in Swedish Municipalities." *International Journal of Public Administration* 28(9-10): 787-795.

Lunday, S. 2001. "Old-Fashioned Doctoring Keeps Cubans Healthy." *Los Angeles Times*, 9 July.

Lutgendorf, S.K. et al. 2005. "Social Support, Psychological Distress, and Natural Killer Cell Activity in Ovarian Cancer." *Journal of Clinical Oncology* 23(28): 7105-7113.

Maloney, W.A., G. Smith and G. Stoker. 2000. "Bringing the State Back into Civic Engagement." In *Social Capital: Critical Perspectives.*, eds S. Baron, J. Field and T. Schuller. Oxford: Oxford University Press.

Mann, M. 1993. *The Sources of Social Power: Vol 2—The Rise of Classes and Nation States 1760-1914.* Cambridge: Cambridge University Press.

Marmot, M. and R.G. Wilkinson. 1999. *Social Determinants of Health.* Oxford: Oxford University Press.

Marquis, C. 2000. "Medical School for Latins Earns Cuba Goodwill." *The Miami Herald*, March 13.

Marsh, D. 2002. "Marxism" In *Theory and Methods in Political Science*, eds D. Marsh and G. Stoker. London: Palgrave Macmillan.

Marx, G. 2006. "Does her Brain Belong to Castro, too? Cuba Claims State 'Patrimony' to Keep Physician on Island." *CubaNet News*, 5 March.

Marx, K. [1887] 1999. *Capital Volume One: The Process of Production of Capital.* Moscow: Progress Publishers (via marxists.org).

Marx, K. [1894] 1996. *Capital Volume Three: The Process of Capitalist Production as a Whole.* New York: International Publishers (via Marx.org).

Mays, G.P. 2002. "From Collaboration to Coevolution: New Structures for Public Health Improvement." *Journal of Public Health Management and Practice* 8(1): 95.

McGeough, P. 2005. "Children of the Revolution: As Castro Ages, What Next for Cuba?" *Good Weekend: The Sydney Morning Herald Magazine*, 19 February.

McGuire, J.W. and L.B. Frankel. 2005. "Mortality Decline in Cuba, 1900-1959: Patterns, Comparisons, and Causes." *Latin American Research Review* 40(2): 83-116.

McKinlay, J.B. and L.D. Marceau. 2002. 'The End of the Golden Age of Doctoring." *International Journal of Health Services* 32(2): 379-416.

Medina, F. 2004. *Interview 13, 21 September*. Havana.

Mendoza, T. 2006. *Interview IV, 9 December*. Brisbane.

Mendoza, T. 2007. *Interview IV, personal e-mail communication, 31 January*. Brisbane.

Mesa Lago, C. 1969a. "Availability and Reliability of Statistics in Socialist Cuba (Part One)." *Latin American Research Review* 4(1): 53-91.

Mesa Lago, C. 1969b. "Availability and Reliability of Statistics in Socialist Cuba (Part Two)." *Latin American Research Review* 4(2): 47-81.

Mesa Lago, C. 1998. "Assessing Economic and Social Performance in the Cuban Transition of the 1990s." *World Development* 26(5): 857-876.

Mettler, S. 2002. "Bringing the State Back In to Civic Engagement: Policy Feedback Effects of the G.I. Bill for World War II Veterans." *American Political Science Review* 96(2): 351-365.

Miliband, R. 1983. *Class Power and State Power*. London: Verso.

MINSAP. 2004. *The Cuban National Health System*. Havana: Ministerio de Salud Pública (MINSAP).

MINSAP. 2006. "Anuario Estadístico de Salud." Havana: Ministerio de Salud Pública (MINSAP).

MINSAP. 2007. "Estadísticas de Salud de Cuba." URL: <http://www.dne.sld.cu/index.htm>.

Molina, H. 2005. "Carta de la Dra Hilda Molina." La Habana: Revista Hispano Cubana. URL: <http://www.hispanocubana.org/revistahc/>.

Molina, H. 2006. "Cuban Medicine Today." Civita. URL: <http://www.civita.no/civ.php?mod=news&id=299>.

Molinero, L. 2004. *Interview 17, 30 September*. Havana.

Muñoz, E. 1998. "The Effect of Travel Restrictions on Scientific Collaboration between American and Cuban Scientists." Washington: AAAS Science and Human Rights Program. URL: <http://shr.aaas.org/rtt/report/report.htm>.

Moore, Michael. *Sicko*. <http://www.michaelmoore.com/sicko/index.html>

Murberg, T. and E. Bu. 2001. "Social Relationships and Mortality in Patients with Congestive Heart Failure." *Journal of Psychosomatic Research* 51(3): 521-527.

Mustafa, D. 2005. "(Anti)social Capital in the Production of an (Un)civil Society in Pakistan." *The Geographical Review* 95(3): 328-347.

Najman, J. and L. Callaway. 2007. *Personal e-mail communication with experts on maternal-infant health Professor Jake Najman and Dr Leonie Callaway*. November-December.

Navarro, V. 1993. "Has Socialism Failed? An Analysis of Health Indicators under Socialism." *International Journal of Health Services* 23(2): 407.

Nayeri, K. 1995. "The Cuban Health Care System and Factors Currently Undermining it." *Journal of Community Health*. 20(4): 321-334.

Newman, L. 2000. "Cuban Doctors Seeking Opportunities Abroad Due to Low Wages at Home." *CNN*, 9 July.

NewsMax. 2004. "Media Silent over Imprisoned Cuban Doctors." NewsMax.com. URL: <http://www.newsmax.com/archives/ic/2004/4/17/210308.shtml>.

Newton, K. 1997. "Social Capital and Democracy." *American Behavioral Scientist* 40(5): 575.

Nigenda, G. et al. 2003. "'Womens' Opinions on Antenatal Care in Developing Countries: Results of a Study in Cuba, Thailand, Saudi Arabia and Argentina." *BMC public health.* 3(1): 17.

Nordlinger, J. 2007. "The Myth of Cuban Healthcare: Michael Moore Gives it a Powerful Boost." *National Review Online.* July 30. <http://nrd.nationalreview.com/>

Obaid-Chinoy, S. 2005. "Kashmir Diary." Bissian, Pakistan: World Volunteer Web. URL: <http://ennews.worldvolunteerweb.org/e_article000509735.cfm?x=b11,0,w>.

O'Brien Caughy, M., P.J. O'Campo and C. Muntaner. 2003. 'When Being Alone Might be Better: Neighborhood Poverty, Social Capital, and Child Mental Health.' *Social Science & Medicine* 57(2):227.

O'Donnell, G. 1993. *On the State, Democratisation and Some Conceptual Problems: A Latin American View with Glances at some Post-Communist Countries (Working Paper).* URL: <http://www.ereserves.nd.edu/~kellogg/publications/workingpapers/WPS/192.pdf>.

OECD. 2001. "Human and Social Capital." Organisation for Economic Co-operation and Development (OECD). URL: <http://www.oecd.org/>.

OECD. 2003. "Poverty and Health in Developing Countries: Key Actions." URL: <http://www.oecd.org/dataoecd/39/62/18514159.pdf>.

Oppenheimer, A. 1993. *Castro's Final Hour: An Eyewitness Account of the Disintegration of Castro's Cuba.* New York: Touchstone.

O'Reilly, K. 2005. *Ethnographic Methods.* London and New York: Routledge.

Orth-Gomer, K., A. Unden and M.E. Edwards. 1988. "Social Isolation and Mortality in Ischemic Heart Disease. A 10-year Follow-up Study of 150 Middle-aged Men." *Acta Medica Scandinavica* 224(3): 205-215.

PAHO. 2001. "Country Health Profile: Cuba." Pan American Health Organization (PAHO). URL: <http://www.paho.org/english/sha/prflcub.htm>.

PAHO. 2006. "Sustainable Development and Environmental Health: Healthy Settings." Pan American Health Organization (PAHO). URL: <http://www.paho.org/English/ad/sde/espacios.htm>.

Partido Comunista de Cuba. 2007. "El Partido y Las Organizaciones de Masas y Sociales." La Habana.URL: <http://www.pcc.cu/pccweb/organizaciones/>.

Pax Christi Netherlands. 1999. "Cuba: a Year after the Pope." URL: <http://www.ikvpaxchristi.nl/>.

Paxton, P. 1999. "Is Social Capital Declining in the United States? A Multiple Indicator Assessment." *American Journal of Sociology* 105(1): 88-127.

Pearce, N. and G.D. Smith. 2003. "Is Social Capital the Key to Inequalities in Health?" *American Journal of Public Health* 93(1): 122-129.

Penié, J.B. 2005. "State of Malnutrition in Cuban Hospitals." *Nutrition* 21(4): 487-497.

Perez, A. 2002. "Cuban Maternity Homes: A Comprehensive Study." Paper presented to The 130th Annual Meeting of America Public Health Association (APHA), Philadelphia, 9-13 November.

Perez, T. 2005. *Interview 2005(1), 18 August.* Brisbane.

Perez, T. 2006. *Interview 2006, 29 May.* Brisbane.

Perez-Lopez, J.F. 1995. *Cuba's Second Economy: From Behind the Scenes to Center Stage.* New Jersey: Transaction.

Perez-Lopez, J.F. 1997. 'The Cuban Economy in the Age of Hemispheric Integration." *Journal of Interamerican Studies and World Affairs* 39(3): 3-47.

Perez-Lopez, J.F. 2006. "The Cuban Economy in 2005-2006: The End of the Special Period?" *Cuba in Transition* 16:1-13.

Perez-Stable, M. 2007. "Sooner or Later the Fidel Show Will End." *Cubanet News*, 2 February.

Pietroni, P. 2001. *Cuban Health Care Systems and its Implications for the NHS Plan.* London: UK House of Commons Health Select Committee.

Polidano, C. 2001. "Don't Discard State Autonomy: Revisiting the East Asian Experience of Development." *Political Studies* 49(3): 513-527.

Ponthieux, S. 2004. "The Concept of Social Capital: A Critical Review." Paper presented to 10th ACN Conference-Paris, 21-23 January.

Portes, A. 1998. "Social Capital: Its Origins and Applications in Modern Sociology." *Annual Review of Sociology* 24: 1-24.

Portes, A. and R. Schauffler. 1993. "Competing Perspectives on the Latin American Informal Sector." *Population and Development Review* 19(1): 33-60.

Portes, A. and Haller. 2005. 'The Informal Economy." In *Handbook of Economic Sociology*, eds N.J. Smelser and R. Swedberg. Princeton: Princeton University Press.

Portes, A., M. Castells and L.A. Benton, eds. 1989. *The Informal Economy: Studies in Advanced and Less Developed Countries*. Baltimore: John Hopkins University Press.

Poverty Net, W.B.G. 2004. "Social Capital and Education." The World Bank Group. URL: <http://www1.worldbank.org/prem/poverty/index.htm>.

Punch, K.F. 1998. *Introduction to Social Research: Quantitative and Qualitative Approaches.* London: Sage.

Putnam, R. 1995. "Economic Growth and Social Capital in Italy." *Eastern Economic Journal* 21(3): 295-307.

Putnam, R. 2000. *Bowling Alone: The Collapse and Revival of American Community.* New York: Simon & Schuster.

Putnam, R.D., R. Leonardi and R.Y. Nanetti. 1994. *Making Democracy Work: Civic Traditions in Modern Italy.* Princeton: Princeton University Press.

Ramírez, P. 2004. *Interview 9, 6 September*. Havana.

Ramos, E. 2004a. *Interview 10, 6 September*. Havana.

Ramos, G.S. 2004b. "Participación Social en el Campo de la Salud." *Revista Cubana de Salud Pública* 30(3).

Rios, M. 2004. *Interview 16, 23 September*. Havana.

Ritter, A. 2005. "Survival Strategies and Economic Illegalities in Cuba." *Cuba in Transition* 14: 342-359.

Rivera, J. 2004. *Interview 1, 14 July*. Havana.

Rivero, R. 1999. "Daily Life in Cuba." *Le Monde*, 2 January.

Robles, F. 2003. "Venezuelans Cheer and Protest Presence of Doctors from Cuba." *CubaNet News*, 13 August.

Rodriguez, A. 2008. "Cuba Releases Economic 'Survey of Prices in the Informal Sector' Report." *Havana Journal* March 21.

Rodriguez, F V, N B Lopez and I Choonara. 2008. "Child Health in Cuba." *Archives of Disease in Childhood* 93(11): 991-993.

Rosendahl, M. 1997. *Inside the Revolution: Everyday Life in Socialist Cuba.* New York: Cornell University Press.

Rundle, M.L.B. 2001. 'Tourism, Social Change, and *Jineterismo* in Contemporary Cuba." *The Society for Caribbean Studies Annual Conference Papers* Vol. 2. ed., Courtman, S. URL: http://www.caribbeanstudies.org.uk/papers/2001/olu2p3.pdf

Sæbø, J. 2007. *Personal e-mail communication with Johan Sæbø, who spent a year of action research in Cuba in 2001 working on a collaborative Norway-Cuba project aimed at improving the country's health information system.* February-March.

Sæbø, J. and O. Titlestad. 2003. *Developing Health Information Systems in Cuba—An Effort to Transfer the HISP Approach from South Africa to Cuba.* Masters thesis, University of Oslo.

Sæbø, J. and O.H. Titlestad. 2004. "Evaluation of a Bottom-up Action Research Approach in a Centralised Setting: HISP in Cuba." Paper presented to The 37th Hawaii International Conference on System Sciences, 5-8 January.

Salloum, H. 1996. "Cuba's Underground Economy on Guardalavaca Beach." *Contemporary Review* 269(1566): 1-5.

Sánchez, J.F. 2007. "Salarios Son Insuficientes Para Comer en Cuba." *Diario Digital*, 26 Febrero.

Sánchez, R. 2004. *Interview 5, 23 July*. Havana.

Saney, I. 2005. "Five Reasons Why the People Rule." Cuba Solidarity Campaign. URL: <http://www.cuba-solidarity.org/cubasi_article.asp?ArticleID=53>.

Santana, S. 1988. "Some Thoughts on Vital Statistics and Health Status in Cuba." In *Cuban Political Economy*, ed. A. Zimbalist. Boulder, CO, and London: Westview Press.

Scanlon, C. 2004a. "What's Wrong with Social Capital?" *Arena Magazine* Blue Book Number Eight: Australian Fabian Society.

Scanlon, C. 2004b. "Social Capital and Social Form (Working Paper)." *RMIT University*.

Scarpaci, J.L. 1995. "The Emerging Food and Paladar Market in Havana." *Cuba in Transition* 5: 74-84.

Schmidt, V. 2003. "How, Where and When does Discourse Matter in Small States' Welfare State Adjustment?" *New Political Economy* 8(1):127-146.

Schwab, K. 2003. "Capitalism Must Develop More of a Conscience." *Newsweek*, 24 February.

Schweimler, D. 2001. "Cuba's Medical Success Story." *BBC News*, 10 September.

Scott, J.C. 1990. *Domination and the Arts of Resistance: Hidden Transcripts*. New Haven: Yale University Press.

Seeman, T.E. 1996. 'Social Ties and Health: The Benefits of Social Integration.' *Annals of Epidemiology* 6(5): 442-451.

Shaikh, A. 1990. "Capital as a Social Relation." In *Marxian Economics*, eds J. Eatwell, M. Milgate and P. Newman. London: Macmillan.

Simis, K.M. 1982. *USSR The Corrupt Society: The Secret World of Soviet Capitalism*. New York: Simon and Schuster.

Sixto, F.E. 2002. "An Evaluation of Four Decades of Cuban Healthcare." *Cuba in Transition* 12: 325-343.

Skocpol, T. 1985. "Bringing the State Back In: Strategies of Analysis in Current Research." In *Bringing the State Back In*, eds P. Evans, D. Rueschemeyer and T. Skocpol. Cambridge: Cambridge University Press.

Skocpol, T. 1996. "Unsolved Mysteries: The Tocqueville Files—Unravelling from Above." *The American Prospect* 7(25).

Smolowe, J. 1988. "Heroines of Soviet Labor." *Time*, 6 June.

Spiegel, J.M. and A. Yassi. 2004. "Lessons from the Margins of Globalization: Appreciating the Cuban Health Paradox." *Journal of Public Health Policy* 25(1): 85-110.

Stark, D. 1989. "Bending the Bars of the Iron Cage: Bureaucratization and Informalization in Capitalism and Socialism." *Sociological Forum* 4(4): 637-664.

Stepan, A. 1985. "State, Power and the Strength of Civil Society in the Southern Cone of Latin America." In *Bringing the State Back In*, eds P. Evans, D. Rueschemeyer and T. Skocpol. Cambridge: Cambridge University Press.

Stone, W. 2001. *Measuring Social Capital: Towards a Theoretically Informed Measurement Framework for Researching Social Capital in Family and Community Life: Research Paper No. 24*. Australian Institute of Family Studies.

Storper, M. 2005. "Society, Community, and Economic Development." *Studies in Comparative International Development* 39(4): 30.

Streeck, W. 1997. "Beneficial Constraints: On the Economic Limits of Rational Voluntarism." In *Contemporary Capitalism: The Embeddedness of Institutions*, eds J. Rogers Hollingsworth and R. Boyer. Cambridge: Cambridge University Press.

Streeck, W. and K. Yamamura, eds. 2001. *The Origins of Nonliberal Capitalism: Germany and Japan in Comparison*. Ithaca: Cornell University Press.

Streeton, P. 2002. "Reflections on Social and Antisocial Capital." In *Social Capital and Economic Development*, eds J. Isham, T. Kelly and S. Ramaswamy. Cheltenham: Edward Elgar.

Sugarman, J. 2003. "Informed Consent, Shared Decision-Making, and Complementary and Alternative Medicine." *Journal of Law, Medicine & Ethics* 31(2): 247.

Surowiecki, J. 2002. "A Virtuous Cycle." *Forbes* 170(13): 248.

Susser, M. 1993. "Health as a Human Right: an Epidemiologist's Perspective on the Public Health." *American Journal of Public Health* 83(3): 418-426.

Swanson, K. et al. 1995. "Primary Care in Cuba: A Public Health Approach." *Health Care for Women International.* 16(4): 299-308.

Szreter, S. 2002. 'The State of Social Capital: Bringing Back in Power, Politics and History." *Theory and Society* 31(5):573-621.

The Australian. 2009. "Cuban Dissident Wins Freedom." *The Australian.* June 15, 2009. URL: <http://www.theaustralian.com.au>

The Economist. 1999b. "Cuba: Not Here." *The Economist* (US) 351(8118):1.

Thompson, A.G.H. 2007. "The Meaning of Patient Involvement and Participation in Health Care Consultations: A Taxonomy." *Social Science and Medicine.* 64(6): 1297-1310.

Tomaka, J. 2006. "The Relation of Social Isolation, Loneliness, and Social Support to Disease Outcomes among the Elderly." *Journal of Aging and Health* 18(3): 359-384.

Tonkiss, F. and A. Passey, eds. 2000. *Trust and Civil Society.* London: Macmillan Press.

UNDP (United Nations Development Programme). 2006, 2009. *The Human Development Report.* United Nations Development Program. URL: <http://www.undp.org/>.

UNSD (United Nations Statistics Division). 2009. *Millenium Development Goals Indicators.* URL: <http://mdgs.un.org/unsd/>

Valera, D. 2009. "More Cuban Doctors in Venezuela." *Havana Times.* October. URL: <http://www.havanatimes.org/>

Valdes, R. 2004. *Interview 6, 2 August.* Havana.

Valdes, Z. 1997. *Yocandra in the Paradise of Nada: A Novel of Cuba.* New York: Arcade.

Vargas, S. 2004. *Interview 20, 4 October.* Havana.

Vega, J. and A. Irwin. 2004. 'Tackling Health Inequalities: New Approaches in Public Policy." *Bulletin of the World Health Organization* 82(7):482.

Waitzkin, H. et al. 1997. "Primary Care in Cuba: Low- and High-Technology Developments Pertinent to Family Medicine." *Journal of Family Practice* 45(3): 250-258.

Wakefield, S.E.L. and B. Poland. 2005. "Family, Friend or Foe? Critical Reflections on the Relevance and Role of Social Capital in Health Promotion and Community Development." *Social Science & Medicine* 60(12): 2819.

Wallace, C. 2006. "Economic Transformation Outside the Law: Corruption, Trust in Public Institutions and the Informal Economy in Transition Countries of Central and Eastern Europe." *Europe-Asia Studies* 58(1): 81.

Wang, J., D.T. Jamison, E. Bos, A. Preker and J. Peabody. 1999. *Measuring Country Performance on Health: Selected Indicators for 115 Countries.* Human Development Network: Health, Nutrition, and Population Series.

Weekly Telegraph. 2007. "The Decline of Cuba's once Famed Health Service." *Weekly Telegraph*, 21 February.

Weiss, L. 1998. *The Myth of the Powerless State: Governing the Economy in a Global Era.* Cambridge: Cambridge University Press.

Weiss, L. and J.M. Hobson. 1995. *States and Economic Development.* Cambridge: Polity Press.

Weiss, L., ed. 2003. *States in the Global Economy: Bringing Domestic Institutions Back In.* Cambridge: Cambridge University Press.

Whiteford, L.M, L.G. Branch and E.B. Chapel. 2008. *Primary Health Care in Cuba: The Other Revolution.* Lanham: Rowman and Littlefield.

Whiteley, P.F. 2000. "Economic Growth and Social Capital." *Political Studies* 48(3): 443- 466.

Whitney, W.T. 2006. "Cuba Waging Fight against Corruption." *People's Weekly World,* 5 January.

WHO. 2004a. "Population Health and Aggregate Health Expenditure." World Health Organization (WHO). URL: <http://www.euro.who.int/>.

WHO. 2004b. *Approaches to the Management of HIV/AIDS in Cuba.* Geneva: World Health Oganization (WHO).

WHOSIS (World Health Organization Statistical Information System). 2009. URL: <http://apps.who.int/whosis/>

Williams, M. 2007. "Cuba Shares its Medical Expertise: Foreign Patients Receive Free Eye Care." *The Atlanta Journal,* 11 March.

Wolf, H. 2005. "Capital." In *Encyclopedia of Social Theory,* ed. G. Ritzer. London: Sage.

Wolinsky, F.D. 1993. "The Professional Dominance, Deprofessionalization, Proletari- anization, and Corporatization Perspectives: An Overview and Synthesis." In *The Changing Medical Profession,* eds F.W. Hafferty and J.B. McKinlay. Oxford: Oxford University Press.

Woo-Cumings, M., ed. 1999. *The Developmental State.* Ithaca: Cornell University Press.

Woolcock, M. 1998. "Social Capital and Economic Development: Toward a Theoretical Synthesis and Policy Framework." *Theory and Society* 27(2): 151-208.

Woolcock, M. 2000. 'Social Capital in Theory and Practice: Where Do We Stand?' Paper presented to 21st Annual Conference on Economic Issues, Department of Economics, Middlebury College, 7-9 April.

Words Without Borders. 2007. "Raúl Rivero." URL: <http://www.wordswithoutborders. org/>.

World Bank. 2002. *The World Development Report: Building Institutions for Markets.* Washington: Oxford University Press for the World Bank.

World Bank. 2004a. "Why Invest in Health, Nutrition, and Population?" The World Bank Group: Health, Nutrition, and Population. URL: <http://www.worldbank.org/>.

World Bank. 2004b. "Spotlight on Costa Rica and Cuba." In *World Development Report: Making Services Work For Poor People.* Washington: Oxford University Press for the World Bank.

World Medical Association. 2004. "World Medical Association Pleads for Doctors and Dentists Imprisoned in Cuba." URL: <http://www.wma.net/e/press/2004_4.htm>.

Yin, R.K. 1994. *Case Study Research.* Second ed. Applied Social Research Methods Series: Volume 5. London: Sage.

Yudkin, J.S, G. Owens, F. Martineau, M. Rowson and S. Finer. 2008. "Global Health Worker Crisis: The UK Could Learn from Cuba." *The Lancet.* 371(9622): 1397- 1399.

Zaglul, H.F. 2002. "Medical Ethics: An Overview of Clinical Ethics." *Heart Views* 3(2): 92-99.

Zunzunegui, M.V. et al. 2003. "Social Networks, Social Integration, and Social Engagement Determine Cognitive Decline in Community-Dwelling Spanish Older Adults." *The Journals of Gerontology Series B: Psychological Sciences and Social Sciences* 58: 93-100.

Index

abortion 11, 29, 90, 95, 121
access to health care xvi, 5, 9, 10, 23, 25, 27, 60, 75, 83-84, 88, 91, 96-97, 99-100, 112-113, 143, 145, 148, 151, 158-159, 161, 171, 173, 177
alternative medicine 59, 111
Anderson, Tim vii, 10, 16, 25, 59, 140
antisocial capital 39, 40, 41
Asamblea del Poder Popular (see People's Power Assemblies*)*
August, Arnold 116-117
Australia 3, 7-8, 10, 40, 68-69, 79, 86, 139
Australian Productivity Commission 37, 38, 41
automedicalisación (see self medication)
autonomy (of the state *see* state autonomy; *see also* patient autonomy)

Barrio Adentro (see Venezuela)
bartering 138-139, 147
Basic Work Groups at Cuban Policlinics (*See* GBT)
Biscet, Oscar Elias 110
black market 132, 135-136, 138-139, 141, 149, 151, 153, 155-156, 171-172; *see also* informal economy, second economy
Blanco, Jose Luis 103
blat 153-157, 174
blockade 74, 99; *see also* embargo
bodies 35
Bourdieu, Pierre 4, 32-33, 48-53, 62, 71, 165-166
Brazil 7, 8, 129
brigade workers 83, 116
brigadistas sanitarias (see brigade workers)
Brotherton, Pierre Sean 24, 25, 75, 92, 111, 145, 149, 163, 178
Burwell, Rebecca 104-105
Bush, George W. 17, 28

capital 3, 4, 10, 32-33, 44-49, 51-53, 54, 57, 61, 64, 71, 125, 133, 134, 152, 165, 174, 177; capital as a social relation 44-48; human capital 2, 32, 33, 44, 47, 61, 152; cultural capital 2, 32; symbolic capital 75, 107; Marx's *Capital* 32, 44, 45-46, 49-50; *see also* social capital
capitalism 134, 152; capitalist contexts 7, 45-46, 61, 120, 125, 132, 133, 134, 158; capitalist production 46, 54, 133, 135; capitalist state 54; capitalist class 55; capitalists 158
casa particular 142
Castro, Fidel xvi, 5, 14, 16, 17, 18, 20, 21, 25, 28, 74, 75, 76, 86, 102, 103, 109, 118, 123, 127, 135, 136, 139, 145, 162, 173, 178
Castro, Raul xvi, 115, 123, 128, 137
Castro government 12, 14, 85, 170, 176
CDR (Committee for the Defense of the Revolution) 82, 97, 104, 116, 119, 128
CEDISAP (Cuba's Centre for the Development of Health Information) 26
CENESEX (Cuba's National Centre for Sexual Education) 98
central institutions of the state 6, 62, 63, 88, 89, 92, 103, 112, 113, 114, 119, 120, 121, 123, 135, 162, 166, 176
central planning 132, 133, 134, 136, 138, 162
Centre for the Development of Health Information (*see* CEDISAP)
Che Guevara (see Guevara, Ernesto "Che")
Chile 127, 129
China 8, 18
childbirth 27, 79, 83, 97, 106, 127
circumvention of formal medical system 98, 115, 124, 131, 153, 171, 175

civic engagement 33, 34-43, 70, 168; *see also* social connectedness
civil society 39-42, 53, 57-59, 62, 71, 89, 115, 125, 126, 128, 159, 160, 162, 175-176, 177
code words (used in black market exchanges) 155
coercion 63, 89, 92, 121
Coleman, James S. 4, 31, 32, 33-34, 39, 42, 48-53, 62, 71, 165
coleros 138
collective decision making 2, 33, 34, 52, 53, 54, 58, 59, 61, 71, 119, 166, 169, 174, 175, 178
collective power 160
COMECON (Council for Mutual Economic Assistance) 24
Committee for the Defense of the Revolution (*see* CDR)
Communist Manifesto, The 54
Communist Party 71, 90, 115, 116, 117, 118, 128, 156, 157
community participation 62, 91
complaints about health services 104-109, 110, 115-119, 122, 128, 162; *see also* problems with health services; frustration with health system
Constitución de la República de Cuba 116
contraceptive use 11, 98, 127
cooperative relationships 4, 48, 50, 63, 81, 83, 85, 104, 119, 166
corruption 40, 56, 70, 107, 135, 141, 148, 155, 157, 163
Council for Mutual Economic Assistance (*see* COMECON)
counterrevolutionary 21, 103, 116, 128; *see also* dissidents, crackdowns on dissidents
Crabb, Mary Katherine 14, 15, 19, 20, 21, 100, 110, 146, 147, 178; *see also* Hirschfeld, Katherine
crackdowns on dissidents 102, 141, 159; *see also* dissidents; counterrevolutionary
cuentapropistas 137, 141, 142
Cuban doctors 25, 75, 90, 101, 126, 143, 144; Cuban doctors in Venezuela 128, 177
Cuban revolution (*see* revolution)
Cubans in Australia 68-69
cultural context 19

data collection 112-113, 128
decision-making xvi, 81, 86, 89, 90, 92-94, 99, 100, 101, 103, 114, 118, 119, 121-124, 161, 162, 164, 169-170, 176; *see also* collective decision-making
democracy 16, 32, 33, 43, 53, 61, 115
dengue fever 13, 60, 106, 109-110
dependency on the medical system 98-101
deprofessionalisation (of medical profession) 125
De Soto, Hernando 133, 134, 135, 157, 158
despotic state power 57, 58, 63, 115
development xiii, 1, 2, 5, 9, 10, 15, 17, 28, 29, 31, 32, 39, 43, 46-48, 49, 51-59, 61, 62, 64, 70, 71, 74, 85, 86, 88-89, 101, 111, 114, 118, 122, 131, 132, 134, 154, 163, 165, 173, 175; development of Cuba's health system 22-25, 67, 76-80; developmental statism 54, 127
diarrhea 13, 24, 82, 84, 111, 128
DNE (Cuba's National Office of Statistics) 114
doctor/patient ratio 7, 13, 121
doctor-patient relations 5, 78, 101-103, 167
doctors (*see* Cuban doctors)
dual discourses 19, 71
Durkheim, Emile 32
Diaz-Briquets, Sergio 12, 13, 14, 75, 83, 87, 90, 102, 111
dissidents 59, 68, 102, 109; *see also* counterrevolutionary

Eberstadt, Nick 12, 13
Eckstein, Susan E. 25, 145
ECLAC (United Nations Economic Commission for Latin America and the Caribbean) 25
Edwards, Jorge 103, 127
elections 43, 52
embargo (US embargo on Cuba) xiii, 1, 9, 16, 24, 28, 106; *see also* blockade
embedded state capacity 4, 6, 57, 58, 62, 63, 89, 92, 120, 123, 166, 169, 175
ethnographic methods 70
Evans, Peter 42, 53, 54, 168

Family Doctor Program 24, 25-26, 76, 77
family doctors 3, 5, 13, 23, 25-26, 29, 63, 76-79, 82, 84, 95, 96, 97, 104, 105,

107, 108, 110, 111, 116, 128, 144, 145, 146-147, 167
Federation of Cuban Women (*see* FMC)
Feinsilver, Julie M. 1, 9, 14, 59, 60, 75-76, 78, 95, 103, 107, 112, 115, 118, 119, 144, 167
fetishism 47, 92
fieldwork 65, 68
FMC (Federation of Cuban Women) 65, 66, 67, 82, 83, 90, 96, 97, 116, 119, 128, 167
foreign researchers in Cuba 15, 16, 19, 65, 72
free health care 2, 124, 140, 148, 158, 161; *see also* universal health care
frustration with health system xvi, 24, 99, 104-109, 110, 124, 127, 150, 152, 153, 156, 172; *see also* problems with health services
frustrated states 160
Fukuyama, Francis 31

GBT (Basic Work Groups at Cuban Policlinics) 79
GDP (Gross Domestic Product) 2, 8, 10, 24, 28, 129, 157, 163
Giddens, Anthony 46
gift-giving to Cuban doctors 109, 127, 147-151, 171, 172
Guevara, Ernesto "Che" 17, 128

Haiti 8
Havana University 135
HDI (Human Development Index) 2, 28
health battlefield 75
health information 112, 113-115, 120, 122
Health Information Systems Program (*see* HISP)
health expenditure 2, 8, 10, 28, 35, 77
health tourism 108-109, 123, 127
Henken, Ted 132-133, 134-135, 137, 153, 160
herbal medicine (see *alternative medicine*)
hidden transcripts 28, 163
hierarchy 6, 73, 79, 87, 89, 120
Hirschfeld, Katherine 19, 21, 78, 92, 95, 102, 110, 153, 178; *see also* Crabb, Mary Katherine
HISP (Health Information Systems Program) 113, 115, 122

HIV/AIDS 8, 94
Hollander, Paul 18
human rights 16, 90, 103, 110, 127
hurricanes 67
hypertension 96

ideology xv, xvi, 12, 14, 17-19, 54, 59, 74, 75, 92, 102, 103, 105, 132, 153, 158, 172; ideological subversion of formal systems due to underground practices 153-157
IMF (International Monetary Fund) 2, 55, 56
Imperialism 17, 75, 76, 117
implementation of health policy 3, 4, 5, 6, 50, 59, 62, 63, i87, 88, 89, 112, 115, 119, 123, 160, 162, 164, 166, 168, 169, 170, 174, 176, 178
inefficiency 11, 24, 53, 55, 98, 107, 110, 118, 122, 127, 128, 135, 144, 150
inequality 24, 40, 53, 61, 136, 140, 158
infant mortality 2, 3, 8, 10, 12, 13, 14, 25, 27, 35, 73, 74, 79, 81, 84, 85, 86, 88, 89, 95, 102, 111, 178
infectious diseases 10, 11, 26, 76, 79
informal economy 7, 100, 122, 131-164, 171-172, 174-175, 177; *see also* informal exchange practices in the health sector, second economy, black market
informal exchange practices in the health sector 7, 131, 132, 143-153, 172, 177
infrastructural power of the state 53, 57, 63, 166, 175
institutional cooperation 80-85, 91
inter-sectoral cooperation 5, 68, 80, 81-85, 90, 91
international Monetary Fund (*see* IMF)
institution building 3, 56, 123, 166, 178
interpenetration between the state and civil society 58, 59, 62, 89, 166, 175
interviews xi-x, 3, 13, 19, 21, 22, 26, 64, 65-70, 72, 73, 80, 81, 95, 96, 100, 108, 145

Jessop, Bob 53, 55

Latin America 7, 9, 10, 14, 17, 28, 56, 90, 104, 106, 107, 129, 134, 159, 163
Lawnton Foundation for Human Rights 110
Ledeneva, Alena 139, 153-154, 157
left wing intellectuals 18, 127, 162

legitimacy of the state 7, 74, 120, 123, 129, 132, 153, 155, 162, 169, 171, 176
liberalism xiii, 2, 3, 16, 17, 25, 32, 41, 49, 50-51, 53, 54-61, 71, 77, 104, 129, 133-134, 157-158, 165
libretas (*see* ration books)
living costs 22, 141, 144, 163, 171

machismo 127
Mann, Michael 57-59, 115, 151, 159-160, 175
Marxists 3, 54-55, 125
Marx, Karl 32, 44-48, 109
mass organisations 2, 26, 63, 82, 86, 110, 115-116, 128, 167
maternal-Infant health xvi, 3, 5, 6, 15, 26-28, 35, 64, 73-74, 81, 84, 85, 86, 87, 89, 90, 95, 98, 105, 110, 111, 167, 169
Maternal-Infant Health Program (*see* PAMI)
maternal mortality viii, 7, 8, 21, 25, 27, 28, 65, 82, 96; disparity between infant and maternal mortality 10-11
maternity homes 66, 79, 84, 87, 95-98, 150
maternity hospitals 3, 66, 96, 105-106, 126, 127
McGuire, James.W 14
medical decision-making 92-100, 121, 129, 149, 161, 164, 170
medical diplomacy 75-76, 107
medical profession 76, 125-126, 129
medical scholarships 9, 76
Mendoza Rivero, Dessy 109
meningococcal B 9
Mesa Lago, C. 12, 13, 17, 24, 112
Mexico 7-8, 10
Ministry of Public Health (*see* MINSAP)
MINSAP (Cuban Ministry of Public Health) 3, 11, 13, 23, 26, 27, 29, 63, 65, 66, 79, 80, 81, 83, 91, 95, 102, 103, 108, 116, 118, 119, 145, 151, 157
Misión Barrio Adentro (*see* Venezuela)
misrepresentation of health outcomes 12-15
Molina, Hilda 108-109
moneda nacional 141
Moore, Michael 1

National Centre for Sexual Education (*see* CENESEX)

National Office of Statistics (*see* DNE)
National School of Public Health 84, 119
negotiated power 6, 57, 63, 92, 163, 174
neoliberalism 56, 71, 158
neo-statists 57-58, 62, 63, 89, 166, 168, 169, 174, 175, 176; *see also* statists
networks (*see* social networks)
Norway (collaboration with Cuba to improve health information systems) 113-115, 120, 122

OECD (Organization for Economic Co-operation and Development) 10, 31, 37, 80
OPJM (Jose Marti Organization of Young Pioneers) 128
Oppenheimer, Andres 25, 74, 77, 102

PAHO (Pan American Health Organization) 14, 25, 118
PAMI (Maternal-Infant Health Program) 3, 5, 26-28, 63, 64, 66, 67, 70, 73, 74, 77, 80, 82, 84, 86, 87, 89, 91, 167, 168
Pan American Health Organization (*see* PAHO)
pap smears 26, 98
participation xvi, 3, 4, 6-7, 26, 40, 42, 58, 59, 61, 62, 86, 87, 137, 143, 162, 166, 169, 170, 174, 176, 178; exclusion and non-participation 91-124
Partido Comunista de Cuba (*see* Cuban Communist Party*)*.
paternalism 6, 93-95, 98-103, 117, 119-124, 129, 135, 170-171, 176
patient autonomy 92-98, 101, 121, 146
Pax Christi Netherlands. 90, 128
penetrative power (of the state) 57, 63, 89, 151, 168
People's Power Assemblies 115, 118-119
Perez-Lopez, Jorge 133, 136, 137, 139, 140, 141, 155, 156, 159
Perez Roque, Felipe 109, 136
Perez-Stable, Marifeli 141
Periodo Especial (*see* Special Period)
pharmaceuticals 9, 23, 24, 100, 118, 139, 144, 147, 150, 153, 159, 177
Pinos, General Rafael 69
policlinics 3, 23, 26, 63, 66, 79, 99, 103, 112, 118, 149, 150, 167
policy implementation xiv, 3, 4, 5, 6, 50, 59, 62-63, 87-89, 112, 115, 119, 123, 160, 162, 166, 168, 169, 170, 174, 176, 178

problems with health services xvi, xv,
7, 28, 83, 99, 100, 103, 104-111, 118,
121-127, 128, 131-132, 138, 143-147,
150, 160-161, 163, 170-172, 173, 176,
178; *see also* complaints about health
services
pro-poor policies 10, 80
pregnancy 5, 11, 27, 29, 77-79, 82, 90,
93, 95-97, 106, 126, 167-168
preventive healthcare xvi, 5, 25, 26, 73,
76, 77, 82, 87, 90, 91, 95-98, 116
privacy 20, 172; lack of privacy in Cuban hospitals 104-109
professional dominance 125
proletarianisation (of medical profession) 125, 129
polio 9
Polidano, Charles 54, 56-58
political dissidents 59, 68, 102
Political Pilgrims 18
political prisoners 110, 127
political will 5-6, 64, 73, 85-87, 90
politicization of health xvi, 14, 15, 95,
121-122, 129, 147, 161, 169, 170
Portes, Alejandro
punishment of doctors 109-113, 120,
159, 169
Putnam, Robert 31, 33-34, 37, 42-43, 47,
48, 168

qualitative research 3-4, 65, 67, 92, 173

ration books 60, 77, 90, 138-140, 141,
144, 150, 163, 168
rationing system (*see* ration books)
real estate market in Cuba 142
relative autonomy of the state (*see* state
autonomy)
remittances 149, 163, 171
research (conducting research in Cuba)
xiii, xiv, xv-xvi, 3-5, 15-22, 35, 60,
64-70, 71-72, 92, 121, 131, 137, 145,
157, 162, 165, 166, 171; recommendations for future research 172-178, 126;
Norwegians conducting research in
Cuba (*see* Norway)
research questions xv, 5, 62-64, 65
resource sharing 5, 40, 83-84, 87, 88,
90, 177,
revolution 12, 13, 15, 16-22, 28, 74, 75,
86, 95, 102, 103, 108, 129, 136, 138,
143, 145, 151, 155, 156, 157, 169

Ritter, Archibald 132, 137, 138, 140,
141, 144, 153, 156, 159, 160, 163
Ritzen, Jo 1
RRC (Process of "Rendering Accounts")
116-117
Rosendahl, Mona 139
Russia 81, 153; *see also* Soviet Union
Rwanda 39

Sæbø, Johan viii, 80, 102, 111, 112-113,
120, 122, 128
salaries 22, 103, 108, 122-123, 128, 133,
139, 140, 141, 144, 146, 149, 150, 151,
152-153, 158, 161, 163, 171
Santana, Sarah 1, 14
Scott, James C. 28, 163
second economy 7, 131-164, 171; *see
also* informal economy, black market,
informal exchange practices in the
health sector
self medication 98-100
sexual health 77, 79, 100, 106
sexually transmitted disease 11, 104
shortages 2, 9, 16, 24, 62, 63, 64, 83, 88,
106, 107, 117, 121, 135, 140, 143, 144,
147, 149, 153, 154, 165, 168, 172, 178
Skocpol, Theda 42-43, 53, 54, 55, 168
small business (*see* cuentapropistas)
smallpox 9
Smith, Adam 44-45, 49
social capital xiii, 2, 4-5, 6-7, 28, 31-
53, 60, 61, 62, 63, 64, 66, 67-68,
71, 88, 91, 123, 132, 162, 165-166,
167, 168, 169, 172, 174-175, 178;
problems with prevailing treatments
of social capital 34-44; measuring
social capital 37-38; *see also* social
connectedness
social connectedness 4, 32, 34-44, 60,
72, 174, 175
socialism xii, 7, 12, 14, 15, 17-18, 19,
25, 54, 60, 61-62, 66, 68, 74, 75, 76,
104-105, 120, 132, 133, 134-137, 143,
147, 149, 152, 153-154, 158, 163
social networks 26, 31, 33, 35, 36, 37,
40, 41-42, 47, 49, 50, 52, 61, 66, 82,
113, 131, 132, 147, 154, 166, 172,
174-175; *see also* social capital, social
connectedness
social workers 3, 5, 98, 140
sociolismo 66, 146
solidarity 49, 52, 104-105, 148-149, 151

Sources of Social Power, The (*see* Mann, Michael)

Soviet Union 14, 24, 28, 126, 135, 149, 153, 154; collapse of the Soviet Union xiii, 1, 24, 140

special period, the xiii, 1, 24-25, 55, 71, 81, 111-112, 140, 143, 153, 162, 163, 171

spending on health (*see* health expenditure)

Stark, David 133, 134, 151, 152, 158

state autonomy 57, 62, 89, 175; relative autonomy 54-55

state capacity viii, 2, 3, 4-5, 6-7, 28, 31-32, 53-64, 65, 66, 87, 88, 91, 116, 132, 166, 169, 175, 176, 178; *see also* infrastructural power, penetrative power, extractive power, negotiated power, state autonomy, statists, state strength, state-led development, Mann.

state-led development 53-54, 90, 133, 175; *see also* state capacity

state strength 57, 175, 176; *see also* state capacity

statistical fetishism 92

statistics xiii, xiv, xv, 35, 65, 75, 80, 92-93, 95, 104, 112-114, 121, 124, 137, 145, 170, 173, 178; reliability of statistics 12-15

statists 54-55, 57-58, 60, 62, 63, 89, 127, 166, 168, 174, 175, 176

STDs (*see* sexually transmitted diseases)

Streeck, Wolfgang 53, 71

structuralist approach to the informal economy 133, 134

structure of Cuba's health system (22-25)

Survey of Prices in the Informal Sector 137

sustainability xv, xvi, 4, 6, 98, 118, 122, 124, 132, 162, 170, 173, 175, 176, 177, 178

Sweden 7-8, 80, 94, 126

theft of state property 139, 140, 144, 153, 155, 158

tourism 24, 70, 110, 137, 140, 141, 142, 149, 171; *see also* health tourism

trade union 90, 122, 128, 152-153

trust 6, 21, 31, 33-34, 37-42, 48, 56, 66, 72, 78, 125, 146, 147, 156-158, 167, 175

UNDP (United Nations Development Program) 2, 7, 8, 28, 163

under five mortality 8

underground economy (*see* informal economy)

under-participation of health workers 109-113

United Nations Development Program (*see* UNDP)

United Nations Economic Commission for Latin America and the Caribbean (*see* ECLAC)

United States 7-8, 9, 10, 14-17, 19, 28, 33, 43, 74-75, 77, 86, 102, 126, 129; *see also* U.S. dollar, embargo

universal healthcare xvi, 10, 22, 23, 59, 60, 75, 77, 99, 109, 152, 154; *see also* free health care

Universidad de la Habana (see *Havana University)*

U.S. (*see* United States)

U.S dollar 24, 140, 144

U.S. embargo (*see* embargo)

useful idiots 18, 28

vaccination 76, 79, 83, 116, 167; *see also* vaccines

vaccines 9, 76, 79; *see also* vaccination

Venezuela 13, 28, 76, 107-108, 123, 127-128, 177

voluntad politica (see political will)

Vigoa Martinez, Rodolfo 103

wages (*see* salaries)

Wealth of Nations, The 49

Weiss, Linda 53, 55, 57

WHO (World Health Organization) 8, 27

WHOSIS (World Health Organization Statistical Information System) 8

Wolfensohn, James 1

women 9, 11, 26, 27, 29, 35, 40, 77, 82, 84, 86, 94, 95-98, 100, 105-106, 126, 127, 140, 167; *see also* FMC

Woolcock, Michael 38

World Bank 1, 2, 10, 28, 55, 56, 85, 89

World Development Report 28, 55, 56, 85, 89

World Health Organization (*see* WHO)

World Health Organization Statistical Information System (*see* WHOSIS)